By Design

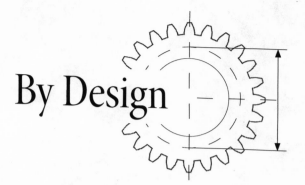

By Design

Ethics, Theology,
and the Practice of Engineering

BRAD J. KALLENBERG

CASCADE *Books* · Eugene, Oregon

BY DESIGN
Ethics, Theology, and the Practice of Engineering

Cascade Books
An Imprint of Wipf and Stock Publishers
199 W. 8th Ave., Suite 3
Eugene, OR 97401

www.wipfandstock.com

ISBN 13: 978-1-61097-479-0

Cataloging-in-Publication data:

Kallenberg, Brad J.

By design : ethics, theology, and the practice of engineering / Brad J. Kallenberg.

xiv + 328 pp. ; 23 cm—Includes bibliographical references and index.

ISBN 13: 978-1-61097-479-0

1. Engineering ethics. 2. Technology—Religious aspects—Christianity. 3. Religion and science. I. Title.

TA157 .K36 2013

Manufactured in the USA

PREFACE

A PREFACE IS A short section of a book to tell readers something before the author tells them other things. In this preface, I want to prepare my readers for possible disappointment!

This book is about Christian ethics and engineering. It does *not* cover U.S. law, federal regulations, lawsuits, or state and city codes. This book does not cover complex, convoluted conundrums. Nor does it offer detailed suggestions for a method for deciding when faced by technological moral quandaries. Nor does it offer a systematic account of right and wrong. Nor does it give much advice about deriving moral duties from moral axioms or natural law. Nor does it contain a catalogue of divine commands. Nor will readers find here any extended treatment of what Catholics call Catholic Social Teaching or of what Protestants call the Social Gospel. What then remains?

What remains is everything else, of course. In fact, there is much, *much* more to what remains than to what I have elected to leave out. But describing all that remains is neither straightforward nor easy. In fact, many of the things I have elected to skip over (e.g., moral quandaries, decisionism, legal positivism, etc.) are the very things that trick us into believing that "ethics" is on the whole quite well defined, just needing a little tidying up around the edges. Not at all! The entire field of Christian ethics is as complex as human living. In a word, ethics is our ongoing quest for the less and less trivial.[1] For that reason, if I do my job, my readers are apt to perceive me as pesky: just when they think they've got "it" (whatever "it" is), I sharply prod them to move on. Of course, we have to start somewhere. So I will introduce a topic and describe it in simple enough terms for us to sink our teeth into. However, just when my readers think some topic or other has been nailed down, I may flit off to the margins and ask, "Okay, but what about *this*?"

There are ten different and progressive "thises" that frame the scaffolding of the book. Once a reader comes to see the interconnections among these ten, "the light will begin for them to dawn over the whole."

Preface

Chapter 1 reminds readers of the differences between engineering and the hard sciences. Engineering happens in the context of systemic unpredictability endemic to the highly messy real world. If there is such a thing as engineering ethics, it has to function within the same context of this extraordinarily messy world. Chapter 2 proposes engineering *design* as the paradigm for thinking about real-world ethics. The analogy turns on the clear similarity between the following two statements:

- "There is no single right answer in ethics. There may be entirely wrong answers. But within the range of roughly acceptable responses, each proposed answer must be evaluated for its relative satisfactoriness."

- "There is no single, correct design. There may be entirely wrong designs. But within the range of roughly acceptable solutions to a design problem, each proposed solution must be evaluated for its relative satisfactoriness."

The murkiness of "satisfactoriness" entails difficulty with the task of defending a given artifact as "good." Thus chapter 3 takes up the question of how value claims—whether about artifacts or about persons—can be justified, at least provisionally. Chapter 4 extends the discussion of justification to the application of professional codes of ethics as warrants for value claims. I argue that treating a professional code of ethics as a collection of clear-cut stipulations is almost as wrongheaded as assuming scientific laws *determine* the outcome of a design process. What is proposed in place of codes-as-stipulations is a strategy for reading codes as *heuristics*.

The notion of "heuristics" is central for this book. Heuristics require a great deal of specialized skill on the part of the engineer to employ well. Many of these skills are "tacit," which is to say, skills that reside in our fingers, our eyes, our ears, our "noses," but cannot be exhaustibly described in words. Tacit skill plays an analogous role in ethics. Thus chapter 5 compares engineering design with what ancient ethicists called "practical reasoning." Chapter 6 shows how the activity of design, a.k.a. practical reasoning, involves human subjects in a way that transforms the way they experience the world. As we shall see, the quality of one's engineering design is a function both of the designer's technical expertise *and* his or her moral character. Chapter 7 extends the discussion of growth in skills (both technical and moral) by looking at the ancient notion of "virtue" through the lens of contemporary neuroscience.

The final three chapters ask about the *social* dimension of engineering. Chapter 8 compares engineering to other morally formative social practices such as medicine. Like medicine, engineering is a morally formative practice; the one who pursues excellence within the practice is more likely to become a better human being than one who is a trifler in the practice. While chapter 8 considers the social nature of engineering within a given era, chapters 9 and 10 consider engineering as a social enterprise *through* time. Chapter 9 asks whether insights for design problems can come from areas *outside* of engineering. This phenomenon is called "cross-domain transfer." In particular, can cross-domain transfer occur from religion to engineering? I shall argue that religion, in general, and Christianity, in particular, may indeed provide insights for doing engineering design well. If that conclusion is plausible, it makes sense to go one step further and ask whether engineering might qualify as a *religious* vocation. In chapter 10 I trace the origins of the high social esteem enjoyed by engineering in the West to the work of a twelfth-century theologian named Hugh of St. Victor. Hugh was the first to show that engineering, by its very nature, makes positive contributions to the redemptive plans of God.

Readers deserve a glimpse of where I come from before trusting me to take them on such a grand tour. I am not an engineer. I am a professor of theology. My outlook is strongly colored by my long-term allegiance to Christian practices and Scriptures. Surprisingly, I rarely teach introductory theology to undergraduates. Instead, I was specifically hired to teach Christian ethics to 120 or more *engineering* students every year. I got my present gig, in part, because my undergrad background was science teaching (physics and chemistry), because my dad was a mechanical engineer, because I did a long stint of campus ministry at Michigan Technological University (where I learned by trial and error how to communicate best with engineering students), and because my doctoral dissertation concerned the impact on theological ethics of the work of an aeronautical engineer-turned-philosopher named Ludwig Wittgenstein.

The work of Wittgenstein is almost as determinative for my outlook as my Christian faith. (I was alluding to Wittgenstein above when I said I hope that, for readers of this book, "the light will begin for them to dawn over the whole."[2]) Readers will learn in chapter 6 that Wittgenstein was a remarkable child who showed promise as a budding engineer by building a working sewing machine out of wood when he was only twelve.³ Exceptionally bright for his age, he attended school in the Austrian town of Linz (he was in the same class as the young Adolph Hitler; Hitler was a year behind the others, while our hero Ludwig had been advanced a grade.) By the age of nineteen Ludwig was enrolled in a graduate program in aeronautical engineering at the University of Manchester in England. The year was 1908, and the Wright brothers had just toured Europe with their flying contraption, piquing everyone's fascination with flying. Three years later Wittgenstein successfully patented a jet-nozzle propeller.⁴ Being fascinated with mathematics, he applied to Cambridge to study mathematical theory. Then came World War I. While in the trenches on the Russian front, he finished a thesis—something like an honors thesis—during his free time. When the war ended he returned to Cambridge, hoping his paper would suffice to finish his degree. The "paper" he had written not only caused a stir in the world of philosophy of mathematics, once he had submitted it, Cambridge University hastily awarded him the highest degree possible, the PhD. Wittgenstein would teach philosophy at Cambridge for several decades. Surprising to many, everything he taught had about it the aroma of his previous engineering experience. His influence in this book is most obvious in my borrowing from him the idea of "dynamical similarity," which is discussed at length in chapter 6. (Readers who are familiar with my published work may catch whiffs of other Wittgensteinian themes as well.⁵)

Unfortunately for my readers, I, rather than Wittgenstein the genius, wrote this book. I did have an enormous amount of help from friends who are as smart as they are charitable. I am particularly grateful for Drew Murray, whose insights about design engineering made all the difference for my understanding of ethics. His comments and objections and suggestions to former drafts of these chapters have made this a much better book. Terry Tilley also has his fingerprints on many early drafts of these chapters. I dare not forget the helpful eyes of Derek Hatch, Aaron James, Ethan Smith, Trecy Lysaught, Kelly Johnson, and Ben Heidgerken, who pointed out the many, many clarifications needed in earlier drafts. Special thanks to Nick Mayrand, who not only made comments on every chapter but also helped typeset the entire manuscript. I also want to thank Bingjue Li, whose skill at CAD transformed the figures from chapter 1 into things of beauty. Finally, I am also deeply indebted to the many engineering students at the University of Dayton who since 2001 have patiently endured my halting attempts to make this material understandable.

NOTES

1. See ch. 8 for discussion of this line from McCabe, *Law, Love and Language*, 99.

2. Wittgenstein, *On Certainty*, 141.

3. For a biography of Wittgenstein, see Monk, *Ludwig Wittgenstein*.

4. Fuel was pumped to a tiny reaction chamber at the tip of each propeller blade. Upon reaction, the jet gas would escape the chamber tangential to the rotation of the blade, thus spinning the blade faster. The idea was eventually put into practice—years later by Doblhoff in a World War II helicopter and more recently by Fairey's Jet Gyrodyne. See McGuinness, *Wittgenstein: A Life*, 68–69.

5. See esp. Kallenberg, *Ethics as Grammar*; Kallenberg, "Praying for Understanding"; Kallenberg, "The Descriptive Problem of Evil"; Kallenberg, "Phronesis and Divine Command Ethics"; Kallenberg, "Teaching Engineering Ethics by Conceptual Design"; Kallenberg, "Dynamical Similarity and the Problem of Evil"; Kallenberg, *God and Gadgets*; Kallenberg, "Rethinking Fideism through the Lens of Wittgenstein's Engineering Outlook."

1

THE MESSY WORLD WE INHABIT

ON AUGUST 1, 2007, the entire truss structure of the I-35W Bridge over the Mississippi River at Minneapolis, Minnesota, collapsed during the morning rush hour.[1] The horrifying catastrophe was over in just seconds. In the end, the disaster claimed the lives of thirteen motorists and injured 145 others. A series of lawsuits followed until finally, two years later, on August 23, 2010, the last lawsuit was settled, to the tune of $52.4 million.

Subsequent to this spectacular engineering failure, no one was surprised that lawsuits were filed, and won or lost. Yet we wished it were not always so. Both engineering designs on the one hand, and their design contexts on the other hand, can be "bad" without there being a question of assigning blame. Granted, sometimes failure *can* be blamed on human error. And we readily admit that once the finger has been pointed and the offending culprit penalized, people tend to feel just a little bit better about the disaster, as though the weight has been lifted just a little. But can blame *always* be assigned? And if not, why do we assume that it can?

The habit of seeking someone to blame for engineering failures springs from a deep-seated temptation to view the world through an ideal lens. This temptation infects engineer and non-engineer alike. Yet for students of engineering, the temptation to think in an ideal mode can be made more acute by their exposure to certain aspects of the first- and second-year engineering curriculum. We will call these features, and the outlook produced, "ideal-world thinking." Eventually, the very best engineering students unlearn ideal-world thinking, or at least learn to temper it with strong doses of skeptical realism. But in the meantime, ideal-world thinking hinders excellence in engineering and misleads ethical conversation. So, before we can get a handle on engineering ethics, we must begin

1

by comparing the ideal world to the "messy world," which is to say, the world in which we actually live.

The Ideal World

Take a good look at Figure 1.1. Gear A rotates at a speed of 3.6π rad/sec. At time t_0, a point (P) is at the position as shown. Where will P be one minute later, at t_{60}?

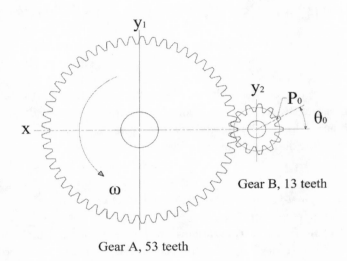

Figure 1.1 Calculating θ for P_{60}^2

For most readers, the calculation is very straightforward. The ratio between the gears is 53:13. Sixty revolutions of Gear A will correspond to (60 × 53)/13 revolutions of Gear B. Since whole revolutions can be discounted (all we're after is the position of P relative to the x-axis), $^{3180}/_{13}$ will produce the same θ value for P_{60} as $^8/_{13}$ rotation. This rotation must be subtracted from θ_0. We can tell from the diagram that P_0 is $^1/_{13}$ of a turn in the counterclockwise direction (2π/13 rad or 360/13°). So, if this were an exam, we could safely predict the final position of P_{60} to be (2π/13) − [8(2π)/13] = -7(2π)/13 rad or 6(2π)/13 rad, if we measure θ in the conventional counterclockwise direction (approx 166°).

But hold on a minute. Haven't we shifted into calculation mode a bit too quickly? Where did this problem come from? Are we so familiar with textbooks that in rushing to find the answer, we may forget that an engineering problem has a specific context in the real world where things can bind, bend, break off, melt, and so on?[3] The diagram *looks* official enough as the above magnification (Figure 1.1b) shows. In fact, it was generated by a program that takes almost no account of the physical limits of actual gear trains as well as the conventions of manufacturing. For example, it is standard to design gears with non-prime numbers of teeth. A gear train with prime numbered teeth can be built, but these are not stock and therefore would have to be special ordered. So why are the numbers of teeth in this particular diagram prime numbers (13, 53)? Is there a very peculiar and particular application behind this problem? (There is, actually. More on that later in the chapter.)

In addition to manufacturing conventions, a kinematician looking at this diagram spotted something else as well. The shape of the teeth is common enough—perhaps a 20° pressure angle. But there turn out to be *physical limits* to how few teeth can be meshed with 53 teeth without interference. For a 20° pressure angle, that number is 16. With 13 teeth as drawn, the interference will be such that the gears lock up.

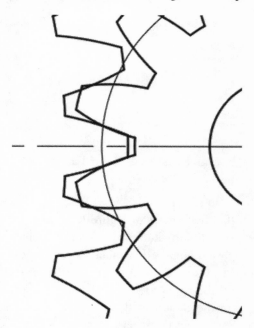

Figure 1.1b Detail of Custom Gear Train (53:13)

To prevent interference, the teeth of the smaller gear must be "undercut"—indented a bit so as to allow the corners of the big gear teeth to rotate past as the gears turn. Undercutting gears may have an effect on load, since the smaller teeth are weakened. Real-world designers must ask, "What does the problem as posed presume about the load to be placed on this gear train?"

Okay, suppose we follow the *standard* methodology for gear train design and replace Figure 1.1 with the following stock gears.

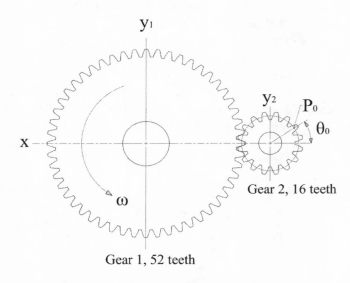

Gear 1, 52 teeth

FIGURE 1.2 A "Stock" Gear Train (52:16)

Are we ready to solve? Maybe. Even the naked eye may be able to see that the "off the shelf" gears of Figure 1.2 appear to need undercutting. Moreover, we still don't know what *kind* of problem we are facing. Is Figure 1.2 simply a thought experiment? Or is it a proposed design for some application in the real world where things bind, bend, break off, melt, and so on? If the application is real, we must ask: is the speed of Gear A at t_0 real or merely assumed? Perhaps a client gave specs on the basis of assumptions rather than facts. This wouldn't be the first client to have insisted on faulty specs! If we are intending to solve on the basis of the unverified assumptions of a client, then we are once again forgetting to be engineers, because *engineers* must pose a *host* of clarifying questions to the client:

- Is the motor that drives Gear A running at t_0 or is it at rest?

- How long does it take for Gear A to achieve 108 rpm (i.e., 3.6π rad/sec)? After how many revolutions can acceleration be ignored?

- How much "play" is in each bearing? If the bearings are liable to human adjustments, is there too much or too little play? Or is the play "just right"—as is the case with sealed bearings? Similarly, if the bearings are adjustable, then are the bearings adequately lubricated? (Or are we using sealed bearings?)

- How great a load is on the motor? After all, 108 rpm is quite slow as far as motors go. Is this a fast motor being made to work slowly by a large load? If so, bearing wear over time may be an important factor as t increases.

- Does the load vary?

- What is the temperature of the surrounding medium? What is the turbulence of the surrounding medium?

- Is the mechanism underwater? Underwater?! The diagram says nothing about the mechanism being underwater. But do clients always volunteer all the crucial details? Or do engineers need to *extract* pertinent information from sometimes unwitting clients?

- And so on . . .

These questions seem like trick questions, even traps. For asking questions like these, engineers are often branded as "glass-half-empty" pessimists. But in the real world, gear trains are not ideal. To think they are ideal would be to make a huge mistake. ("Real" is the actual, everyday world we live in where things bind, scorch, melt, break off, and generally fall apart. Mathematics may be used to *approximate* the real world—and not the other way around.)

For example, in 1986 General Electric switched from reciprocal compressors to rotary compressors in their refrigerators. They made the switch knowing that rotary compressors require more power and operate at higher speeds. But GE presumed that even at these higher speeds, rotary action was inherently closer to an "ideal" than reciprocal action and therefore inherently better. This sounds almost as if GE assumed rotary compressors behave *ideally*, as if they perfectly mimicked a technical

5

drawing of contextless gear trains comprised of frictionless revolute joints. Technicians reported no failures during the testing phase. But when the techs said that something about the new compressors "didn't look right either," GE decision-makers roundly ignored the lowly techs. Eventually these compressors *did* begin to fail. Twelve short months after one million refrigerators had been sold, the long-term effects of operating at higher speeds (and thus higher temperatures) became painfully visible: compressors bound, melted, broke, and burned out. It cost GE $450,000,000 to replace the defective compressors.[4]

Back to our ideal gear train in Figure 1.1. When facing the problem of locating P at t_{60}, one student will answer "$\theta = 6(2\pi)/13$ rad." Another interrupts with a string of questions. *Which student gives the better response to the problem?* Well, doesn't it depend on who is doing the asking and under what conditions? If we are in the classroom, we know that the ideal case *can* be diagrammed: point masses, frictionless bearings, instantaneous acceleration, infinitely solid grounding for revolute joints, etc. The ideal case has a single true answer, "For $\omega = 3.6\pi$ rad/sec, P_{60} is shown to be $\theta = 6(2\pi)/13$ rad." This answer can be delivered with *certitude*, because the ideal mechanism follows mathematically precise *rules*. These rules govern the ideal device with complete authority. In the ideal case, there is no wobble in the bearings because the bearings are completely snug yet frictionless. And yet . . .

IDEAL-WORLD ETHICS?

Some people think, mistakenly in my book, that ethics is like the study of the rules governing the ideal mechanism. For these thinkers, a great deal of effort has gone into explicating the rules—even with mathematical precision, wherever possible. On this view, the job of the professional ethicist is to answer questions such as, "If human interaction is like an ideal mechanism, what *rules* govern person-to-person interactions?" Of course, human beings are not really mechanisms, and they concede that human interactions will sometimes deviate from the ideal, especially when they fail to follow the rules. But can ethics be modeled on the ideal? To find out, let's take a closer look at one of these ideal-world models.

One proposed rule is this: human beings are obligated to behave in the manner that maximizes the likelihood of yielding the most quantifiable beneficial consequence for the greatest number of people. This rule, "maximize net quantifiable goodness," is given by a series of calculations:

$$\text{Net } \overset{x}{\underset{1}{G}} = \overset{n}{\underset{1}{\sum}} \text{(likelihood)(goodness)(significance)}$$

EQUATION 1.1: Calculating *Net Goodness* for course of action *x*, where *n* = the number of outcomes for course of action *x*, and *l* =likelihood, *g* = goodness, and *s* = significance of each given outcome *n*

Suppose the boss has moved up a deadline that I was already struggling to meet. If I'm to stay on pace, I'll necessarily have to work longer hours than I'm already working—longer into the evenings (forget about my kids' soccer games) and big chunks of the weekend (forget about that anniversary getaway). On first thought four courses of action seem possible. I can (*a*) work the hours and take the lumps with my spouse and children; (*b*) appeal to workmates to help with my present task in exchange for the promise to help them out in the future; (*c*) say to the boss, "As you wish!" but in reality make no adjustments and simply fail to make deadline (perhaps I can apologize for this later); or (*d*) stridently refuse the boss's request, underlining my feelings by punching the boss in the nose. If these are my possible courses of action, then in the terms of the formula, $x = 4$.

Each course of action will have consequences of varying degrees of likelihood. For example, we can imagine that *d* (punch the boss in the nose) may result in one or more of the following: (1) I get fired; (2) I'm sued for bodily injury; (3) I break my hand; (4) I feel really good about myself; (5) I'm admired by my colleagues, who go on strike in solidarity with me until the boss is fired and I am promoted as the new boss. For this course of action (punching the boss), the possible number of outcomes listed is five ($n = 5$).

For each of these three outcomes a *likelihood* (*l*) is predicted and assigned a numerical value (such as "a 75 percent chance of occurrence.") The *goodness* (*g*) of an outcome is a simple binary quantity: +1 if it is a good thing, -1 if it is a bad thing.[5] In the case of punching the boss, the first three outcomes listed are bad, or -1, but the last two are good, or +1.

Finally, the *significance* of the outcome is assigned a numerical ranking, say 1 for something trivial and 10 for something of grave importance. Getting fired is pretty serious—but not as bad as dying or being sued. So, perhaps we'll give it an 8. Being sued is worse than getting fired (since

7

it goes on my permanent record), but not as bad as dying. So a 9 seems about right. Breaking one or more fingers is painful and inconvenient, but not as severe as losing the job. Let's give it a significance level of 5. Feeling good about myself is pleasant, but not more pleasant than a broken hand is painful; let's say a 3. Finally, my promotion into the place of my former boss is pretty sweet, maybe even a 9½ out of 10.

The *likelihood* of being fired is probably 90 percent or better; the chance of being sued depends on the boss's personality—let's say 75 percent. And the risk of breaking my hand stands at about 50–50. The chances of feeling temporarily very good are extremely high—the adrenalin rush virtually guarantees (100 percent) a brief elation. But the solidarity of my peers resulting in my promotion is extremely unlikely; let's say on the order of a 2 percent chance. Now we can do the math:

Net G for Action$_4$ = (-1)(8)(.90)+(-1)(9)(.75)+(-1)(5)(.50)+(1)(3)(1.0)+(1)(9.5)(.02) = **-13.26**

Of course we are only one-fourth the way done. If I can only think of four possible courses of action, then $x = 4$ and I will generate four different calculations, four different Net G's. Thus the calculation must be repeated for the other three courses of action. Let's try one more calculation, say for Course of Action$_1$, a.k.a. "do the work but take the lumps at home." Four possible outcomes: keep my job (+8 at 100 percent); my wife takes the kids and leaves me (-9.9 at 10 percent); I am fined by the city for not mowing my lawn in a timely fashion (-2 at 15 percent); and having to cook for myself in my wife's absence, I lose 20 lbs. (+5 at 60 percent).

Net G for Action$_1$ = (+1)(8)(1.0)+(-1)(9.9)(.10)+(-1)(2)(.15)+(1)(5)(.6) = **+0.8**

After having carefully calculated the outcomes for these two courses of action, the obligatory thing to do according to this brand of consequentialism (called "utilitarianism") is to give in to the boss and take my lumps on the home front. Why is this the "best" option? Because 0.8 > -13.26.

One can see that if the scales are the same in each case (i.e., l ranges from 0 to 100 percent, $g = +1$ or -1, and s ranges from 1 to 10), then the goodness of an outcome can be *quantitatively* compared to other outcomes predicted for taking this course of action. The result of summing these values is the net G for *that* course of action. This string of calculations is repeated for each possible course of action; the course of action with the biggest total "wins," which is to say—or so this theory *claims*—the one with the biggest total is revealed to be the *morally obligatory* course to take.

Objections to the Ideal-World Model of Ethics

Of course, there are bound to be enormous problems with the quantification of moral value. After all, *likelihood* is terrifically difficult to predict in advance. Why? Because we do not live in an ideal world, but in a *complex and chaotic* one. "Complexity" and "chaos" are technical terms that mean no physical system, especially no living system, is entirely predictable.[6] This is not the same as saying nothing is predictable. (The flight of a baseball *is* pretty nearly a parabola.) The key term is *entirely*. Saying that no physical system is entirely predictable means that prognostication runs up against a limit.[7] But those who insist on thinking in ideal terms resist this conclusion and instead concoct ways for dismissing *all* the unknowns.

The most common strategy for dealing with unknowns in a decision-making scheme is to restrict the calculation to outcomes with a fixed likelihood, usually those conceded as certain ($l = 100$ percent). This strategy means that the entire burden of comparative reasoning falls upon correctly ranking the relative significance (s) of each outcome. Of course, the idealists must be careful: assigning rankings can itself be a way to beat the odds. Since numerical rankings *mathematically guarantee* the conclusion, one might be tempted to play around with them until one gets what is wanted. In hopes of safeguarding against cheats, the idealists insist that the ranking be performed in the most publicly accessible denominator known to humankind: money.

Remember, the idealists want to perform a calculation of *Net Goodness*. If *goodness* is a simple +1 or -1, and *likelihood* is fixed at 100 percent, then the only remaining difficulty is in measuring *significance*. Unfortunately, in hedging the system against unpredictability and cheats, idealist decision-makers have inserted economics into the fray. The problem is this: Is market value a genuine measure of significance? Philosopher Caroline Whitbeck points out that we regularly do make various kinds of value judgments: "Van Gogh is a good painter," "Gödel's proof is a good one," "Reading the Bible is good for you." No doubt, each of these claims will have its objectors. Nevertheless, each claim is fully intelligible. We readily understand, and just as readily argue over, *aesthetic*, *logical*, and *religious* value claims. But as Whitbeck points out, *none* of these value claims translate into dollar signs. Van Gogh was a good painter *before* his paintings sold for millions.

Here's the rub: Ascribing monetary "value" is really not an ascription of value. Monetary "value" does not reflect value; *it only reflects what the economic market can bear.* That being the case, the reliance on monetary value may lead one astray who attempts to perform a calculation for *Net Goodness* (as per Equation 1.1). Famously, in the late 1970s defense attorneys for Ford Motor Company argued that the corporation was blameless in the burn deaths resulting from exploding gasoline tanks in Pinto cars and light trucks.[8] They employed Equation 1 to make the case that Ford did exactly what the numbers obliged them to do: nothing.

The legal case boiled down to two courses of action: (1) recall and repair 11 million Pintos, and 1.5 million light trucks with the same design, by installing a bladder in the gas tank costing a measly $11, or (2) do nothing and settle each lawsuit for wrongful death and property loss on a case-by-case basis. Let's do the numbers:

Outcomes (n = 3)	Likelihood	Goodness	Significance	Net G$_1$
180 burn deaths	100 percent	-1	$200,000	-$36 M
180 serious burn injuries	100 percent	-1	$67,000	-$12 M
2,100 damaged vehicles	100 percent	-1	$700	-$1.5 M
			Net G =	-$49.5 M

FIGURE 1.3 Course of Action 1: Do Nothing

Outcomes (n = 2)	Likelihood	Goodness	Significance	Net G$_2$
11 million cars	100 percent	-1	$11	-$122 M
1.5 million light trucks	100 percent	-1	$11	-$16.5 M
			Net G =	-$137.5 M

FIGURE 1.4 Course of Action 2: Recall and Repair with $11 Tank Bladder

Astute readers often wonder whether the attorneys lowballed the numbers. And why were only *two* courses of action considered? Surely multiple courses of action were open to Ford once it learned of the design flaw. But for the moment, let's stay focused on whether "value" can be measured in dollars. In the Pinto case, the market supplied the data for both the value of a used Pinto ($700) and human loss of life ($200,000). When adjusted for inflation,[9] the approximate value of life in today's dollars would have been placed at $635,000. This figure pales in comparison to the present market value of human life established by the EPA: $9,100,000![10]

Had Ford used the tenfold higher "value" in its calculations, it would have concluded that the morally obligatory course of action was to recall and repair all the tanks. (Just the 180 burn deaths at $7.9 million produces a negative quantity of $1.4 billion, which is almost ten times more than the cost of fixing the tanks!) As it was, Ford used the 1978 market value for life and concluded that, morally speaking, they were in the clear.

Such discrepancy doesn't sit well with us. My older brother owned a Pinto back in the late seventies. Can I really believe that Ford would have been *blameless* had he died in 1978 but *guilty* if he had died in 2010 simply because the market value for his life had increased? Of course not. Our instinct is completely correct—loss of life is always an inestimably bad thing regardless of the market's price tag. (Nevertheless, culture asks engineering firms to move forward with designs that are merely "safe enough." A maximally safe airplane could never get off the ground.)

Equation 1.1 is called *consequentialist* because it is concerned with the outcomes or consequences of a given moral decision. When one uses it to help make a moral decision, one has to deal frankly with the inherent uncertainties of the equation. The form of the equation used by Ford's attorneys is called cost-benefit analysis. As we have seen, it discounts uncertainty in the *likelihood* column by considering only those outcomes that can be conceded as given ($l = 100$ percent). An alternative strategy for dealing with uncertainty in the equation is to fix the significance column (s) instead of the likelihood. In other words, instead of conceding that certain outcomes are bound to happen and then assign a market value to each outcome, the alternative focuses on only one outcome—for example, loss of life—and then works to give precision to prediction of likelihood. Accuracy in prediction is attainable only when vast pools of data are available. For example, actuaries working for large insurance companies can show that the statistical chance of a red car crashing is slightly higher than the chance of a blue one crashing. No one knows for sure why. But given the millions of crashes by blue and red cars, the statistical difference in their rate of incidence is not negligible. This approach is called risk-benefit analysis. Risk-benefit analysis avoids the problem of "market value" because it is based on real-world data rather than the fluctuation of markets. Unfortunately, risk-benefit analysis cheats on the other end of the spectrum by severely restricting itself to immediate (or at least short-range) outcomes. But is this inherently more fair than the kind of confusion that "market value" injects?

Imagine a biologist considering taking a vacation cruise in the Indian Ocean. Socially minded fanatical friends urge the biologist not to go. Rather, they plead, the biologist ought to cash in her tickets and donate the money to relief efforts for the 1.5 million refugees still (in 2011) left homeless as a result of the 2009 Haitian earthquake. Ordinarily, we would say that the surrender of the price of one's vacation to charity is a noble deed. Such a gift might conceivably save many human lives. By lowering incidents of death, the risk-benefit form of the equation *decrees* that giving away the cruise money is even the *obligatory* thing to do.

But wait a minute. It is also conceivable, though in no way knowable, that a much-needed vacation might have a more beneficial *longer-range* result. Perhaps while the cruise ship is anchored in the bay, the biologist takes a day trip to the coast that brings her into contact with the farming practices of a local people, which in turn redirects her own research, resulting in the production of a pesticide that vastly increases grain harvests and feeds many more people than could have been fed by the surrender of the price of her ticket.[11] What I have done here is reminiscent of the work of ethicist Bernard Williams, who was fond of complicating apparently straightforward ethical calculations by the telling of simple, but realistic, stories about how we really live.[12] All such realistic tales remind us that the very best moral reasoning must consider the intangibles—those factors that we can neither predict in advance nor easily place a value upon, perhaps because they are longer-ranged than can be presently seen.

Williams's point about the importance of including such intangibles becomes persuasive when we consider the messy world that we live in with all its hurly-burly. But if we slip into thinking of the world in terms of ideal mechanisms, we may unwittingly overlook some of the very most important factors. Given the innumerable ways things can bind, melt, or break off, it seems unlikely that a good analogy for real-world ethics is that of an *ideal* mechanism. *Fortunately, there is another way.* As we shall see, this way is much closer to real-world engineering than to an ideal mechanism.

The Messy World

Consider a second mechanical example, that of a Bianchi racing bicycle ridden by a fortysomething male competing in "Ride the Bear," a 105-mile road race over the highest paved road in Southern California. The problem of pressure angle disappears because the gear train has been replaced by chain and sprocket.

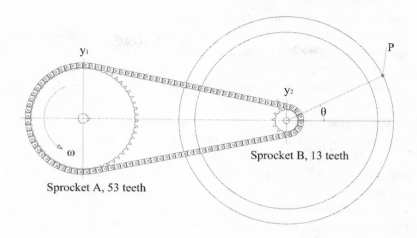

FIGURE 1.5 Bianchi Racing Bicycle with Rear Cassette Ratio 53:13

The ratio between the two sprockets is the same as in Figure 1.1, although in this case another member (the 700 mm wheel) has been added to the train. (In addition, the chain drive means that the rear cassette [sprocket] rotates counterclockwise, matching that of the chain ring.) The front chain ring has 53 teeth, which gives the racer a slight advantage on the flats over rivals who ride models that typically have 52-teeth chain rings. A smaller chain ring is available for climbing hills (it has 42 teeth; real bikers sneer at a 39-teeth chain ring—a.k.a. "Granny gear"—even for steep mountain climbs!).

Owners of racing bikes also have options for the sizes of their rear sprocket set (cassette). An easy set has sprockets with 25-23-21-19-17-15 teeth. The largest sprocket (25) makes for easier uphill climbing. Similarly, a set with much smaller ratios (e.g., 21-19-17-15-13-11-9 teeth) will give the rider more downhill velocity but will be more difficult to pedal. The 23-21-19-17-15-13 set on this particular Bianchi was a good compromise for me. As the owner of this seafoam-green Bianchi, I had the entire middle range of ratios covered and had no problem climbing aggressively (forty-five miles of "The Bear" was uphill). But my top speed was capped at 52 mph. Unless I was in free fall, I could only go as fast as I could spin; and it was physically impossible for my then fortysomething body to exceed a short-burst cadence of 145 rpms (which for 700 mm tires and a maximum gear ratio of 53:13 produced P_{ave} = 52 mph).

Seen from the view of a cyclist, *none* of the interrupting questions raised about the ideal gear train in Figure 1.1 are insignificant. The "load" on the "motor" is constantly varying as terrain shifts. So, "instant acceleration" was impossible, as was steady cadence (ω_{ave} only approximates 220π rad/min.). Friction is *constantly* the enemy. Having one's bottom bracket properly adjusted for optimum range of play was *crucially* important. (Had my Bianchi not been a classic, I'd have opted in a heartbeat for the modern sealed-bearing bottom bracket.) Bearings are *always* in danger of binding and overheating and scoring their races. The ticking noise that developed in my bottom bracket was not only the symptom of its eventual demise; it also reminded me that this was *not* a frictionless system I was pedaling. Air temperature—which in Southern Cal could easily top 100°F—was important data to consider when strategizing how to keep the human "motor" from overheating. (Overheating from lack of water was obviously of greater concern than "bonking," or "hitting the wall," which results from lack of food. When both aerobic and anaerobic fuel have been digested, the body begins to digest itself.) Ironically, when we reached Lake Arrowhead, almost a vertical mile higher than the start, the temperature was in the low 40s). Nor were air speeds negligible. Obviously, if ambient air is still, racers create their own headwind. But with the added bluster of the seasonal Santa Anas, the gusts of which top 50 mph, keeping one's balance was almost as challenging as making headway. (When the Santa Anas swept down Devil's Canyon during an earlier training ride, I had to *stand up in first gear on the flats*.) And stability of the "motor mounts" are of no small consequence: when my head tube tore in half (apparently a failure long in the making) on a particularly steep training ride, my "motor" lost perhaps one-third of its climbing power, since I could no longer pull on my handle bars nor safely throw the frame from side to side.

All questions about context, which rudely interrupt so-called ideal design, are parameters that cannot be ignored if one wants to be a happy biker. "Happy" or "successful" or "good" cycling has only minimally to do with "rules" (obey traffic laws; be courteous to fellow riders by pointing out road debris when they are drafting, etc.). Moreover, happy cycling also has relatively little to do with the principles that have been extrapolated for the ideal mechanism.[13] But it has *everything* to do with real-world messiness: incompletely described scenarios littered with imperfect data and ever-changing conditions. This messiness is the terrain that all human beings share. Mechanical engineering prof Billy V. Koen says that coping with the messiness of the real world makes us all "engineers" of a sort. Human reasoning is none other than the engineering method. Thus Koen describes the engineering method as "a strategy for causing the best change in a poorly understood situation within the available resources."[14]

In this book we are going to scrap the idea of ethics as the ideal case and look at ethics as something messier. Ethics is more like the real-world activity of designing and racing bicycles than it is calculating θ for P_{60} on a technical drawing. But we must be careful! At every step along the way, we will be sorely tempted by the sheer attractive simplicity of the "ideal" case. One way to counter this temptation is to constantly force ourselves to "look and see." We must always ask ourselves, "What is *really* going on here?"

For example, think of how engineering students are initially taught design. At least on the first pass, design is typically taught as a straight-line process. From the textbook diagrams it is easy to imagine that one turns the crank at one end and out pops the innovation at the other end. Consider Figure 1.6 on the following page, depicting the "science" of design from a standard text.

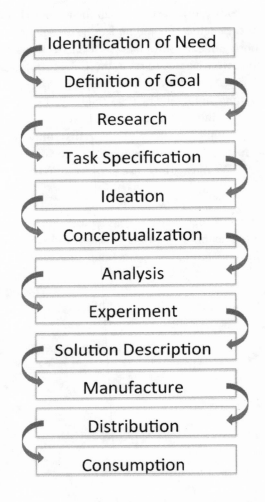

FIGURE 1.6 A Typical Diagram Depicting the "Science" of Design[15]

Now, to be fair to the professors, it is common practice to initiate students into new material with ideal types and later ramp up the complexity of description as students get a more realistic grip on things. (Hopefully, you have already met some of these correctives in your more advanced coursework.) Notice in this diagram that the design process is laid out like a production sequence on an assembly line. Because we are already prone to interpret technical drawings as ideal machines, to use such a diagram of the design process misleads some into thinking that design is analogous to an ideal mechanism (predictable, clear boundaries, etc.).

As they learn, students hopefully graduate to better diagrams, ones that depict the interaction between "stages" as bidirectional, with double arrows indicating feedback loops from subsequent stages.[16] At one point in his publishing, Stuart Pugh used something like the following diagram to convey the design process.

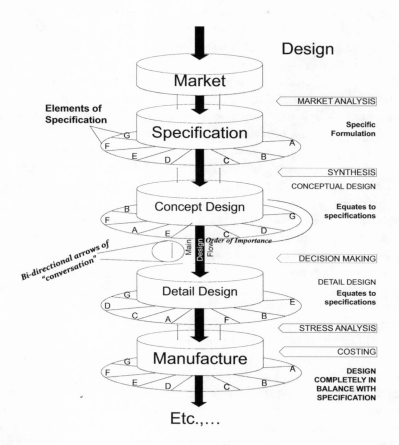

FIGURE 1.7 Design Core[17]

17

You'll notice two things. First, there are bidirectional arrows, which indicate conversation between subsequent stages. Of course, the small size of these arrows relative to the whole seems to suggest that cross-level conversations are at best concessions and at worst interruptions to the overall march toward production, shown by the thick, black downward arrows. Second, the parameters—what Pugh will later call "design boundaries"—are not only rankable, they have been given clear ranking (A through G, "in order of importance"). But of course, in the real world things are *much* messier than this. *All* "stages" have feedback into all other stages. And rankings of design boundaries can only be definitively completed retrospectively. That means it is artificial to say when one stage ends and another begins. Of course, without identifiable stages, the diagram falls apart and ceases to teach anything at all. So the diagram may hint at design as a regular process, but design doesn't really happen this way.

Oddly enough, designers seem to get along just fine despite inhabiting an undiagrammable situation. Real-world design is not straight-line, or even bidirectional; it is "loopy." There are iterations of conversations between various stages. However, these iterations are not inherently convergent, like iterations of the algorithm for calculating the square root of 2. Successive iterations of the square root algorithm give an increasingly precise answer. But in the design process, sometimes further iterations of conversations between stages corrupt, even ruin, a good design. Consequently, teams need to figure out when to *stop* iterating. But the "time to stop" is itself a metric whose optimum cannot be spelled out in advance. Messy, yes?

In addition to the linearity implied about design, there is a second danger lurking in the oversimple diagram. Such diagrams make it look as though the terms in which the project is negotiated are *clear to everyone at each step along the way*. Obviously, there will be disagreements to be sorted out. But the diagram makes it appear that the terms of negotiation are understood by each player: "What problem are we solving? What are we making? How will it function? What metrics ought to be optimized? What issues are open for negotiation? Who has what stake in the outcome?" And so on. But answers to these questions are all achieved—sometimes very slowly and painfully—over time.

So, what is design *really* like? Perhaps design is a bit like a medieval quest, like the search for the Holy Grail. With only the vaguest of ideas about what is sought (What's a "grail"?), a team of relative strangers, whose powers—both singly and together—are untested or uncertain, launch off in some direction. Along the way tests will be faced that will prove mettle, hone skills, clarify what they seek, and reveal how best to keep seeking. A map (or "diagram") could only be constructed retrospectively, *after* the deed is done. In other words, even if a map had been available at the outset of the quest, the nature of a quest is such that, on the front end of the journey, the questers would have been as mystified by the map as they were by the journey itself. (If a group knows where they are going, how to get there, and what they are after, we say they are taking a "trip" rather than going on a quest.) And perhaps engineers often enough require "trips" rather than quests. But we must stay open to the possibility that engineering design often has a quest-like character in order to learn what this is.

The real world is messy. As wonderful and powerful as mathematics and the hard sciences are, they do not perfectly describe the actual world we live in. We live in the messy one. And engineers make the amazing progress they do by remembering that it isn't the real world that approximates math and science. Rather, *math and science are the approximations.* Don't misunderstand: math and science are the very best approximations we can possibly have. In fact, we ought to work hard to mathematically model not only, say, general principles of kinematics, but also all the imperfections involved, such as acceleration (dv/dt) and friction (μ) and so on. And of course, advanced models *do* begin to account for these deviations.[18] But the important difference between scientists and engineers is that whereas science aspires to express an ideal world, engineers *use* both math and science *as tools* for approximating *the real world we actually live in*. That is why the final bar for the engineer is never a theory or a mathematical model, but "look and see": Does it work? Does it work well *enough*? This is not to say that idealized models ought to be completely ignored. Most often, an ideal picture clears the workspace for design; proposals that *defy* the ideal picture do not even make it onto the table. Most often—but not always. For there are cases in which engineering *precedes* science. James Watt had a functioning steam engine long before the first thermodynamics text was written. And centuries before Bernoulli, Eilmer of Malmesbury glided six hundred feet wearing homemade bird's wings![19] (He was quite possibly the only one ever to succeed. Sadly, he broke both legs in landing and remained crippled the rest of his life.) An infamous episode in the history of civil engineering illustrates the bewitching mystique of the ideal picture.

Early in the twentieth century, road building, like many other fields in engineering, depended on a "look-and-see" approach. That is, the skilled eye and trained hand of the experienced practitioner constituted an "empirically derived understanding of nature."[20] In other words, what counted as expertise *inside* civil engineering resided in the know-how of the expert practitioner. Unfortunately, what outsiders wanted was numerical proof.[21] Without "proof" people mistook engineering for a "low-tech" enterprise, forever destined to be less respectable than the more quantitative and "scientific" fields such as electricity (for which the mathematical ideal governs more closely). Some civil engineers felt the urge to "keep up with the Joneses" and tried to justify the expertise they already possessed in their fingertips by collecting numerical data to prove to outsiders what they themselves already knew. This turned out to be a wild goose chase. So, for a time, the federal Bureau of Public Roads (BPR) scrapped the field-testing of new road materials and designs. Rather, they moved the data gathering into a controlled lab environment in the search for repeatable numerical results. For example, the BPR devised a complex machine for simulating the way a truck pounds pavement. The device numerically measured the impact made by a heavy weight falling two inches (the sort of blow a truck delivers when it drives off a two-inch plank). The device was then complexified to simulate any size truck. Yet in order to keep the experiment properly "scientific," only one variable (weight of vehicle, height of drop, thickness of pavement, the type of underlying soil, etc.) could be altered per trial. After months, even years, of testing, the BPR had collected exhaustive data—but only for *a single* kind of subsoil! Drainage of the soil was not even on the radar. Nor was the effect of the recoil action of truck springs initially considered. Still, federal road builders doggedly followed the BPR data and began constructing roadways that were thick at the center—where the wheels touched most often—and thin at the edges.

Fortunately, a number of states, perhaps too poor to afford the equipment and too much in a hurry to wait for yet more federal experiments, simply laid down sixty-eight sections of road, each about fifty yards long, with various designs, thicknesses, materials, soils, and drainage patterns, and then assigned a fleet of trucks (from 2,500–13,500 lbs.) to drive on it nonstop. Eventually, fifty of the sections were pounded into failure. The surviving eighteen sections were deemed superior designs. Some of the results were intuitive (e.g., concrete outperformed brick). But one result was startling: the best road design was one that was thick at the edges and thin in the middle, the very *opposite* of the conclusion demanded by BPR's theoretical ideal.

The lesson to be learned? Don't succumb to the bewitchment of thinking you have the ideal answer. In an ideal picture, or an idealized model, there is always the implication that if we look hard enough, we'll find the single correct solution. But in the messy world, things are different. This is not to say that anything goes. In the absence of a single correct solution, we are not thereby free to do whatever pleases or amuses us. No! Some proposals are clearly wrong. (For example, those that simply do not work or cannot be built.) However, *there may be more than one right solution*. In all fields of engineering the activity taken in response to the messiness of the actual world, when no answer is to be found in the back of the book, is the real field of *engineering design*.

CONVERSATION IS CRUCIAL TO DESIGN

In this book we shall discover that *engineering ethics is analogous to real-world engineering design*. There is no substitute for actually doing design work en route to learning what design is. But short of field experience, we shall have to rely on the observations of those who have taken the trouble to "look and see." Louis Bucciarelli, professor at MIT, has done just that. After shadowing three different teams doing three unique projects for three separate firms, Bucciarelli was able to spell out why design was neither straight-line nor ideal. His short answer is that *design is a social enterprise that at its core is a conversation spoken in a language of its own invention*. How thoroughly does conversation impinge on good design? On Bucciarelli's view, to the extent that designers talk unwillingly or incompletely, design will inevitably succumb to entropy, or "design degradation." We know that degradation certainly enters through *manufacturing* stages of engineering.[22] But Bucciarelli observed that degradation can result not only from short cuts in manufacturing, but also at the design table. This is plausible if we remember that designers are neither omniscient nor morally perfect. Perhaps one designer unwittingly competes with others.[23] Or perhaps another's emphasis on cost reduction conflicts with someone else's goal of going green. Only in the classroom does the assigning of weights for evaluation happen *a priori* (which is to say, prior to looking and seeing). In the real world these metrics must be *negotiated*.[24] Sometimes these negotiations are both risky and painful.[25]

Depending upon student maturity, design may be introduced to the students by any number of helpful first-order approximations: there are straight-line models, ones that describe overlapping phases, ones governed by computational algorithms, and so on. Whatever pedagogical model is employed, novice students first encounter "design" in the abstract, cut off from actual persons who do actual design work. But real-world engineering design doesn't happen in the abstract any more than it happens by itself. So, engineering students must graduate to the realization that design is something that *people* do. It doesn't make sense to talk about "design" without at the same time talking about people. Each person at the table brings his or her unique blend of skills to the task. But people also complicate things.

Bucciarelli observed that at the outset, each designer, whatever the team, conceives the to-be-completed "object" in ways that differ from her compatriots. In Bucciarelli's words, each team member inhabits her own "object world." The activity of design means bringing our object worlds together by talking long enough until the worlds begin to blend. But at the outset, team members are almost consigned to speak foreign languages with each other.[26]

Perhaps Plato can help us understand Bucciarelli's point. Plato once told a parable about blind persons each describing one part of an elephant by touch and then drawing conclusions about the whole elephant! Feeling a stout leg: "This beast is like a tree!" Feeling the long nose: "This beast is like a snake!" The same sort of thing might happen if each participant spoke a different language in addition to being blind. It would take a very long time to come to terms if everyone were describing the elephant's parts spoke a different language. But Bucciarelli is not talking about French or English. He isn't even thinking about different dialects. He is referring to *sublanguages within* English. Since none of us know the half-million or so words in the English language, it seems likely that entire conversations go on without us being able to understand a single sentence. So, there may be many, many more sublanguages that might be in play than we might first imagine. Still, it's hard to believe Bucciarelli when he says that even within a design firm, like IDEO or OXO, each designer speaks a language unique to her. But perhaps the best policy for our investigation is to "look and see."

For example, in the now famous five-day redesign of a shopping cart, the design firm IDEO utilized a team in which engineers were outnumbered by non-engineers (such as linguists, biologists, marketers, psychologists, etc.). Some will say that IDEO takes this mixed sublanguage approach to the extreme. But Bucciarelli observes that the multiple-languages problem plays out even in ordinary engineering firms in which every designer is

and Peacocke, *Chaos and Complexity*. See also Juarerro, *Dynamics in Action*; Mitchell, *Unsimple Truths*.

7. The French mathematician Henri Poincaré showed that even in simple linear systems like billiard balls colliding, an error in the *nth* decimal place leads to total uncertainty after *n* collisions. "Linear" does not mean "traveling in straight lines," although billiard balls tend to do this. "Linear" here means solvable with simple algebra. Conservation of momentum, equations using *mv*, does not require differential equations to solve. See Polkinghorne, *Science and Providence*, 28–29.

    Systems of physical measurement inevitably run up against Heisenberg's uncertainty principle. Given Planck's constant, Poincaré's work leads to the conclusion that linear systems—those solvable by simple algebra rather than differential equations—become entirely unpredictable after something on the order of 30–40 or so collisions. How then do Rube Goldberg devices work? (For example, see Honda's "The Cog": http://www.youtube.com/watch?v=_ve4M4UsJQo.) I suspect that such devices have moments of "re-start"; rather than being actual pre-predicted chains of 50+ collisions, they are groups of shorter chains, each ending with a binary event rather than a continuation of the series. For example, a good pool player may be able to regularly pocket a ball after three collisions. The pocketing completes the chain. The act of falling into the pocket is not unpredictable as if instead of falling into the pocket, a fourth precise collision needs to happen.

8. The details of this case are easy to find. See, for example, Hoffman, "Ford Pinto."

9. The conversion factor for 1978 dollars is 0.314. Inflation adjustment data from the Web site maintained by Oregon State University: http://oregonstate.edu/cla/polisci/individual-year-conversion-factor-tables.

10. The numbers vary: the federal Transportation Department uses a figure close to $6 million, whereas the FDA has declared a life was worth $7.9 million. Appelbaum, "As U.S. Agencies Put More Value on a Life, Businesses Fret." See also Fahrenthold, "Cosmic Markdown."

11. This story has precedent. The Neem tree has been used for centuries by continental Indians as a pesticide. In 1992 W. R. Grace tried to establish a patent on the active ingredient derived from Neem, *azadirachtin*. See Severance, Spiro, and Werhane, "W. R. Grace & Co. and the Neemix Patent (a)," 399–409.

12. Perhaps the most famous of these involves a botanist named Jim who stumbles upon a village in the Amazon basin while looking for flowers. "Jim finds himself in the central square of a small South American town. Tied up against the wall are a row of twenty Indians, most terrified, a few defiant, in front of them several armed men in uniform. A heavy man in a sweat-stained khaki shirt turns out to be the captain in charge and, after a good deal of questioning of Jim which establishes that he got there by accident while on a botanical expedition, explains that the Indians are a random group of inhabitants who, after recent acts of protest against the government, are just about to be killed to remind other possible protestors of the advantage of not protesting. However, since Jim is an honored visitor from another land, the captain is happy to offer him a guest's privilege of killing one of the Indians himself. If Jim accepts, then as a special mark of the occasion, the other Indians will be let off. Of course, if Jim refuses, then there is no special occasion, and Pedro here will do what he was about to do when Jim arrived, and kill them all. Jim, with some desperate recollection of schoolboy fiction, wonders whether if he got hold of a gun, he could hold the captain, Pedro, and the rest of the soldiers to threat, but it is quite clear from the setup that nothing of that kind is going to work: any attempt at that sort of thing will mean that all the Indians will be killed, and himself. The men against the wall, and the other villagers understand the situation, and are obviously begging him to accept. What should he do?" Yikes! Cited in Pojman, *Ethical Theory*, 191–92. See also Mulhall, "Mortality of the Soul," 355–79.

13. Remember that mathematical "laws" are unattainable asymptotes for real machines. As such, *math approximates reality* and not the other way around. Math is at best a "rule of thumb" for real-world problems. More on this in chapter 3.

14. We will later consider his more complete definition: "the engineering method is the use of heuristics to cause the best change in a poorly understood situation within the available resources." Koen, *Discussion of the Method*, 9, 28.

15. Adapted from the diagram by Hill, *Science of Engineering Design*, 49. Notice that the book's title pairs engineering with "science" rather than the older understanding of engineering as an art form. *Ars mechanicus* will be explored in chapter 10.

16. Despite drawing the specious analogy between design and the scientific method, Hill does note that, perhaps unlike science, design requires the iteration of some steps along the way. See ibid., 36–38. Similarly, Stuart Pugh acknowledges bidirectional feedback between stages of design. However, Pugh downplays this give and take on grounds that feedback diminishes as design progresses. See Pugh, *Creating Innovative Products Using Total Design*, 267–68.

17. Compiled from various diagrams used by Pugh over the course of his lifetime. See Pugh.

18. However, even here we must be careful. Modelers cannot account for all the imperfections. Every computer model divvies up reality into chunks in order to make the calculations manageable. It is precisely here that engineers are in danger, when they forget to consider the modeler's assumptions. See Ferguson, "How Engineers Lose Touch."

19. White, "Eilmer of Malmesbury."

20. Seely, "Scientific Mystique," 675–702.

21. For an account of math used rhetorically, see Seife, *Proofiness*.

22. For example, the Boston Tunnel was originally designed to be tiled with metal-plated porcelain. Unfortunately, this expensive tile was substituted with cheaper, but much heavier, concrete ones. Famously, five three-ton ceiling sections failed and crushed a car, killing a woman on her way to the airport. Wald, "Late Design Change."

23. Amélie Rorty has written a clever satire showing how blindness sets in among team members. See her "How to Harden Your Heart."

24. Bucciarelli, *Engineering Philosophy*, 20.

25. Ibid., 14. For a much more technical account of design discourse, see Bucciarelli, "Between Thought and Object," 219–31.

26. ". . . different forms of expressions go hand in hand with different ways of thinking about the world, about the existence of conceptual entities—their ontological status—and about the meaning and scope of the principles and requirements of the different paradigmatic sciences that frame thought and practice within object worlds. My framing of design as a social process in which different participants work within different object worlds which, in some restricted sense are incommensurable worlds, leads me to claim they *speak different languages*." Bucciarelli, *Engineering Philosophy*, 15. Whew! That's a mouthful. By

the way, why do professors write in such a complicated fashion? Might it be that sometimes profound or complex ideas can only be expressed in profound or complex ways? Could you explain differential equations to a ten-year-old?

27. Bucciarelli writes about three firms he shadows and their three respective design problems: a photovoltaic array for lighting highways in Saudi Arabia, a problem of dropout in quality for images of a high quantity photo-printer, and an X-ray machine for inspecting large cargo crates. Bucciarelli, *Designing Engineers*.

28. Bucciarelli, *Engineering Philosophy*, 15.

29. ". . . object world language is a *proper* language." Ibid., 16.

30. Ibid., 16–21.

31. In Bucciarelli's terms, "object worlds are incommensurable." Ibid., 20.

32. Wittgenstein, *On Certainty*, §§99, 97, 256.

33. This kind of trust toward others is one example of what Danish ethicist Knud Løgstrup called "the sovereign expressions of life." Or what John Howard Yoder called working "with the grain of the universe." Hauerwas, *With the Grain of the Universe*; Løgstrup, *Ethical Demand*.

34. "Different participants with different responsibilities, competencies and interests, speak different languages when working, for the most part alone, in their respective domains (electrical circuits, kinematics, linguistics, psychology, and so on). For this to ring true, we ought to construe language in the broadest terms—to include the sketch, the prototype, the charts, even a computer algorithm as elements employed in the productive exchange among participants. But individual effort within some disciplinary matrix does not suffice: *Designing is a social process; it requires exchange and negotiation as well as intense work within object worlds.*" Bucciarelli, *Engineering Philosophy*, 21. Emphasis added.

2

ETHICS AS DESIGN

REMEMBER THE AUTOPSY SCENE from the film *Men in Black*? Things were proceeding normally for Dr. Laura Weaver when (suddenly!) the head of the cadaver pops open, revealing a tiny alien (a.k.a. The High Priest of Baltia) surrounded by an array of levers and pedals. The "human" wasn't a human at all, but a robot. And the "skull" of the humanoid did not house a brain but a control room. The little alien's entire world was this control room. Of course, the little alien had to worry about unpredictable contingencies, namely, the theft of his galaxy by a giant cockroach. But its immediate "world" was a sophisticated clockworks; the humanoid host only mimicked something alive. In reality the humanoid was just a complex mechanism. In fact, every movement, down to the smallest twitch, was nothing but an effect caused by a corresponding pull or push of these levers and those pedals.

Sometimes we seem to behave as though *we* live inside a clockworks, like the High Priest of Baltia. His ruse required great diligence—he'd better not fall asleep in the chair! But at least the little Baltian had the advantage of knowing that every action initiated—turn this cog, tense that spring, advance that ratchet, depress this lever—had a fully predictable, mechanically driven outcome.

However, *our* bodies are not machines, nor is our world a clockworks. Our world is something far messier . . . both it and we are *alive*. We respond to our complex and sometimes problematic surroundings *not* as mechanical automatons, but as living, speaking human beings. Each intentional response to life's hurly-burly constitutes an act of *design*.

To do something "by design" is to do something *on purpose*. Sometimes this involves a great deal of planning, other times relatively little.[1]

31

We design parties, research papers, workout schedules, menus, social calendars, travel itineraries, and color schemes for our walls. My children used to spend hours upon hours sorting and re-sorting and *re-re-sorting* baseball cards. This too is an act of design.

In the last chapter, we began to see that design problems are not at all like following an ideal picture. Philosopher Caroline Whitbeck has pointed out three major differences between design thinking and solving for the position of P_{60} (recall Figure 1.1). First, design questions are *open-ended*.[2] They are not brainteasers or puzzles (much less dilemmas) to be "solved." Instead of looking for *the solution*, design problems require a satisfactory *response*, and often an *ongoing series* of satisfactory responses.

Second, *the character of a response is a function of the character of the designer(s)*. The "character" in question involves much more than the sort of creative insight needed to solve, say, $\int dx/(1+e^{-x})$. And in some sense, the character of the designer is expressed in the response. The designed response *embodies* both the technical skills of the designer and the designer's character, which is to say, the designer's moral skill set as well as his or her technical skills. In 2001, American Ken Frantz flew to Ethiopia to build for the villagers of Sebara Dildiy a bridge over the Blue Nile simply because he happened to see a *National Geographic* special that showed their rickety, often washed-out bridge. His gift of a stable bridge that could withstand spring flooding was welcomed with great joy by the villagers. This was the beginning of Bridges to Prosperity, a nonprofit dedicated to constructing well-made bridges for people who are too poor to afford them. Since Sebara Dildiy, Frantz has built more than forty bridges in seven countries—and counting. Each bridge is a satisfactory response that embodies both technical prowess and kindness. But Frantz's first response, his first act of design, happened because *he detected a need and took it personally*. In other words, in addition to displaying both *technical expertise* and *kindness*, the bridge at Sebara Dildiy also embodies Franz's *openness to others* (the opposite of self-centeredness). In fact, the moral quality of openness to others is part of what Whitbeck means by saying that good design is "open-ended."

Third, design problems are entirely unlike problems of the form "Predict θ for P_{60}." In the words of Rittel and Webber, design problems are "wicked" problems.[3] Don't be misled by the humorous label. For Rittel and Webber, "wicked" is a technical term. Here are their top ten reasons why design problems are rightly called "wicked":

1. "There is no definitive formulation of a wicked problem." In other words, design becomes tricky because differing solutions will emerge as a function of *how the problem is described*. There may be a functional expert who calls the shots (namely, the supervisor). But no designer is so omniscient as to give the only and exhaustively true description of what is going on and of what is sought.[4] No such description is possible. Wicked!

2. "Wicked problems have no stopping rule." In other words, there are no clear-cut criteria for saying the problem is solved well enough to stop working on it. Solutions can always be tweaked and improved. So, when does one stop? Wicked!

3. "Solutions to wicked problems are not true-or-false" but better or worse. And since good and bad come in shades of grey, there is no right answer to be found in the back of the book. "Solutions" must be compared to each other on grounds that require judgment calls over something's relative "goodness." Since "goodness" is unique to each sublanguage that employs it, the term's meaning is not static. Instead, criteria for measuring good must be negotiated. Wicked!

4. "There is no immediate and no ultimate test of a solution to a wicked problem." Unlike mathematical solutions, there is no way to "prove" that the response is the right answer (although putative "proofs" are often craved for their rhetorical power[5]). We only know for certain when a response is *un*satisfactory, and then only retrospectively, when it fails. Wicked!

5. "Every solution to a wicked problem is a 'one-shot operation'; because there is no opportunity to learn by trial-and-error, every attempt counts significantly." For example, one cannot build a trial dam and then change the design once the dam has failed—costing the lives of hundreds of people—and designers have had the chance to learn from their mistakes. Wicked!

6. "Every wicked problem is essentially unique." In other words, one cannot consistently generalize from one satisfactory response to a one-size-fits-all template. Wicked!

7. "The planner has no right to be wrong." Real-world design is no longer school; the stakes are high and, as they say, the bullets are real. You only have one shot to make sure the bear-strap on the airplane fuselage fits properly[6] or the hydraulic ram shears the pipe.[7] Wicked!

8. "Every wicked problem can be considered to be a symptom of another [wicked] problem." In other words, each design solution is itself "proactive" and thus alters the conditions of the problem. Consequently, designs have unforeseeable consequences that become the occasion for the need of another design response, and so on—*endlessly.* Wicked!

9. "The existence of a discrepancy in representing a wicked problem can be explained in numerous ways. The choice of explanation determines the nature of the problem's resolution." In other words, that there are debates over which way to solve a given problem is itself a design problem. For example, if a problem can be solved either mechanically or electronically, then once that choice is made, the rails are laid down for one class of solutions (and its correlative class of problems) but not others. Yet how to decide which set of rails to lay down?[8] Nevertheless, decisions must be made. Wicked!

10. "Wicked problems do not have an enumerable (or an exhaustively describable) set of potential solutions, nor is there a well-described set of permissible operations that may be incorporated into the plan." In other words, one can never be sure that the set of proposals currently under consideration constitute *all* the good possibilities that might be feasible. If a team knew with certainty that there was a finite number of solutions—say, six of them—then they could calculate how much stock to place in any one solution. But, in fact, no one knows even the number of possibilities that can be dreamed up. This is a double-edge sword. If a team doesn't take with utmost seriousness the current idea on the table (which is to say, if they don't treat it as if it were their last hope), then they won't develop the full potential of the idea. On the other hand, if they treat whatever is on the table as the last hope, they may blind themselves to an entirely different class of possible solutions. Wicked!

So then, when faced with substantive (nontrivial) design problems, we would be silly to pine for a uniquely correct answer. Of course, there are innumerable *wrong* answers. Just because a problem has no one right answer doesn't mean that anything goes. Some proposals will be clearly and flatly wrong. Moreover, there may be many more than one satisfactory response. How does one decide between rival proposals? That is the tricky bit. As Whitbeck observes, the *advantages and disadvantages are relative to a given idea*; each roughly satisfactory response will have its own distinctive pros and cons, with the result that comparing two possible responses may be as difficult as comparing apples and orangutans.

Now notice the similarity that can be drawn between design problems and moral problems:

- "There is no single, correct design. There may be entirely wrong designs. But within the range of roughly acceptable solutions to a design problem, each proposed solution must be evaluated for its relative satisfactoriness."

- "There is no single right answer in ethics. There may be entirely wrong answers. But within the range of roughly acceptable responses, each proposed answer must be evaluated for its relative satisfactoriness."

In another seminal article, Whitbeck argues that "solving actual moral problems is not simply a matter of choosing the 'best' of several possible responses. It is also a matter of *devising* possible responses."[9] When issues are researched and described in ways that are thick enough to capture the uncertainties of a particular situation together with the dynamic, open-ended character of the problem, then the complex nature of an appropriate response becomes evident.[10] A satisfactory response may involve either *solving* or *coping*, or aspects of *both*. But if one response is "satisfactory," then, as we have already seen, there are bound to be any number of other satisfactory responses.[11] It is not the case that there is only one right answer in design. Nor is it the case that there is always a single right response in ethics. But also like design, each response to a moral problem may not be as good as another: "Although there is not a uniquely correct solution, nonetheless some possible responses are clearly unacceptable—there are wrong answers even if there is no unique right answer, and some solutions *are* better than others." Importantly, this does *not* imply that there is a single "best" answer: Whitbeck notes that "for interesting or substantive engineering design problems there is rarely, if ever, a uniquely correct solution; nevertheless two solutions may each have advantages of different sorts, so it is not necessarily true that for any two candidate solutions one must be incontrovertibly better than the other."[12] If this comparison holds, then moral reasoning within engineering is not an exercise in problem solving or plug-and-chug theoretical reasoning. Whitbeck adds: "Because engineering recognizes the importance of engineering design as well as engineering theory, it appreciates the importance of practical as well as theoretical problems and of synthetic as well as analytic reasoning. Devising a good response requires *synthetic reasoning*. Ethics has paid more attention to analytic reasoning and the analysis of ethical problems and possible answers to them. Analysis is important but it is not sufficient to devise responses."[13]

We will return to what is meant by "synthetic reasoning" in chapter 5. Surprisingly, not only does ethics offer correctives to design, *design* offers a corrective to ethics: "most of recent ethics and applied ethics have neglected the perspective of the moral agent. Instead, ethics has exclusively emphasized the perspective of the judge or that of a disengaged critic who views the problem from 'nowhere' and treats it as a 'math problem with human beings.'"[14]

But ethics, like design, is not a math problem. It cannot be solved from afar. Rather, the designer/ethicist must become involved, not only with the specifics of the situation on the ground, but also deeply enough so that his or her own perspectives begin to change. (This means that design is self-involving, a topic that we will take up in chapter 6.) It is natural to draw the following lesson from Whitbeck's essay: issues of moral responsibility are issues of "response-ability." In other words, moral reasoning involves actual subjects engaging a particular situation, learning to see, learning to ask questions, learning to brainstorm—in short, learning to design.

So then, from here on out we can compare features of ethical reasoning profitably with features of design thinking. Often the resemblance is so striking that we can treat these two modes of reasoning as synonymous. These similarities enable us to describe both ethics and design in terms of three family resemblances: *heuristics, design periphery*, and *practical reasoning*. We'll not get to practical reasoning until chapter 5. But heuristics and the design periphery will occupy the rest of this chapter.

1. Heuristics

Let's return to the problem of describing design to someone who has never done it or seen it done. We saw that some diagrams of the design process (e.g., the "science" of design, Figure 1.6) give the false impression of design as a very straightforward process with tidy boundaries for each phase: here designers commence "identifying the goal," next they stop "identifying the goal" and begin "research," now they cease "researching" and begin "task specification," then comes "ideation" (whatever *that* is), and so on. We then examined a slightly more nuanced diagram from Stuart Pugh that is somewhat more faithful to the gritty and iterative character of real-world design. The gist of Pugh's diagram has been reproduced as Figure 2.1.

Remember some of the observations we made in the last chapter. A couple of changes in Figure 2.1 are improvements over Figure 1.6, but still do not yet quite line up with the actual messiness of design. First, Pugh allows for give and take between the phases, represented by pairs of vertical double arrows. In comparison to the entire diagram, these arrows are admittedly very small, a visual suggestion that the give and take between phases is either infrequent or not very disruptive. In general, the diagram seems pretty optimistic: the bold downward arrows indicate things march confidently onward until the manufacturing phase achieves the impossible: "Design completely in balance with specification"! Second, the "Elements of Specification" (listed as A through G) appear to hem in as well as express the order of the process of design thinking. In other words, the diagram seems to imply that design work happens within the tidy perimeter set up by these specs. Each specification is assigned a letter that will be used to signify its respective "order of importance." The ranking of these specs appears to happen early on in the process and makes it look as though negotiating priorities is already complete from the beginning of the "Concept Design" phase. This is more than a bit misleading. According to Bucciarelli and others, loud and hot negotiation may haunt the design process until the bitter end.

In real life, the so-called phases of design have fuzzy boundaries. That being the case, we would do better to identify the phases by their conversational *centers* rather than trying to define them by their boundaries. Consider: Young children can be forced to stay in a particular play area by fencing (a boundary). Or, one can set up an ice cream stand in the middle of the play area. Both the ice cream and the fence succeed in keeping the children on location. But the ice cream stand works differently than the fence. A conversational center is like the ice cream; it reins in conversation *as if* there were a fence, but no coercion is involved.

A reminder: We must not be too hard on the authors of these diagrams. It is a mark of our inexperience that we tend to read a design diagram as if it were the ideal picture and then chastise the author for our wrongheaded approach! An experienced reader knows that these diagrams, like technical drawings, are approximations within the real, messy business of design work. The diagrams are not standards against which design is measured. Rather they are teaching tools to acclimate novices to an activity for which they have limited experience.

The impossibility of concocting an ideal picture of design process is one indication that design does not happen with mathematical tidiness. But that doesn't mean design is *non*rational. The actual activity of design may not be tidy or linear, but it is nevertheless completely rational—provided we understand "rational" in the right way. Design is not governed by ideals, as though each designer closes his or her eyes and sees in the mind's eye a finished product with photographic clarity. Rather, designers *construct* their designs with others over time. Designers make headway in this constructive process in the most rational way possible: by means of time-tested "tips," or "rules of thumb," or "heuristics."

Some of the "tips" extrapolated from expert design may strike us as a bit trivial. For example, consider the maxim "At the appropriate time, freeze the design and go into production."[16] Is this reliable advice? Well, yes, of course. If a team never freezes the design, the thing will never get built. Alternatively, it is equally true that one can move too quickly and end up manufacturing an inferior design. So the maxim is a good one.

What makes the maxim a "tip"—or what we shall from now on call a *heuristic*—is the ambiguity of the phrase "at the appropriate time." *When* is this? Because there is no ideal picture involved, the notion of "the appropriate time" cannot be specified in advance or with mathematical precision. Still, *some* kind of knowledge is involved, because outsiders and novices can only *guess* at the time. Those who do not have the foggiest idea when the appropriate time is do well to defer to those who do know. The ones who actually know are not simply those who have the power to *dictate* the timetable (although some supervisors do simply follow a predetermined schedule). The ones who actually know are those who are most experienced in design; they possess skilled judgment or "know-how" (or in this case, "know-when").

1.1 Optimization and Heuristics

The heuristic "at the appropriate time" is an example of an optimization heuristic. Optimization heuristics express the two (or more) terms that must be balanced against each other in a maximal way. Here is another: "Allocate resources so long as the cost of not knowing exceeds the cost of finding out."[17]

In January 2006, the roof of an indoor ice rink in the German town of Bad Reichenhall collapsed under the weight of recent snow. Fifteen skaters were killed, twelve of whom were children. The outcry was immediate:

"Could this disaster have been averted?" Since the question could apply to every public building, within two weeks of the tragedy, scholarly engineering journals began to publish recommendations for how to proceed. Consider two sets of recommendations:

- Christian Grosse (UC Berkeley) and Markus Krüger (University of Stuttgart) recommended combining four techniques of monitoring public structures: (1) visual examinations, together with (2) a wireless sensor network—for example, micro-electric mechanical systems (MEMS); together with (3) radar; together with (4) impact-echo techniques.[18]

- Udo Peil (Technology University of Braunschweig) offered somewhat contrasting advice that took seriously the need to accept a realistic lifetime for buildings as a way to control spiraling costs involved in extending the life span of aging buildings.[19]

Although both articles recommended monitoring, one can get a sense of the need to balance two opposing values. The use of MEMS and radar and impact-echo techniques may indeed have succeeded in spotting structural faults in a roof designed to hold 150 kg/m^2 of snow (admittedly low by today's standards, but still 10 percent more than needed for the actual snowfall of this storm[20]). So what prevents the immediate implementation of these for *all* of Germany's public buildings? Sheer lack of *Deutsche Marks*! No municipality has funds for renting (much less owning) high-tech equipment and for paying a team to install and monitor the data. Clearly the heuristic in play is "Balance safety and cost." Here we can see what Whitbeck means by saying that "best" doesn't mean the same thing on every occasion. We can compare two proposals with respect to safety and say which one is "best." And we can compare two proposals with respect to cost and say which one is "best." But how does one begin to use "best" when the safety is evaluated against cost?

What makes "Balance safety and cost" a *heuristic* is the fact that the statement contains reference to a balance point that cannot be specified in advance. We saw with the Ford Pinto case (see chapter 1) that the value of safety cannot be expressed financially. But even if "safety" could be quantified, the balance point is not calculable by taking the arithmetic average. We are right to suspect that the balance point is *more* on the side of safety than in the middle, but how much to this side? This is a determination that *requires skilled judgments* to be made (a judgment of value is the function of experience in such matters) and for those making such judgments to negotiate some kind of consensus for this time and place.

According to ancient Greek ethics, Aristotle's Golden Mean expresses the same concept of rational balancing. It was possible to have too much of a good thing as well as not enough. The optimal amount was what Aristotle called the Golden Mean.

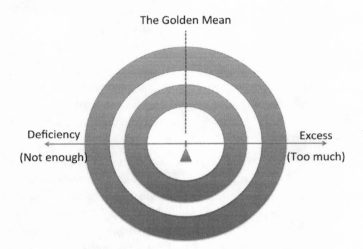

FIGURE 2.2: Aristotle's Golden Mean

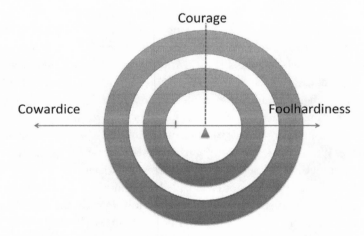

FIGURE 2.3 Courage as a "Mean"

Consider, for example, the virtue of courage. Is it possible to be *overly* courageous? Of course. Someone who is too courageous is said to be rash or foolhardy. But the opposite is also true; it is possible to be not courageous enough. Such a person is called a coward. So where does courage lie? Not on the arithmetic midpoint between rashness and cowardice, but rather *a little to the side of foolhardiness*. In other cases, the Golden Mean is pinned to one pole. For example, there is no optimum midpoint between fidelity and infidelity in marriage! The Golden Mean lies at the extreme end of the continuum. One can be deficient in fidelity. But there is no way—in Aristotle's mind, at least—no way to be *too* faithful to one's spouse.

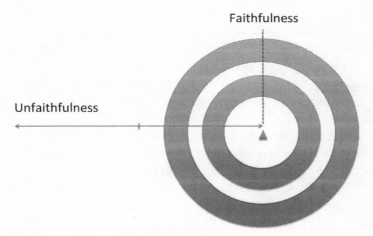

FIGURE 2.4 Fidelity as a "Mean"

Aristotle was not writing about engineering heuristics. But he might as well have been. For Aristotle, not everyone can rightly judge the location of the Golden Mean (or "middle"). On his view, the one who alone is able to recognize the Golden Mean is the one who habitually exemplifies the Golden Mean in daily living. Those who are not yet courageous are puzzled as to where courage lies on the spectrum. But those who are habitually courageous, do know.

The same is true for the expert practitioner of engineering. Of course, no one is fully developed in his or her expertise; but one may be developed "enough" to begin practicing the making of particular, small-scale, low-risk decisions. (And, as you probably guessed, figuring out this "enough" is itself a heuristic.) The experienced practitioner already has a sense of where that balance point is and so does not need the advice of the heuristic "Balance safety and cost." Unfortunately, those who need the heuristic the most, those who are still inexperienced and therefore unskilled in making judgments, are the very ones who are ill-equipped to use the heuristic. Consequently, expert practitioners keep careful watch over the novices they are mentoring. But since no mentor can watch everyone all the time, expert practitioners have *codified* a number of balance points, which is to say, turned them into black-and-white stipulations so that newbies don't get it wrong. For example: "For elevated walkways, use a safety factor (SF) of 2.0." However, in the case of airplanes, SF is 1.5 (since 2.0 will be too heavy). In the case of leaf springs, SF is 1.2. But in the case of a cast-iron flywheel, SF is 13.0![21] These are not magic numbers that can never be improved upon. Nor are they stipulations that correspond to an ideal world. Nor are they exceptionless commands. Rather, these SF numbers are rough summaries of best engineering practice today and are therefore crucially helpful to novices, who, being new to the field, have no clue what SF to use. Because of the nature of heuristics, there will be cause for variance from time to time.[22] And it is very likely that future engineering practice will revise some SF numbers. But for now, they are helpful tips, good places to begin.

Heuristics, then, are rough-and-ready tips that help the inexperienced know how to proceed in imitation of best practice, since no ideal answer can be calculated. Heuristics also identify the terms in which optimization is negotiated. In the current example, the problem is maximizing safety within available resources. Unfortunately, too often "resources" function *de facto* as a hard-and-fast cap. Thus, facing a cost cap may *not* be an optimization problem at all. Perhaps a better example of optimization is close at hand.

One summer my granddaughter (then two years old) beckoned me to "swim" with her in the kiddie pool. The extended family was all vacationing on a piece of largely undeveloped wooded property that had been in the family for generations. I had just returned after clearing a fallen tree from a hiking trail on this northern Minnesota property and was very hot from the chainsawing. To her delight I immediately jumped in—clothes and all. No sooner had I jumped into the kiddie pool than I jumped back out. The pool had just been filled with North Woods water drawn from thirty feet underground and was *freezing* cold![23] Much too cold for a toddler to enjoy herself! (She *stood* gleefully watching me: "Funny Grampa!!") So the optimization problem has these two parts: If the pool is too deep, it stays too cold too long. If the pool is too shallow, it is no fun. In this case the parameters *can* be expressed numerically. The speed of warming up is a function of the surface area, the depth of the pool, the specific heats of air and water, the radiant energy of the sunshine (about 1,350 watts/m^2 on a sunny day), and the difference between the respective temperatures of air and water. (The last term makes the problem one that requires calculus to solve.) The principal variable, water depth, might be anything between one and eighteen inches. Of course, one inch will not be fun "enough." And deeper than eighteen inches means that the pool won't get warm "enough" today for a child to swim. It is the presence of "enough" in the parameters that indicates the need for skilled judgment that marks heuristics. (Of course, the experienced mom cuts through all the calculus and fills the pool halfway early in the day, long before it gets hot, knowing it will be just right by mid-afternoon.)

1.2 Procedures and Heuristics

In addition to optimization problems, another common place one finds heuristics in play is when experts coach novices on how to do something. Sometimes the rationale behind an *operational heuristic* is obvious to the uninitiated: "Measure twice, cut once." Other times the rationale is more mysterious. Consider this heuristic from medicine: "Before surgery, each person in the Operating Room shall introduce himself or herself by first name to all present."[24] This heuristic is the product of a study of hospitals that excel in surgery. The result surprised even the researcher (himself a surgeon): when everyone is on a first-name basis, there is a 35 percent reduction in surgical complications and deaths! Amazing! Perhaps the idea is that when a mistake is about to happen, someone on the team is more likely to speak up if he or she knows others' names. Whatever the reason, the heuristic "Introduce yourself by name before operating" gives a reliable tip to practitioners who are more likely to be preoccupied with complicated technical details than with attending to relational matters. Even when we are unsure of the explanation, the heuristic can be relied upon to work.

On the face of it, of all the heuristics imaginable, the ones having to do with procedures sound most like black-and-white commands. But always keep in mind that these do not depict an ideal picture but tell us something about the needs of the novice for concrete direction. The novice will outgrow them soon enough. Did you catch that? *Some heuristics are for leaving behind as one matures.* For this reason, some expert practitioners make poor teachers. The greater their expertise, the more completely they have internalized heuristics, and therefore they may no longer remember how to give concrete tips that a novice can follow. It is the particular plight of the novice that he or she cannot yet distinguish which heuristics are permanent and which are provisional and temporary.

Many practices are learned by initially taking heuristics *as if* they were permanently binding stipulations. One cannot tell a beginning chess player to "control the center" until he or she has first learned to open up the board by "moving each piece only once in the early game" and "Castle on the king's side ASAP." Or consider the game of soccer. Young children are issued commands like "Don't bunch!" and "Pass the ball!" and "Move the ball away from our goal!" and "Stay wide!" Only as they mature in knowledge and leg strength will they be able to "cross the ball!" Only later will they be able to appreciate the instruction to "look for angles rather than lanes!" It is a waste of time to try to teach five-year-olds the offside trap or to explain a bangoo to children who don't yet obey the offside rule!

Billy Vaughn Koen (professor of mechanical engineering at the University of Texas at Austin) has given us this rough definition of "heuristic": "*A heuristic is anything that provides a plausible aid or direction in the solution of a problem but is in the final analysis unjustified, incapable of justification, and fallible.*"[25] As Koen gleefully admits, the previous sentence is not a definition but rather is itself a heuristic(!), since skilled judgment is required for navigating the built-in ambiguity. Still, several features of heuristics can be summarized:

- First, heuristics tend to greatly reduce the time needed to achieve a satisfactory solution. In this regard heuristics not only rival theoretical reasoning, but often *outperform* theoretical reasoning. Those interested in mastering engineering would do well to give the greatest respect and attention to learning heuristics.

- Second, no heuristic guarantees a solution. Heuristics do not constitute an ideal mechanism, so that after one turn of the crank out pops the solution.

- Third, the acceptability or applicability of any given heuristic is always a function of the immediate context. No absolute standard or ideal picture governs whether a particular heuristic is relevant any more than it could dictate with precision how the heuristic is to be applied. Experience, know-how, and skilled judgment are needed all the way down.

- Finally, any given heuristic may run against the grain of other relevant heuristics, even to the point of contradiction! We must guard against thinking that problems end once we are armed with a handful of heuristics.[26] Rather, once heuristics are in hand, then the design discourse begins in earnest.

One might object that all this blather about heuristics doesn't sound like it makes anything clearer. To this I can only say that if the water is muddy, it only makes things worse to pretend it is clear. Dealing with murky problems is what engineering is all about. In Koen's words, "The engineering method is the use of heuristics to cause the best change in a poorly understood but particular situation within available resources."[27]

2. Design "Boundaries" versus Centers of Design Discourse

Some time ago I had a psychotic friend who couldn't be depended on to take his medication regularly. One time he phoned me out of the blue to advise me (among other things) never to live in Denver because the city planner's middle name had six letters. Hmm . . . "Ed, have you stopped taking your meds?"

My friend's "advice" was built on a true observation—the city planner's middle name *did* have six letters. But as a piece of advice, it was random and unhelpful. In his book *Shop Class as Soulcraft*, Matt Crawford tells the story of the random and unhelpful advice he received concerning ignition trouble in his 1963 VW. When he mentioned it to his dad, his dad simply said, "Ohm's law!" Of course, in a contrived way Ohm's law (*voltage = current × resistance*) is relevant: if resistance is very high (or infinite), voltage *will* be negligible (or zero). That goes without saying. But Crawford complains in his book that the theoretical absolute $V = I \times R$ does *nothing* to help him begin to look for the actual source of failure in this particular car. The story is humorous because his father, something of an abstract intellectual, offered this piece of "advice" with all seriousness. But it was so off topic and wide of the mark that it came across like the ravings of a lunatic!

Design reasoning—and, as we shall see, ethical reasoning—may presume the truth of statements like $V = I \times R$, but not deliberate about them. What *does* receive attention and may comprise the bulk of all assorted design conversations—from memos to napkin sketches, from brainstorming

45

sessions to watercooler chats—is the problem of meshing a particular problem-in-context with best practice heuristics that are most relevant to proposed solutions. Stuart Pugh has characterized features of context as constituting the perimeter within which design thinking happens. If all the possibly satisfactory proposals are "on the table" (the unsatisfactory ones being "on the floor" or "in the trash can"), then parameters of design thinking are represented by the edges of the table. Now, we have seen reasons for taking issue with Pugh's idealistic model of how design happens through time. Recall that Pugh's diagram seems to suggest that "elements of specification" (see Figure 2.1) are clearly ranked very early in the process. Nevertheless, his observations about the design boundary can be appreciated so long as we remember to take each "boundary" to be a *center of conversation*—like an ice cream stand rather than a section of fence. For example, "safety" is a design boundary in the sense that a great deal of conversation is given to it and/or that safety considerations have a great deal of heft in design conversations. Another way of putting it might be to say that a family of heuristics having bearing on safety is relevant to this design and frequently dots the landscape of the team's deliberations.

It is very difficult to diagram these centers of conversation. Some of the topics, like safety, are of greater concern than others. Some of them, like materials, are physical in nature. Others are very black and white and leave little room for conversation, like government regulations. Still, all of these conversation centers create the linguistic space within which design reasoning takes place. We might say these conversation centers give shape and direction to our design discourse. As we proceed, we shall have occasion to analyze the following diagram carefully and put it to much good use.

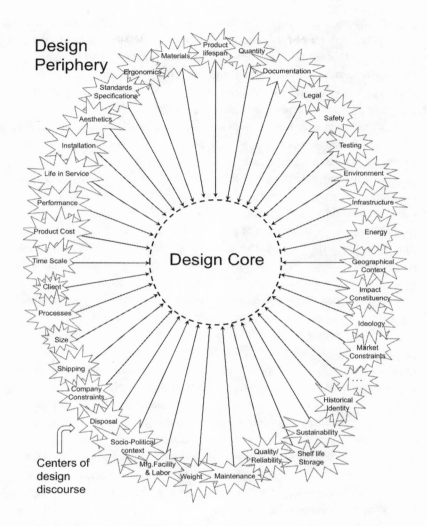

Figure 2.5 Design Periphery and Centers of Discourse[28]

Ethical "Boundaries" versus Centers of Ethical Discourse

Before turning explicitly to practical reasoning in chapter 5, it is worth answering a mystery regarding the relation of ethical reasoning to design periphery: "Doesn't morality function as a boundary around design?" After all, we certainly don't want to produce immoral designs! That being so, why isn't "ethics" (where "ethics" means reflection about rightness or wrongness) listed as one of the conversational centers?

The answer is as important as the question. First, ethics is not the sort of thing that has tidy boundaries. Second, ethics does *not* enter the design process as its own stand-alone conversation center. Figure 2.5 does *not* contain a little starburst with the word *ethics* in it. That is not to say that ethics doesn't show up in design conversation. Of course it does. Rather, ethics is inherent to *every* sub-conversation that constitutes the design process. If you like, ethics is not a little starburst in Figure 2.5, but is more like the color of the paper that Figure 2.5 is printed on—ethics permeates *every* conversation. Moreover, ethics is not always sophisticated and technical. It does not always involve highfalutin terms like *categorical imperative* or *teleological*. Ethics is simply our talk about genuine moral values. As such, ethics permeates ordinary conversation in the most ordinary of ways. Every time we remark "Nice job!" or "You should have clamped that before drilling!" we are showing the fact that value, *moral value*, is already present, even if it is unnoticed. In chapter 3, and again in chapter 5, we will see why this is so. But for the present, we can explain the ubiquitous presence of *morality talk*, a.k.a. *ethics*, by the claim that every intentional action—as opposed to unintentional actions, like absentmindedly scratching my chin—*every intentional action is already moral*.[29] Morality is not a feature that gets added on; we cannot dissect an act into *movement + intention + morality*. These things are inextricable from each other. So it is better for us to think about morality as ever present in the form of "a good that is sought." Granted, an action may be moral in a trivial way. (To seek a Snickers bar will temporarily quench my hunger, and quenching hunger is a good thing because it answers the genuine and legitimate human need for calories.) But so long as some good (or evil) is aimed for, the action is inherently moral and the *talk* about the act is inherently ethical.

This means that ethical questions—here, I am using "ethics" to name all the conversations that have to do with moral action—can be asked for *each* of the centers of design conversations. Each little starburst on Figure 2.2 has one or more ethical questions that are germane to the conversation. For example, suppose we are designing a large-scale dishwashing unit capable of high temperature and high pressure water. The "materials" conversation may consider tubing made of PVC or of copper. Suppose the team leans toward using copper tubing. An example of an ethical question might be, "Where will the copper come from?" Forty percent of industrial copper is imported, and some of it (12.4 percent) comes from large Peruvian mines.[30] These mines are notoriously unsafe and colossally polluting. Consider the mining town of Ilo, Peru, where the air quality is so poor that cars must use their headlights at midday to cut through the soot, and many children suffer long-term lung damage from inhaling SO_2—which becomes H_2SO_4 in the moist environment of the human lungs.[31] In the design conversation about materials, most people will sympathize with the objection, "We shouldn't use copper imported from Peru" and even, "We shouldn't use copper at all if we cannot guarantee excluding from the manufacturing all the copper that comes from Peru."[32]

We are beginning to see that ethics is not its own self-contained design boundary. But wait a minute! If ethics is not its own self-contained design boundary, then what are we to think of professional codes of ethics (PCOE)? If government regulations are listed as a design boundary, should not a PCOE also be listed as a sub-conversation of design? The short answer is that neither ethics, in general, nor PCOE, in particular, "governs" design from "above"—which is to say from outside and above—in the ways that laws and government regulations do. Rather, ethical reasoning is already inside of, and everywhere within, the entire design process. This suggests that the most fruitful way to approach PCOEs is by seeing them as belonging to the family of all relevant design heuristics. We'll pick this up in chapter 4. Of more immediate interest is the nature of ethical argument. In saying, "The Jaws of Life are good," we are using the term *good* both in reference to the device's design (it works well) and in reference to the morally good role this device plays in human life. Since we've already seen that ethics and design resemble each other, we shouldn't be surprised to learn that *good* can be used equally well as ethical vocabulary and as a design term. How to properly employ this term persuasively without becoming tangled is the point of the next chapter.

Discussion Questions

1. Why isn't "Ethics" one of the centers of discourse listed in Figure 2.5?

2. What is a "wicked problem"? Which of the ten symptoms of wicked problems bothered you most? Can you devise an illustration for this symptom?

3. What is design? How does it relate to the person designing?

4. What are "heuristics" and what do they have to do with (a) engineering and (b) ethics?

5. Why should stages of design be thought of as "conversational centers" rather than boundary conditions for doing design?

Notes

1. Examples of the use of the word *design*, both as a noun and a verb, can be found in the *Oxford English Dictionary*. For example, compare the difficulty of *planning a battle* (from 1848, "Grey . . . had concurred in the *design* of insurrection") to the relative ease of *planting an evergreen shrub* (from 1779, "I have glazed the two frames, *designed* to receive my pine plants"). As noun it had been used to indicate *a mental plan or intention* (1734, "with design to besiege"); a *scheme to harm* another (1704, "to have design upon a woman, [is] a modish way of declaring war against her virtue"); a *final perhaps unattainable end or goal* (1711, "Happiness is the natural design of all the world"); *craftiness* (1719, "a faithful . . . servant . . . without passions, sullenness, or designs"); a *decoration* (1863, "To admire the designs on the enameled silver"); a *preliminary set of plans or sketches* (1703, "'Tis usual . . . for any person before he begins to Erect a Building, to have Designs or Draughts drawn upon Paper"); and *the adaptation of means to ends* (1802, "The machine, which we are inspecting, demonstrates, by its construction, contrivance and design"). Ironically, this last use occurs in William Paley's so-called Design Argument for the existence of God-as-Designer, which begins with the questionable notion that the world is a machine.

2. Whitbeck, "Teaching Ethics to Scientists and Engineers."

3. Rittel and Webber, "Planning Problems Are Wicked Problems."

4. Adequate "specification" of the problem is itself an action of practical reasoning. See chapter 5. For something more technical on "best specification" in Aristotle, see Wiggins, "Deliberation and Practical Reason," 228.

5. See Seife, *Proofiness.*

6. Bear-straps strengthen the fuselage around cargo hatches and exits. Whistleblowers accused Boeing assemblers of using "bash to fit" to correct unaligned holes. Kaplan, "Boeing Whistleblowers Say Planes Must Be Grounded." For the FAA's study of Boeing Model 757-200 Series Airplanes, see Federal Aviation Administration, "Airworthiness Directives."

7. The reference is to the massive oil spill that followed the explosion and sinking of the Deepwater Horizon oil rig, leased to BP Oil by Transocean, in April 2010.

8. A similar problem faced Søren Kierkegaard when he observed that how one explains "I have a good job" not only means something different for the hedonist than for the saint, but the two cannot even exchange reasons, since the saint's criteria for "good" are unacceptable to the hedonist and the hedonist's criteria are likewise unacceptable to the saint. For discussion, see MacIntyre, *After Virtue*, 39–45.

9. Whitbeck, "Ethics as Design," 9. Emphasis added.

10. Ibid., 13–14.

11. Ibid., 11.

12. Ibid.

13. Ibid., 10. Emphasis added.

14. Ibid., 15.

15. Pugh, *Creating Innovative Products Using Total Design.*

16. See discussion of Billy Vaughn Koen below.

17. Koen, *Discussion of the Method*, 35. Koen discusses a large number of examples of heuristics in engineering and in other fields.

18. Große and Krüger, "Inspection and Monitoring of Structures in Civil Engineering."

19. Peil, "Life-Cycle Prolongation."

20. Krabbe, "Senseless Deaths in Bad Reichenhall."

21. Koen, *Discussion of the Method*, 67–69.

22. Notice that it would be misleading to refer to these variances as "exceptions." The word *exception* implies that the SF numbers comprise an ideal picture.

23. The permafrost level in mid-Minnesota is somewhere around five feet.

24. Inskeep, "Atul Gawande's 'Checklist' for Surgery Success."

25. Koen, *Discussion of the Method*, 28. Emphasis added.

26. Ibid., 29.

27. Ibid., 28.

28. Adapted from Pugh, *Creating Innovative Products Using Total Design*, 357.

29. St. Thomas Aquinas, writing in the thirteenth century, may have been the first to spell this out. See Pinches, *Theology and Action*.

30. Workman, "Us Copper Exports and Imports in 2007."

31. For a heartrending tale of pollution and disease in Ilo, Peru, see Kim et al., *Dying for Growth*, 192.

32. Admittedly, ethical consideration may seem outside the bounds of designer control. But even if there are one hundred degrees of separation, one is still complicit in the goods and evils that are done more directly by others. And to claim ignorance may not render the designer guiltless if consequent ignorance is involved. For example, see Binswanger, "Challenge of Faust," 640–41.

3

ARGUING ABOUT GOOD DESIGN

IF ETHICS RESEMBLES DESIGN, and good design requires talking with each other, it should not surprise us that ethics too involves talking. And while our society often uses "moral" and "ethical" interchangeably, ethicists will sometimes distinguish between them this way: morality has more to do with what is right and wrong; ethics has more to do with those conversations in which we defend what is right and wrong.

Before we begin thinking about ethics as argument, there are a few cautions to attend. First, I will generally follow the above distinction between morality and ethics. But this distinction is not hard and fast. If a person is a whiz at constructing ethical arguments but lives like a schmuck, such a person would be a double failure—both a failure at morality and a failure at ethical argumentation. This is because, as it is commonly assumed, solid ethical reasoning ought to be self-persuasive. If someone is unconvinced by their own ethical argument and so lives like the devil, we rightly assume that something is wrong—wrong with the individual and quite possibly wrong with their arguments. Granted, our intuitions about human nature obviously prevent us from taking this too far, that is, from thinking that solid ethical argument will compel people to be good. After all, we say, "We're only human!" (We'll see in a later chapter that our intuitions are correct on this point.) Yet we also intuitively reject the idea that ethical argument has no connection whatsoever with how we live. So, as important as it is to be clear about what makes for good ethical argument, ethics-as-argument is only a small part of a much bigger story about how to live well.

Second caution. Arguments—the kind that can be spoken or written—are generally evaluated along three lines: completeness, soundness, and validity. The test of completeness asks, "Have we forgotten any relevant premises?" The criterion of soundness asks, "are all the premises true or factual?" And the metric of validity inquires, "does the logical linkage between premises work correctly?" Beginning students often think that the most difficult task is ferreting out the logical form of an argument and discerning whether this linkage is valid or invalid. But in fact, a more common way to go astray is failing to ask, "Have we forgotten any relevant premise?" This is difficult because getting it right depends on a combination of the sharpness of one's moral eyesight and how well formed one's moral imagination is. Here, then, is the second caution: Don't become so enamored with constructing ethical argument that you neglect the more important task (to which the middle and later chapters of this book are devoted), namely, embarking on the journey of clarifying your own moral vision and educating your own moral imagination. One can begin to master ethical argumentation in a matter of weeks or months, but moral vision and imagination is a much longer journey.

A Provisional Paradigm for Arguing about Good and Bad Design[1]

The most concise form of an ethical argument is called a Value Statement.[2] Here is an example:

> *Value Statement*: "Professional Engineering (P.E.) licensure[3] will land you a government job."

There are two parts to this statement. First, there is a *value claim*. A *value claim* is an implicit or explicit claim that something is *good/bad, obligatory/permitted/forbidden, right/wrong*, etc. The italicized terms, as well as others such as *should/shouldn't* and *ought/oughtn't*, are generally thought to constitute moral vocabulary. In the above statement, we can easily detect that the speaker of this Value Statement is "thumbs-up" about getting one's P.E. license. Although the moral term is implicit, we might rewrite the Value Statement in these ways:

> *Value Claim*: "You *ought* to pursue P.E. licensure because . . ."
> *Value Claim*: "Achieving one's P.E. license is *good* because . . ."
> Etc.

Here the moral terms have been made explicit. We can tell the speaker approves of getting P.E. licensure because the Value Statement uses words like *ought* and *good*.

The second part of the Value Statement is the *ground(s)* or *reason(s)* supplied in defense of the *claim*. In the initial statement, the *reason* has to do with securing stable employment with the government.

> *Value Statement:* "Achieving one's P.E. license is *good* because it will land you a government job."

In this sentence, we are tipped off to there being some sort of special relevance or logical link between "Achieving one's P.E." and "landing a government job" by the word *because*.

| Value Claim | --logical link--
(because) | Reasons |

FIGURE 3.1 Parts of a Value Statement

We might reverse the order of the terms and achieve the same effect:

> *Value Statement:* "Earning one's P.E. license will land you a government job, therefore, achieving one's P.E. is *good*."

But notice that the tip-off term is no longer *because*, but rather *therefore*.

| Reasons | --logical link--
(therefore) | Value Claim |

FIGURE 3.1a Parts of a Value Statement

Whichever order we write them, we see clearly that the two parts—the *claim*, the *reason(s)*—are linked together by words like *therefore* or *then* or *because*. These linkage words show the logical movement of the Value Statement. Since the *reason(s)* is often said to "support" the *claim*, we say that the logical flow moves from *reason(s)* to *claim*. This is usually represented by an arrow.

Figure 3.1b Diagramming the Flow of Logic

For the sake of consistency, we will diagram ethical arguments as moving from left to right.

Evaluating Ethical Arguments

We said at the outset that there are three kinds of questions for evaluating arguments in general. These three also work for evaluating ethical arguments in particular.

1. Completeness: Are all the relevant *reasons* present? Are all the *reasons* related to moral good rather than merely instrumental good?

2. Soundness/Veracity: Are all the *reasons* factual, true, reliable?

3. Validity: Does the logic flow correctly? Does the argument employ proper logical form?

Let's take these in order and ask them of ethical arguments.

Completeness

First, we can ask whether all the relevant premises are listed. In the case of achieving one's P.E., perhaps landing a government job (R_1) isn't the only good *reason* for undertaking this rigorous four-year process. If it is statistically true that P.E.s earn more money on average than their noncertified counterparts (I do not know if this is true), then we could add a second *reason* (R_2):

"... and because you'll earn more money."

I've also heard it argued that achieving one's P.E. will improve the moral fiber of the engineer's character. Again, I don't know whether this is true or false. But supposing it is true, it can be added as a third *reason* (R_3). Perhaps it can also be shown that P.E.s have better-looking spouses.

This sounds suspicious, but if the data bears this out, then our provisional Value Statement can be stated more completely:

Value Statement: "Achieving one's P.E. is *good* because it will land you a government job (R_1), you'll earn more money (R_2), it will improve the moral fiber of your character (R_3), and you will be more likely to have an attractive spouse (R_4)."

Notice how the strength of the argument currently stands. If someone wanted to attack this Value Statement, how would you expect them to proceed? The strength of the conclusion ("Achieving one's P.E. is good") is linked to the *reasons*. If the *reasons* are strong, the conclusion will be strong, too. If one or more *reasons* are untrue, then the conclusion may be likewise weakened. Sometimes a lone *reason* can carry all the weight. More frequently ethicists look for a cumulative case: all else being equal, the argument with the greatest number of reasons often (though not always) is taken to be stronger.

For all we know, there may be a dozen additional *reasons* that support the wisdom of pursuing P.E. certification. But for the sake of simplicity, let's say these four are all the relevant possibilities. We can diagram the logical flow this way:

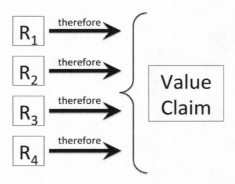

FIGURE 3.1c Diagramming the Flow of Logic

Soundness

This brings us to the second test: Is each *reason* "sound" or "factual" or "true"? All of a sudden the task of evaluation becomes very tricky. R_1 (government job) and R_2 (higher pay) are worded in such a way that we might possibly estimate their truthfulness by means of simple numerical data. But R_3, moral fiber, is very difficult to assess. One possible correlative measure might be data about white-collar crime: do P.E.s less frequently than non-P.E.s embezzle, steal intellectual property, and so on? But, of course, not every bad character commits a crime or gets caught when they do. So the data might turn out to be only crudely representative.

Now notice something else. As it stands, R_3 (moral fiber) *is itself a claim*. In other words, R_3 needs its own set of *reasons* before it can play a trustworthy role in our argument. This problem is not uncommon. Remember, like design work, we expect ethics to be an *ongoing* conversation. So if the arguer is pressed by an opponent, he or she must supply an additional level of *reasons*:

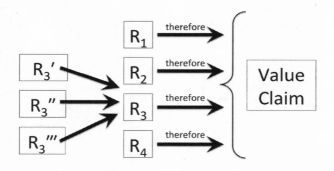

FIGURE 3.1d Second-Order Reasoning

If there are no second-order *reasons* for R_3, then R_3 must drop out of the argument. If secondary *reasons* (R_3' etc.) can be found then R_3 stays—at least it stays until someone can mount a serious rebuttal. Imagine that we know of a study that shows there really is a significantly lower incidence of white-collar crime among P.E.s. This R_3' means that R_3 (moral fiber) can stay. On the other hand, if the study that we hope will back up R_3 turns out to have used a flawed method of data sampling, then R_3' is out the window, and R_3 may need to be abandoned for sheer lack of support.

The fourth *reason*, R_4 (attractive spouse), presents a different kind of problem. Suppose a group of listeners is willing to concede that P.E.s have more beautiful spouses. "But what of it?" they ask. Does spousal beauty really make for a *better* spouse? Is having a beautiful spouse really a *significant reason* compared to qualities that outweigh beauty on the goodness scale?

In contemporary Western society, marriage for beauty *alone* is looked down upon, because beautiful people are not necessarily nicer, harder working, more faithful, and so on. So the beautiful person who is married for beauty alone is called a "trophy"—something easy to look at, but possibly having very little functionality. Since a trophy spouse is not necessarily a "better" spouse, R_4 might indeed fail the test of soundness at the outset, not because we know R_4 to be false, but because we are correct to doubt that R_4 is a *morally significant reason*. To say the same thing differently, R_4 may be true, but somewhat beside the point. Of course, someone may one day concoct a good case for why trophy spouses are morally significant. But this would have to be argued out. And until the day a strong argument is presented, R_4 must be discarded as trivial in comparison to other goods.

One of the difficulties with analyzing for soundness is the fact that "moral" tends to be a *relational* term rather than the name of a property. For example, we say that the ability of grass to reflect green light (say, 5500Å) makes for its green color. This would be true no matter what country the grass is growing in. Green is thus a property of the grass. But moral terms are more like *spatial relations* than inherent properties. A grassy field is green in and of itself. But the grassy field is "to the south of" only in virtue of whatever is to the north. If a lake is to the north and a parking lot to the south, then "to the south of" can be said of the field *with respect to* the lake but cannot be said of it with respect to the lot. In other words, "to the south of" is not an inherent property of the field, but a property dependent upon context.

Frequently, though perhaps not always, a moral term functions more like "to the south of" than "green." Consequently, understanding a moral quality requires describing the wider context, usually by telling a story, just as the surrounding context of the grassy field must be described in order to understand the truth of the property "to the south of."

Let's return to our argument about P.E.s. A common way to ask about wider context of "good" is: "Good *with respect to what*?" One audience mistakenly thinks that R_1 (landing a government job) is an *inherently* good thing. But we would be right to inquire *why* is a government job a *good* thing? Good *with respect to what*? A reasonable response may be "a government job is good with respect to stability of income." That may settle the question and the argument then can proceed. But a skeptic can push to the next level by asking whether stable income is necessarily a good thing. Again we ask, "Good *with respect to what?*" If the protagonist is a parent of very young children, the supervision of whom requires one parent to stay at home, then getting a stable job *is* a moral good that aims at providing for children during the years when only one parent can work. On the other hand, perhaps the job seeker wants a stable income to support an illegal drug habit rather than to support young children! Or perhaps the person wants the government job because the government gives out the most stylish ID badge. Okay, this seems silly. But if either of these were *reasons*, nether would be a good reason—an illegal drug habit is an evil rather than a good, and the stylish ID badge is only good in the most trivial sense. The landing of a government job would be instrumentally good, in the sense that landing a government job helps one achieve what one craves—illegal drugs or a cool ID badge. But what one craves does not appear to be tied to a good that has moral significance. In telling the rest of the story, R_1 (land a government job) is exposed as a distraction to the logical flow of the real ethical argument.

At this stage, you may be frustrated both at the tediousness of ethical argumentation as well as its highly contingent nature; an ethical argument can rarely, if ever, deliver a knockout punch. When, say, doing a d-e proof in calculus, the answer is categorically irrefutable. *But ethics, like almost all of life, is not like mathematics. One must employ skilled judgment within a whirl of contingencies at every step, knowing one might be challenged and shown to be wrong.* This is not to say that every ethical argument is endless (though some appear to be). No. It really is possible to make a strong enough case that the audience—the boss, clients, coworkers, etc.—move toward consensus. But to understand ethics-as-argument is to realize that every consensus is provisional and liable to challenge and revision on another day or by another audience.

Validity

The third and final class of measures for assessing arguments has to do with logical structure. The simplest way to ferret out the invalidity of an argument is to demonstrate that one or more *reasons* are simply irrelevant. But there are more complex ways that an argument can fail the test of validity. In logical terms, the validity of an argument has to do with its *form*. Most of us have met the logical form called *modus ponens*, or "the mode of putting." The idea is that if we "put" the antecedent "P" into a conditional "If P then Q" we are guaranteed "Q" as the consequent.

If P then Q	If it is pouring rain, then it's cloudy	P => Q
given P	It is pouring rain	given P
therefore, Q	therefore, it is cloudy	∴ Q

FIGURE 3.2 Modus Ponens

Logicians spend their careers identifying and proving valid forms of argument just as geometers identify and prove various corollaries in Euclidian geometry. But unlike geometers, logicians also expose certain attempts at argument as flawed, fallacious, or invalid.[4] Consider the fallacy called "affirming the consequent." A child knows that if it is pouring rain, then it must be cloudy outside. But even a child would not *claim* from the fact that it is cloudy outside that it must therefore be pouring rain at this present moment.

FIGURE 3.3 The Fallacy of Affirming the Consequent

The fallacy of "affirming the consequent" tries to squeeze a guarantee for the existence of P out of "Q" and "P implies Q." But it cannot be done. My dog, Angie, is decidedly not a cat.[5]

The logical flow of an argument is sometimes compared to the way movement is thought to be constrained by the material conditions of a mechanism. The direction and flow of an argument's logical "mechanism" is symbolized by the arrow. In addition to "affirming the consequent," four of the more common ways the "logic arrow" can go awry include *ad hominem* (attacks on the speaker rather than on what is said); *denying the antecedent* (If P then Q; not-P, therefore, not-Q);[6] *generalizing an anecdote* (thinking that one example proves a general rule); and *post hoc ergo propter hoc* (confusing temporal succession with causality). Many of these faulty ways of arguing are well known to us from political campaigns and advertisements. As important as it is to be able to spot fallacious arguments, our focus will be more positive, namely, learning how ethical arguments succeed rather than fail. So, we will set aside issues of improper form. But before we can do some constructive work, we must deal with one enormously important objection philosophers once leveled against the logic of ethical arguments. As we shall see, this philosophical worry, though once widely held, can be set to rest by good engineering thinking.

Moving from Is to Ought by Means of Functional Definitions

At stake is whether arguments that move from "fact" to "value" can work. Enlightenment period thinkers (circa eighteenth-century Europe) began to say there is no legitimate way to infer statements of value from statements of fact, or statements of "ought" from statements of "is." The work of British empiricist David Hume (d. 1776) led philosophers to claim in all seriousness that the move from "*is* to *ought*" constitutes a logical fallacy. They called it "the naturalistic fallacy." It is still believed in some quarters. But since the late 1950s, beginning with the work of Cambridge philosopher Elizabeth Anscombe and expanded upon by Notre Dame philosopher Alasdair MacIntyre, there has been growing acknowledgment that movement from "*is* to *ought*" under some conditions may be not only perfectly legitimate, but also extremely important for ethical argumentation.[7]

The legitimacy of moving from "*is* to *ought*" should not surprise those who live in the engineering world. We know that from an engineering perspective, there are very good reasons for linking "ought" to "is." The simplest way to see this is by considering an artifact like, say, the wrist-watch. If I say, "This is a good wristwatch," people will understand me to mean that it keeps time accurately. Why do people assume I mean this? Because we all know what wristwatches are *for*. To ask what something is for, is to ask about its intended purpose or intended function.[8] When we say, "Wristwatches are for keeping accurate time," we are stating the *functional definition* of the artifact. A functional definition is simply an answer to the question, what is this thing *for*? A functional definition enables us to easily move from statement of fact—"This watch keeps accurate time"—to a statement of value: "This is a *good* watch." Notice, also, that from the functional definition we can easily infer how a watch *ought* to behave: "A wristwatch *ought* to keep accurate time." Both descriptive and prescriptive moral vocabulary—both "is good" and "ought"—follow directly from the functional definition.

The reason Hume denied a passage from "*is* to *ought*" in ethics was that he *denied* the possibility of there being a functional definition for human beings. Thoughtful people from time immemorial have been asking the question, what is human life *for*?—and have not produced a univocal answer. But wait a minute. Isn't this like design? Just because there is no perfect answer does not mean there is no answer at all! It doesn't matter that our answers are always provisional or hotly contested. The point that confounds Hume is that very few people say that *no* answer is possible. So long as there is the possibility of local, provisional agreement about what life is *for*, there is a way for us to say how we *ought* to live. Had Hume said human beings do not have an unambiguous functional defini-tion he would have been right. It is true that there is no single, universally accepted explanation of what human life is for. Nevertheless, as in good design, there are a number of proposals on the table. Many of these pro-posals are religious proposals; but atheists, too, have proposals regarding what life is for. So long as we keep arguing about this question, we must concede that the concept of a functional definition is at least intelligible. And if a proposed functional definition is intelligible, the question about its counterpart, the *ought*, will also be intelligible.

The detour into Hume's so-called naturalistic fallacy has taken us far afield. All that engineering ethics needs is for the concept of functional definition to be intelligible. This gives us the leverage we need to move from facts to value, or in our lingo, from *reason(s)* to a value *claim*.

While the philosophers and theologians debate what human life is for, our task will be much easier. We are about the business of constructing arguments (admittedly provisional ones) in defense of some value *claim*. So, we argue about whether "this bridge is good" or "that video game is bad," by saying so and supplying supporting *reasons*.

WARRANTS

The technical term for moving from a factual *reason* to a value *claim* is *warrant*. You'll notice that *value claims* employ moral vocabulary: *good/ bad, obligatory/permitted/forbidden, should/shouldn't, moral/immoral*, and so on. This vocabulary—whether implicitly or explicitly expressed—is what distinguishes the sentence as containing a *value claim*. You'll also notice that *reasons* given are shorn of any such special vocabulary. (This absence is what led Hume wrongly to think that there is no way to draw conclusions about value from statements of fact.) *Reasons* use everyday terms—for example, "Government jobs pay more than nongovernment jobs." The role of what we are calling here the *warrant* is to make explicit how the link is made between factual *reasons* and the moral vocabulary that appears in *value claims*. We have already met one of these logical links: the functional definition. A functional definition belongs to the class of logical links called "warrants."

The following example is so very obvious that no one would bother diagramming it. But because it is obvious, it can help us see the *warrant* in action. We are all familiar with the hydraulic cutter/spreader called "The Jaws of Life" that rescue workers use to extract trapped persons from wrecked automobiles. As an artifact, we can state the value *claim* without hesitation: "The Jaws of Life are morally good." Here the word *morally* indicates that "good" means more than simply "it works efficiently" (although effective performance is included in "good" design). This device is good both with respect to its *means* (it works effectively) and with respect to its aim or *end* (it aims to extract trapped human beings from danger).

If someone asked, "Is the thing called Jaws of Life good?" you could reply, "Yes! Because it saves lives." So the obvious Value Statement is:

Value Statement: "The Jaws of Life are good because they save lives."

We'd be shocked if someone pressed us further: "Sure they save lives, but are they *good*?" We'd think that they were being sarcastic or perhaps that they do not speak English fluently. Nevertheless, the clearest rebuttal to their wrongheaded question is simply: *"Anything that saves human lives is morally good."*

This is the warrant. The *warrant* links the fact ("Jaws of Life *save lives*") with the moral vocabulary of the *value claim* ("is *good*"). A more complete diagram, therefore, of ethical argumentation is as follows:

"[it] saves human lives"   therefore   "the Jaws of Life are good"

"Anything that saves human lives is morally good."

FIGURE 3.4 *Warrants* **Support the Logical Linkage**

In the example just given, the *warrant* is so obvious few would consider asking for it to be spelled out. Nevertheless, a *warrant* must be implicit in the argument in order for the argument to succeed. This *warrant* works, as it were, behind the scenes and out of view. But it is still in play.

We now see that an ethical argument can be analyzed into three primary parts: the *value claim* (the conclusion), the *reasons*, and the *warrant* that links the *reasons* to the conclusion. The strength of an argument is a function of these three parts. In an earlier illustration we said that the strength of the conclusion ("Achieving one's P.E. is good") is dependent upon the strength of the *reasons*. We can now say that the strength of the conclusion is also related to the relevance of the *warrant*. If someone wanted to challenge a Value Statement, he or she might question one or more of the *reasons*. But they might also challenge the *warrant*. On such occasions, *warrants* need to be defended. (See the section below called "Backing.") Let's see how *warrants* function in everyday discussions concerning design and technology.

Types of Warrants

As an example of a morally good artifact, the Jaws of Life is a nice and tidy example that few would oppose. More typically, ethical arguments about the moral worth of an engineering project will be messier and more complex. For that *reason*, it is important that we understand the full complement of acceptable ways of moving from factual *reason(s)* to a *value claim*. For our purposes, there are four classes of *warrants*.

A. Moral Definition

The above defense of the Jaws of Life uses a *warrant* that we will call a *moral definition*: "Anything that saves lives is morally good." It is a definition because it is universal in scope ("anything"). This definition is constructed in unambiguous, black-and-white terms that virtually anyone can understand. Not all definitions are like this. Some may be more analogical in nature, requiring skill to make the application. The more skill required, the more likely we are dealing with a *heuristic* than with a definition that anyone can understand. In many cases, a functional definition works like a moral definition. In other cases, the functional definition works like a *heuristic*. More on this ambiguity later.

B. Stipulations

There is much, *much* more to living well than following rules. Nevertheless, from time to time, clear-cut rules that we will call *stipulations* do play a role in ethical argument. While definitions are *warrants* that use descriptive moral vocabulary such as *good*, stipulations often use *modal* moral vocabulary, words like *ought* and *should*. Unsurprisingly, people argue about rules: Which rules are binding? To what extent? Under what conditions? Are there any exceptions? And so on. But here are some common stipulations whose authority is widely acknowledged:

- The Ten Commandments, the Code of Hammurabi, and the Golden Rule

- U.S. federal and state and city laws—because these are far from perfect, the laws of the land are not the place to end ethical argument, but the place to begin. Laws are best thought of as something like the ground floor, a level beneath which we'd best not sink.[9]

- Discipline-specific federal regulations (e.g., building codes, material codes, licensure policies, etc.)

- Professional codes of ethics such as the NSPE Code, the ASME Code, etc.[10]

In 2008 an engineer working for San Jose–based software firm Quantum3D was found guilty of selling fighter pilot training software to the Chinese government.[11] Here is one possible Value Statement: "Mr. M's act was wrong because selling his firm's software is intellectual property theft." The *value claim* is thumbs-down; what Mr. M did was wrong. The *reason* supporting this *claim* is that his act was a form of stealing. In this instance the logical movement from "theft" to "morally wrong" is *warranted* by a *stipulation*—in particular, the eighth commandment (or its equivalent from other cultures), "Thou shalt not steal." Of course, prohibitions against stealing are found in many more places than the Hebrew Bible—that is why the prohibition is widely accepted. We only need to quote one form of this warrant to make explicit how the argument works:

FIGURE 3.5 Stipulation *Warrant*

C. Principles

A third class of *warrants* is called the "principle." To the untrained eye, principles look like definitions. For example, one common principle is the utilitarian formula explained in Equation 1.1, namely that the *Net Goodness* calculates the product of *(goodness)* × *(likelihood)* × *(significance)*. But principles, more than definitions, require sophisticated judgment to use appropriately. For this *reason*, principles may be thought of as a kind of heuristic. But principles differ from heuristics in scope—principles often appear to have universal application and seem to *claim* universal assent. Whether moral principles have universal applicability and assent is a matter of scholarly debate. For our purposes, a given principle's applicability, like the usefulness of a given design, has to be decided on a case-by-case basis.

One must be careful when *warranting* an ethical argument by means of the principle of utilitarianism. This principle requires not only skill in its application, but it also requires *data*; the utilitarian conclusion holds only when actual numbers are supplied for calculating outcomes. As we saw in chapter 1, this may be extremely difficult to do. For example, sixty-five years ago it was argued that fluoridation of the public water supply would result in a marked decrease in tooth decay. This was a very heated political debate, because no one knew the long-term ill effects of regularly ingesting very small amounts of fluoride. But today, sixty-five years later, the Center for Disease Control can say with confidence: "For 65 years, community water fluoridation has been a safe and healthy way to effectively prevent tooth decay. CDC has recognized water fluoridation as one of the 10 great public health achievements in the 20th century."[12] The CDC Web site houses all the statistical data one could wish for. So from *today's* vantage point, we can compose the following Value Statement: "Fluoridation of the public water supply is good, because it improves human health." What *warrants* the move from the *reason* ("Fluoridation improves human health") to the value *claim* ("Fluoridation of the public water supply is *good*") is the net gain in human health. We know this net gain—a marked decrease in tooth decay, and undetectable negative side effects—to be real rather than imagined because someone along the way did the math and calculated *Net Goodness* $=\Sigma$ *(goodness)* $\times$ *(likelihood)* $\times$ *(significance)*. The calculation—easy enough today, but difficult in 1950—is a *warrant*, because the calculation translates fact ("improved health") into quantified units of value. (As we shall see below, the function of R' is called "*backing*.")

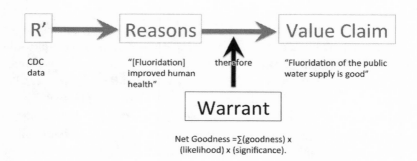

Net Goodness $=\Sigma$(goodness) x (likelihood) x (significance).

Figure 3.6 Principle *Warrant*

D. Heuristics

The term *heuristic* was introduced in chapter 2. As you remember, Koen defines a heuristic as "anything that provides a plausible aid or direction in the solution of a problem but is in the final analysis unjustified, incapable of justification, and fallible."[13] There is no straightforward way to apply heuristics to an ethical argument because proper understanding of heuristics depends upon proper development of the skills of the persons employing them. In this regard we are each and always in progress. Yet we can't wait around until our training is finished before undertaking ethical argumentation. In point of fact, doing ethical argumentation, even imperfectly, is itself part of the training regimen for improving our skills in using heuristics well. As they say, "Anything worth doing is worth doing . . . *poorly*, until one can learn how to do it better!" Let's see how a heuristic might *warrant* an ethical argument about an engineering artifact, in this case, a bridge.[14]

In 1936, Robert Moses (1888–1981) was awarded the Cornelius Amory Pugsley Gold Medal Award for his work in developing the parks and parkways in Greater New York City. Moses held as many as twelve different New York City and state jobs simultaneously and earned a reputation for being "the man who gets things done." During his reign, he more than tripled the number of playgrounds in NYC—a good thing. But by all accounts he was a power-hungry, egocentric, violent, and racist man capable of great harm.[15] Under Moses' watch, clumsy intersections were replaced by scenic overpasses and elegant throughways that allowed traffic to flow smoothly. Two hundred of these overpasses were constructed over the beautiful parkways that led to the parks and beaches. Now the nefarious part: these two hundred overpasses were built with a maximum clearance of only nine feet. Because city busses were twelve feet tall, low bridges effectively *excluded* those who rode busses—namely, poor people, especially blacks and Latinos—from having access to the posh public parks and beaches. Let's be clear: racial discrimination is evil. Moses *intended* these overpasses for evil and the *use* to which they were put *was* evil. Moses is long dead, but the overpasses remain standing, perpetuating moral evil without any living human agent willing it so. One can almost imagine these overpasses as perpetual minions forever carrying forward the evil designs of their maker.[16]

We understand that these two hundred overpasses are a mixture of good and evil. In terms of safety and aesthetics, they are good: they work well and look beautiful. Yet upon reflection, we instinctively recoil against them as evil. In addition to finding Moses guilty of both evil intention and evil action, the artifacts themselves can be called morally evil, regardless of who designed and built them.

Value Statement: These two hundred overpasses are evil (in part), because they effectively deny the poor access to public parks and beaches.

The structure of this value statement is clear: the value *claim* is thumbs-down—these overpasses are "evil." The *reason* provided has to do with their discriminatory work: people are prevented access to public parks and beaches simply because they were poor.

What *warrant* links "preventing beach access" with the moral vocabulary "evil"? We can't say that Moses' designs were illegal, because they were built before the Civil Rights Act of 1964. We might hazard a moral definition: "denying beach access to the poor is evil." But this definition doesn't seem quite right. In the first place it is too specific, too *ad hoc*.[17] If we call *this* a moral definition, we will need to concoct an *ad hoc* definition for absolutely everything we want to call evil. The resulting moral system will be crystal clear, but infinitely large—too large to learn, much less write down! In the second place, this moral definition might be opposed by Moses himself. Moses might employ the utilitarian principle against our questionable definition by insisting, "The greatest good for the greatest number of the public is to keep the riff-raff off the beaches." Here we smell a rat; we should immediately and forcefully counter this utilitarian claim by arguing that "the poor" cannot be blithely equated with "the riff-raff." But, alas! Do we have the sociological data at hand to show the utilitarian argument is flawed? Remember, if we're doing utilitarian consequentialism, *we must have the numbers.* Since sociology is *not* our expertise (assuming we are engineers rather than sociologists), our argument might not turn out to be very powerful. So we have two choices. We can either enlist a sociologist for help in gathering data to prove that Moses' use of the utilitarian principle is flawed, or we can look for another way of *warranting* our *claim* that these two hundred overpasses are evil. There is an alternative; it uses heuristics. To explain how a heuristic can *warrant* our Value Statement, we'll need a quick detour to sharpen our skilled judgment.

As I wrote this paragraph, there was a blip in the news that I'm sure will be quickly forgotten. House Speaker John Boehner (R-OH) gave the 2011 commencement address to Catholic University of America in Washington, DC. Eighty-one Catholic academics signed a letter of protest. Why did they object? They were protesting Boehner's voting record;

Boehner repeatedly and consistently opposed the interests of the poor, disenfranchised, and marginalized persons of society—including children, minorities, and women. Thus, these eighty-one professors claimed that "Boehner ought not address the graduating class." A short time after the brouhaha died down, a political pundit invited two of the signatories, Dr. Vince Miller (University of Dayton) and Dr. Steve Schneck (Catholic University), to "explain" themselves on national television.[18] Of course, talk shows don't really want rational explanation; they want a spectacle. So at one point the pundit interrupted whoever was talking and demanded to know, "Are you *socialists*?" Without blinking, Dr. Miller replied, "No—we are *Catholics*." If we pause here a moment, we can consider whether "We are Catholics" might function as a *heuristic warrant* in the implied ethical argument. I think so. For sake of illustration, consider the way social identity functions in Amish moral life.

We can imagine an Amish child asking his mother, "Why can't we wear zippers?" And we can imagine the parent's reply: "Because we are Amish." This may sound like a dodge to me, but remember, I am not Amish. And because I am not Amish, I don't have a very deep understanding of who the Amish are or how they think. I mean, what if there is a powerful and convincing explanation of why they don't wear zippers, and what if the explanation *cannot* be spelled out in a sentence or two? Hmm. Perhaps if I study Amish life and culture carefully and come to know in a deep way who they are as a people, I may eventually begin to get a handle on why the use of zippers is a big deal.[19] Since the explanation of the no-zipper policy is complex and involved, the answer given to the child—"Because we are Amish"—is true and *not* trivial. When the Amish astounded the world by forgiving the murderer of five Amish children in Nickel Mines, Pennsylvania, they could explain their marvelous, but strikingly odd, response by appeal to this very same heuristic: "Because we are Amish."[20] The sentence "because we are Amish" is a heuristic, a sentence that requires skill and knowledge and hands-on experience to unpack fully.

As a *warrant* in ethical arguments, Amish identity is a heuristic because it requires skill—namely, a certain kind of fluency in Amish practices, history and theology—to understand it. Similarly for Catholic Christians, their religious identity functions as a heuristic *warrant*. Granted, being a Catholic Christian may not seem as odd to most Americans as being Amish. But there still is *some* oddness. At any rate, the conservative pundit interviewing Drs. Miller and Schneck clearly did not share this understanding (or else appeared willfully to misunderstand them), since he mistook the theologians for socialists (*socialist* is a dirty word to most Americans). So Miller clarified his *warrant* by appealing to something that Catholics like John Boehner and the political pundit should know about Catholic Christianity: Catholics have a deep and abiding commitment to "the preferential option for the poor." This phrase encapsulates Jesus' teaching and is the cornerstone of Catholic Social Teaching. The basic idea is that the extreme poor, the marginalized, the disenfranchised are so disadvantaged that they can never catch up. It is too late to go back in time and grow up again with better nutrition to help brains and bodies develop; it is too late to go back and attend better schools; it is too late to go back and move into an area with better houses and better neighbors and a lower crime rate. Therefore, enabling the impoverished to survive requires more than merely a *level* playing field. A level playing field would still give the rest of us a huge edge. Rather, Catholic Christian compassion requires the field to be *tipped in favor of* the poor.[21]

This *warrant*, the preferential option for the poor, is certainly contestable—the interviewer thought it blatantly ridiculous, and probably many viewers did too. Nevertheless, it is undeniably the Catholic position, and in fact, the Christian position in general.

We can, at last, complete our simple argument against Moses' two hundred overpasses. The link from "denies beach access" to the moral conclusion "are evil" is *warranted* by the Catholic identity heuristic: "We are the ones who give preferential option to the poor."

FIGURE 3.7 Heuristic *Warrant*

This chapter has aimed to introduce the practice of ethical argumentation in order for us to argue fairly about engineering design. The examples have been intentionally simplified so that we can more easily see the template for justifying value statements. We expect that real-time justification will be more complex. The next level of complexity of ethical justification is called "*backing*."

BACKING

Every ethical argument, once made explicit, has the three working parts with which we are now familiar: One or more *reasons* supply "support" for a *claim* about something's value or *goodness* (thereby obliging humans to behave in certain ways) or its *badness* (thereby prohibiting certain human behaviors); the character of the "support" is spelled out in the *warrant*. As we have seen, the paradigm case is spelled out by Figure 3.4. But this diagram looks suspiciously simplistic. Surely there is more to ethics than three boxes and two arrows! And there is: the *reason* and *warrant* are often themselves the conclusions of other supporting arguments (Figure 3.1d).

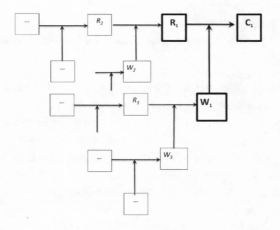

FIGURE 3.8 A Nearly Endless Regress of Justification

Theoretically, nothing prevents this process of justification from extending to the left *forever*. Practically speaking, however, real-time conversations between two people rarely extend backwards more than a step or two. Nor can printed "conversations"—that is, book-length treatments of a moral issue—go on forever. While an ethics book can extend justification many more steps to the left than can ordinary conversations over coffee, even a book truncates justification eventually. But where to stop? If a Value

Statement is first-order justification, we will call everything else second-order justification.

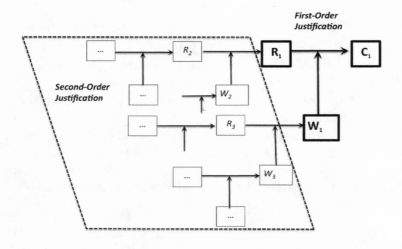

FIGURE 3.9 First- and Second-Order Justification

We know that questions can *always* be raised against one or more parts of an argument; there simply is no such thing as knockdown proof in discussions about moral goods. The key heuristic for knowing when to stop adding more support is this: "Supply sufficient justification to adequately address legitimate questions raised against a given Value Statement." Rather than diagram second-order justification in all its detail, we will adopt a conventional shortcut regarding all these steps to the left, whether one or one hundred, and simply fold them under the term *backing*. As a result, the heuristic in play can be clarified: *"Supply sufficient backing to answer legitimate questions raised against a given Value Statement."*

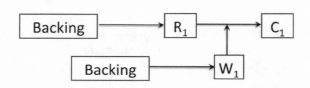

FIGURE 3.10 Backing

As illustrated in Figure 3.10, *backing* is shorthand for the whole process of settling questions raised against the original *reasons* and *warrants*. In sum, ethical arguments have not just three but four primary parts: *claim, reason(s), warrant(s)*, and *backing*. Before concluding, let us examine how *backing* works.

Recall the above illustration, "The Jaws of Life are morally good." The *reason* supplied was that "the Jaws of Life save lives." Can this statement be questioned? Of course. But the question can also be answered. A convincing response to someone who doubts the efficacy of the Jaws of Life will require some research. Yet before doing research we can imagine what *sorts* of answers will work. For example, in this instance *empirical data* might provide *backing* for the stated *reason*, "The Jaws of Life save lives." A simple Google search takes us to the company Web site where we read that the Jaws of Life have saved "thousands" of lives since first introduced by Hurst Performance, Inc., in 1972.[22] Do these data ("thousands") constitute adequate *backing*? Well, is this a reliable source? Maybe. Then again, maybe not. After all, we realize that Hurst wants to sell its product, so it is in their best financial interest not to mention the failure rate of the device in their marketing. But let's suppose for the sake of illustration that the data ("thousands") is reliable. We can still ask, is "thousands" specific enough to quell all objections about whether the device saves enough lives to *back* the stated *reason*? Admittedly, "thousands" is pretty vague. But perhaps a more important number is the statistic that thirty-five thousand rescue teams carry the portable Jaws of Life.[23] Here the *backing* is not data about the number of lives saved, but an inference drawn from expert opinion: "Thirty-five thousand teams of rescue experts carry Jaws of Life because *they* (the experts) think the device is likely to save lives." Both the number of rescue teams (thirty-five thousand) and their status as experts supply *backing* to the *reason*. A third possible *backing* might be found in the fact that the sheer value of a single human life is so great that we do not need a large number but only a single instance of a life saved to *back* our *reason*. The same Google search reveals testimonial of a woman whose life was apparently saved by a rescue team employing the Jaws. Generally, argument by anecdote is in poor form.[24] But one testimonial is better than no testimonial. In 1972, Hurst faced the same difficulty as those dentists who wanted to convince cities to put fluoride in the water in the 1940s. Months before the first life was actually saved, Hurst likely *claimed* that the Jaws will in the near future save lives. While the prophecy turned out to be true, it was not a *claim* that was *backed* by data. Notice how much stronger the argument becomes once that first life has been saved. From that moment on, a testimonial in the form of "so-and-so's life was saved by the Jaws of Life on (day/month/year)" may function as convincing *backing*.

The previous paragraph supplied three possible strategies for *backing* the *reason*. The *reason* is not the only part of the argument that can be challenged by a doubter. The *warrant* also can be criticized. The stated *warrant* for moving from "saves lives" to "is morally good" is the *moral definition*, "Anything that saves lives is morally good." Surely this is a *warrant* to which everyone subscribes. Or is it? Notice that the definition leaves some stones unturned. Suppose that the manufacturing of this device requires rare minerals the mining of which statistically shortens the lives of the miners. Doesn't their human suffering and shortened life spans undermine our confidence in the "anything" of "*Anything* that saves lives is morally good"? In other words, the objector can legitimately ask, "What does it actually cost human beings (in terms of human lives shortened or physical suffering incurred) to produce this device that perhaps only occasionally saves lives? Might there be collateral damage that comes close to outweighing the value of saving a life?" At stake is whether the manufacturing process resulting in thirty-five thousand Jaws of Life now in the field *may cost more lives* than are saved by use of the device. The form of the challenge is *logical*, a denial of the universal ("*Anything* that save lives . . .") on grounds that we live in a messy world where mechanical gains come at a price: the production of this device has real-world costs in terms of energy consumption, greenhouse-gas emissions, health risks to those who mine the metals and breath the fumes, etc.

An adequate *backing* for this attack on a widely accepted *warrant* could conceivably take an *empirical* form. If we could provide real-world data that demonstrate that the costs of production are "acceptable" relative to the number of crash victims saved by the Jaws of Life, then the original universal moral definition still stands as *warrant* for the argument. Alternatively, the *backing* could conceivably take a *logical* form, observing that costs may detract from the relative weight of thing's goodness, but costs are unable to change the nature of the thing's goodness. Since the aimed-for end of the Jaws of Life is indeed the saving of human lives, it is morally good. High costs of production may make its context of use "morally tragic" (i.e., a legitimate good that entails unavoidable negative aspects), but may not make the device itself morally bad. If this kind of instrumentalist argument works (why it does *not* need not distract us here), then sufficient *backing* derives from the logical point that costs do not alter the basically good nature of the device.

CONCLUSION

Ethical argument is an important part of ethics. (Remember, it is only *one* part.) Ethical argumentation would be easier to do if clear-cut definitions, stipulations, and principles were ready at hand. Perhaps sometimes they are. But more often than not we find ourselves enmeshed in conversations that are murky, and the only *warrants* at hand are those slippery critters we've dubbed "heuristics." We already know heuristics to be tricky things. But discarding heuristics in favor of something more cut-and-dried would be a grave mistake. Increasingly, scholars are realizing Koen's right: definitions, stipulations, and principles are only clear-cut when all the mess is trimmed off and a problem is reduced to the *ideal* case. In the real world, where the mess cannot be trimmed away, *pretending* things are crystal clear won't help a bit if things are irreducibly murky all the way down! When we take the messiness of the world seriously, we see that *definitions*, *stipulations*, and *principles* function "heuristically." Ergo, we need to attune ourselves to the sort of difference it makes when ethical argumentation is approached through the lens of heuristics. In the next chapter we will look specifically at the difference it makes to read professional codes of ethics "heuristically." Then, in chapter 5, we'll tackle the really big topic in ethics, which is not ethical argumentation but something called "practical reasoning."

DISCUSSION QUESTIONS

1. What do you think makes a *reason* a *moral reason*? Why?

2. What is a *warrant*? How do *warrants* function in ethical arguments?

3. What kind of utilitarianism is the calculation represented by Figure 3.7? (Recall that in chapter 1 we read about two forms of utilitarian consequentialism, namely, cost-benefit and risk-benefit analyses.)

4. Give examples of possible *backing* for the *reason* listed in Figure 3.7.

5. What kind of approach would you recommend for supplying *backing* for the *warrant* in Figure 3.8?

NOTES

1. For a crystal clear introduction to ethical reasoning, see Murphy, *Reasoning and Rhetoric in Religion*, chs. 1 and 8.

2. I am indebted to the discussion of these concepts in the opening chapter of Whitbeck, *Ethics in Engineering Practice and Research*.

3. Professional Engineering (P.E.) licensure requires four years of practical engineering experience after the university degree plus at least two exams: the Fundamentals of Engineering (the "F.E.," two four-hour portions covering 180 discipline-specific questions) and the Principles and Practices of Engineering (the "P.E."). Achievement of licensure subsequently qualifies one to belong to the National Society of Professional Engineers and be governed by the NSPE Code of Ethics.

4. For a simple place to begin sorting out valid and invalid logical forms, see Weston, *A Rulebook for Arguments*.

5. If you thought hard enough, you might be able to come up with an example in which the affirmation of a consequent seems to work. But as logicians are keen to point out, those cases where it seems to work are either (*a*) accidental coincidence of effects (rather than Q causing P) or (*b*) instances of P being a "necessary" condition for Q. But in the latter case, we are no longer dealing with a simple conditional.

6. For a very concise and helpful book on the logic of argumentation, see Weston, *A Rulebook for Arguments*.

7. Anscombe, "Modern Moral Philosophy." See also the works of MacIntyre, especially *After Virtue*.

8. The Greeks called a thing's intended purpose its *telos*; hence this kind of moral reasoning is known as *teleological* reasoning. This can be confusing; one kind of teleological reasoning looks for expected outcomes (e.g., utilitarianism). But Aristotle's much earlier version of teleological reasoning derives "ought" from the thing's intended function or purpose.

9. We also know some laws are downright immoral—there were once laws protecting slaves as the property of their holders. The difficulty

with overturning immoral laws is that to do so will require "revolution" rather than reform. For insightful discussion, see McCabe, *Law, Love and Language*.

10. See the Online Ethics Center for Engineering and Research, http://www.onlineethics.org/Resources/ethcodes.aspx.

11. Associated Press, "Engineer Becomes First Sentenced under Economic Espionage Act."

12. http://www.cdc.gov/fluoridation/

13. Koen, *Discussion of the Method*, 28.

14. The following paragraph is borrowed from ch. 1 of Kallenberg, *God and Gadgets*.

15. For some of the more shocking details, see Caro, *Power Broker*.

16. The suggestion I just made—that technology can take on a life of its own—was very much at home in the NT. I will take up this discussion in more detail in chapter 5.

17. To solve a problem *ad hoc* means to do something that only works in this case. Good design aims to avoid the need for *ad hoc* fixes once the artifact is in circulation.

18. The interview can be found on YouTube: http://www.youtube.com/watch?v=x02b9dRWlfQ.

19. See, for example, Kraybill, *Riddle of Amish Culture*.

20. See Kraybill, Nolt, and Weaver-Zercher, *Amish Grace*.

21. McCarthy, *Heart of Catholic Social Teaching*.

22. See company Web site: www.jawsoflife.com/About.

23. Ibid.

24. For examples of bogus and poorly formed argumentation, see Weston, *A Rulebook for Arguments*.

4

READING PROFESSIONAL CODES OF ETHICS THROUGH DESIGN[1]

IN 2004 A SENIOR Air Force official, Lieutenant General Druyun, left the military and took a prestigious job at Boeing (vice president in charge of missile defense). How does one land a prestigious job in industry? In this official's case, it apparently helped that *before* she retired from the military, she had procured a $23 billion Pentagon contract for her new employer (Boeing) to supply one hundred tanker planes for in-flight refueling! That hardly seems fair, does it? In ethics we call this *conflict of interest*. Lieutenant General Druyun had a stake in finding the best contractor for the Pentagon *and* she had a stake in finding a good civilian job. These two interests (finding a new job and finding a contractor) were in danger of "conflicting" because one interest might cloud her judgment in the other. And apparently the new job at Boeing *was* the reward for procuring the $23 billion contract. She tearfully pleaded guilt in U.S. District Court.[2]

There are laws against such things. And, as we know, laws can function as warrants in ethical arguments. We learned from chapter 3 that stipulations can warrant ethical arguments by supporting the link between a factual claim (reason) and a value claim. This might be diagrammed this way:

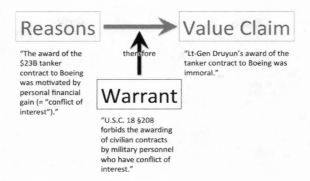

Reasons

"The award of the $23B tanker contract to Boeing was motivated by personal financial gain (= "conflict of interest")."

therefore

Value Claim

"Lt-Gen Druyun's award of the tanker contract to Boeing was immoral."

Warrant

"U.S.C. 18 §208 forbids the awarding of civilian contracts by military personnel who have conflict of interest."

FIGURE 4.1 U.S. Law as Stipulation Warrant

As you might imagine, appeal to U.S. law is not the only way to defend the claim that what Druyun did was immoral. We can also appeal to an engineering professional code of ethics (PCOE) as warrant for this claim. The most common reading strategy for professional codes of ethics is to approach a code as a kind of stipulation that warrants value claims like laws do. In the National Society of Professional Engineers (NSPE) Code of Ethics, we read that "engineers shall not be influenced in their professional duties by conflicting interests." To be even more specific, "Engineers shall not accept financial or other considerations . . . from material or equipment suppliers for specifying their product" (NSPE Code, "Professional Obligations," §§5 and 5a). This section of the NSPE Code is worded very much like a law. As a stipulation warrant, the ethical argument against Lieutenant General Druyun can be diagrammed as on the following page.

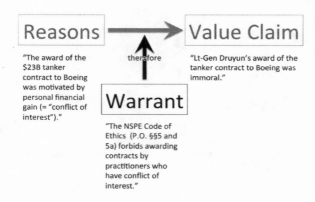

Figure 4.2 Code of Ethics as Stipulation Warrant

This argument works. It is sound, valid, and complete. While professional codes of ethics are often thought to function in just this way, it is not the only way PCOEs can function.

Reading Professional Codes of Ethics "Heuristically"

In order to understand a PCOE as functioning in ways other than as a stipulation warrant, think back to the Design Periphery diagram (Figure 2.5), the one with thirty-six examples of conversation centers, each of which is (possibly) relevant to design. Each starburst (✶) on the diagram represents a topic around which designers chatter like children around an ice cream stand. Notice also that among all the examples, there is an unnamed conversation center marked simply by an ellipsis (. . .). This ellipsis is trying to show that the diagram has been left intentionally *incomplete*. Not every topic relevant to the ethics of a design project can be predicted in advance. There is bound to be one relevant topic, maybe more, that ought to be talked about but hasn't made it onto this diagram. Much like in a mathematical series {2, 4, 6, 8, . . .}, the ellipsis signals that we are to "go on in the same way." Once designers get the hang of relating various conversations to design, they will be able to figure out which design topics ought to be added to the conversation. For example, "competition" is not mentioned on the diagram. Might "competition" be important to design? Might ethics impinge on relationship with and between competitors? Of course! So we must remember that even if a new angle for discussion dawns on the design team late in the game, it may be important to hash it out.

It helps to be clear about what *cannot* go into the circle marked by the three dots, namely, "ethics." Remember, "ethics" is not a stand-alone topic. Nor is ethics an ingredient that gets added *after* the design work is done. We saw in chapter 2 that ethics is more like the color of the paper that Figure 2.5 is printed on, because "ethics" is inherent in each and all of the sub-conversations that constitute the design process. This fact makes the role of PCOEs in design a little confusing, because a code of ethics is a stand-alone document. It seems very tempting to complete the design and then, almost as an afterthought, check the design for violations against the PCOE. But perhaps there is a way that the PCOE can be helpful earlier in design conversations. How this works can be seen if a PCOE is read *heuristically.*

We first met the term *heuristic* in chapter 2. By now you should instinctively think two things when you see the term *heuristic.* First, you should think of a heuristic as a shortcut ("anything that provides a plausible aid or direction in the solution of a problem . . ."). Second, the term *heuristic* ought to remind you that skilled judgment is needed (". . . but is in the final analysis unjustified, incapable of justification, and fallible"[3]). As we learned, there are design heuristics and ethical heuristics. Both kinds of heuristics are useful in design reasoning. In this chapter, the word *heuristic* is turned into an adverb, *heuristically,* which, as we shall see, points to *a special kind of reading strategy.* While every professional code of ethics is necessarily imperfect, even the most imperfect of codes may still be useful in the hands of those who have been adequately trained to use them well.

Many professional codes of ethics are very short. The Institute of Electrical and Electronics Engineers (IEEE) Code can fit onto a single page.[4] The ones that are longer than a page typically begin with seven or eight "fundamental canons" followed by explanation in outline. The very brevity of these codes creates problems if we expect too much of them. As philosopher John Ladd has shown, the complexity of engineering practice means that a one-page code cannot be of much help in solving complex moral conundrums.[5] It isn't even clear who is a code's intended audience. Is a code for assuring *the greater public,* for training the *novices* in a field, or for policing *engineering practitioners?* Is it for defending practitioners from lawsuits or for solving moral dilemmas? If a professional code of ethics is supposed to do any or all of these things, shouldn't it be longer than a page?

The brevity of codes also leaves open the possibility that a code might be used for nefarious purposes as well as honorable ones. Some firms employ codes as a form of image management and advertising: "Trust us! Give us your business! Look, we have a code of ethics!" Some ethicists are suspicious of the fact that codes almost always originate from the side of *management*. Could this mean there might be a hidden agenda lurking in some codes? Apparently so—at least sometimes. The U.S. Department of Justice successfully sued the National Society of Professional Engineers for the way the 1974 version of the NSPE Code of Ethics was exclusionary and monopolistic.[6] Did you catch the irony? The 1974 version of the NSPE Code of *Ethics* was guilty of propagating *unethical* practices to the point of breaking the law! Moreover, the brevity and ambiguity of PCOEs are likely the reason that practicing engineers by and large don't pay much attention to codes; many are even unaware of their existence. An ethics survey conducted by the American Institute of Chemical Engineers (AIChE) discovered that fewer than six of the 4,318 completed surveys (about 0.001 percent) referenced the AIChE Code of Ethics when formulating their responses to posed conundrums.[7]

Some of these shortcomings may be avoided if we adopt the proper reading strategy. We must admit, in the first place, that it is hard *not* to think of PCOEs as a kind of picture of a perfect world. But we already know that in engineering, *ideal* pictures aren't always useful and sometimes lead us astray. So, despite the fact that PCOEs can function as binding legal requirements, this kind of function isn't particularly helpful in design conversation. Moreover, PCOEs can indeed be read as expressing stipulation warrants for ethical argumentation. We saw this illustrated above with the conflict of interest case for Lietenant General Druyun. As another example, the NSPE Board of Ethical Review utilizes its PCOE as stipulation warrants when ruling on specific cases.[8] As common as these two reading strategies are, a third and less familiar strategy for reading PCOEs is to approach them like we do other engineering *heuristics*. Learning this reading strategy may require us to break some bad habits and develop some new ones.

If we resist the habit of reading PCOEs as stipulations, we may discover our moral imagination is awakened by reading PCOEs as *emblems*, *expert consensus*, *covenants*, *conversation-starters*, and *prescriptions*.

1. Emblem rather than Uniform

In 1994, the Long Beach (California) Unified School District started a trend that swept California: mandatory school uniforms for middle and elementary schoolchildren. Of course, private religious schools had been using uniforms for decades. So why did public schools only now find it urgent to make the switch? Part of the urgency stemmed from the fact that gangs were attracting younger and younger members, even among children in elementary school. Given the fact that gangs identified themselves to each other by means of tattoos and garments (hats, clothing brands, shoes, etc.), if these markers could be removed or homogenized, then (or so it was hoped) students would be unable to spot their "enemies" and thus less likely to commit violence in the schoolyard. Compulsory uniforms for schoolchildren aim at imposing one form of equality by means of conformity to a dress code.

As you can imagine, compelling uniformity doesn't work all that well. But now consider a different sort of distinguishing mark: an *emblem*. When a soldier is decorated with an emblem—say, of the Rangers or Delta Force or Navy Seals—the mark does not *compel* uniformity but *identifies* one as a constitutive member of an elite combat unit. The emblem itself gestures to the identity that the wearer has *already* attained. As a result, a far greater degree of unity is associated with an emblem than with a mere uniform. Of course, there is nothing magical about the patch itself. Rather, it is the hard-won group identity behind the patch that makes the patch function as an emblem. Let's see how this might play out in another context.

In late September 2001, Rev. David Benke found himself helping lead a national prayer service in Yankee Stadium just days after the 9/11 terrorist attacks. Benke, a bishop within the Lutheran Church Missouri Synod, shared the stage with a rabbi, a Muslim imam, a Roman Catholic cardinal, and Sikh and Hindu holy men. Greeting everyone present as brothers and sisters, he prayed, "The strength we have is the power of love, and the power you have received is from God, for God is love . . ."[9]

So far, so good. When tragedy strikes, it is proper and good for people of faith to gather and to pray. Now the shocker: Benke's participation got him in trouble with his church's hierarchy. For this action Benke was at risk of losing his ordination. Members of Benke's denomination raised formal charges of "tolerating syncretism" (the mixing together of various religions) and opened a "heresy trial" against him. "Heresy" amounts to a serious breach of group identity. Thus, heretics are reprimanded, put on probation, reduced to lower status in the group, or even kicked out altogether.

It is my view that these proceedings against Benke were ill-conceived.[10] And perhaps another decision would have been rendered had Benke's denomination deliberated longer. But I want to stay with this illustration to help us see how one's group identity functions in moral reasoning. As it turned out, Benke *was* defrocked (that is, he lost his ordination, so he could no longer rightfully preside over religious functions), and like many others, I question the intentions of those behind such a decision. It seems so scandalous to our democratic sensibilities to censure Benke for his efforts to be inclusive. Such a decision only raises our suspicions of a behind-the-scenes coup against Benke. Nevertheless, let me retell the story in a slightly different way, because even as an unpleasant example, it illustrates what I mean by the logical force of an emblem.

At the time, the Lutheran Church Missouri Synod (LCMS) was the nation's ninth-largest Christian denomination. In Benke's case it matters *who* it was that brought charges against him: Benke was accused of heresy *by his own denomination*. The LCMS has a number of identity documents (a.k.a. "emblems") that together function as the terms of their hard-won group identity. Like a Delta Force tattoo or patch, these identity statements assured fellow teammates of what they could count on from pastors like Benke. For example, the 1996 "Reaffirmation of the Synod's Position on Closed Communion" (published five years *before* 9/11) states that faithful confession and catechesis requires pastors to maintain a form of congregational life that stands as a living alternative to "an increasingly pluralistic and secularized view of the Christian faith."[11] In other words, if you signed on with the Missouri Synod Lutherans, you intentionally aimed at being different from the rest of society and pledged *to maintain that difference*, right or wrong. This is simply who LCMS understand themselves to be. Benke's action, reasonable enough to us, nevertheless *compromised the identity this group pledged themselves to maintain*. To outsiders, maintaining this "difference" amounts to being peculiar; to insiders it amounts to being "distinctive."

Part and parcel of becoming a Ranger or Green Beret or Navy Seal—or an LCMS pastor—is learning to think like one. Those who stand outside these respective units cannot see the totality of what insiders see. Consequently, many onlookers were horrified to read of Benke's dismissal from the clergy of the LCMS. Benke's "court martial" seems downright uncivilized to outsiders. But like it or not, those who are insiders to *this* tight-knit group understand the inseparable relation between their "emblem" (namely, identity documents such as the Missouri Synod "Statement of Faith," which, like the Navy Seal patch, reminds them who they are) and the engagement in those behaviors that constitute their distinctive form of life.[12] These behaviors and activities (like refusing to participate in a mixed religious service with non-LCMS persons) both shape how the members of the "unit" see and constantly reminds them of their unique identity. And, as strange as this may sound to some, maintaining a distinctive *group* identity is protected under the U.S. Constitution in some of the same ways individual rights are protected. (In January 2012, the U.S. Supreme Court, in a 9-0 decision, ruled in favor of the "ministerial exception," which gives LCMS and all other religious congregations freedom "to choose and dismiss their leaders without government interference."[13])

Think of it this way. A child wants to become a Boy Scout. However, the child refuses to wear what he considers a "dorky" uniform, insists on playing Wii games rather than working on merit badges, can't stand camping and so never goes, neglects paying dues, and avoids the National Jamboree like the plague. Understandably, this child would be denied the privilege of wearing the emblem. If the boy stole someone's Eagle Scout patch and sewed it to his sleeve, he still wouldn't be an Eagle Scout. The emblem is incapable of forcing the child to conform. The "force" of the Boy Scout emblem is simply that of an identity marker; it stands for an association within a form of life that this young person has chosen *not* to share, but one day may—if, and only if, he adopts *their* form of life.[14]

We ought not be surprised that PCOEs do not *compel* engineers to stay in line. However, if it is possible to conceive of engineering codes of ethics as *emblems*, then it stands to reason that codes may play an important role in the shaping of how an engineer "sees." So long as codes are mistaken for consumer protection devices, codes will be interpreted in terms that anyone can understand and thus be virtually worthless for the sort of character formation that Scouts or Navy Seals or LCMS pastors undergo. However, *if codes are allowed to function as emblems of a particular social role and group identity, they may also play a role in the training of newcomers to the field.*

How might that formation play out in engineering? Here is a simple positive example that comes from the wise authors of the fairly recent code of ethics for software engineering. After insisting that engineering codes of ethics are *not* simple algorithms for decision-making, the Software Engineering Code of Ethics advises software engineers "to consider broadly *who* is affected by their work."[15] Such consideration includes not only the usual suspects—clients and colleagues, employers and consumers—but also, and this is important, "how the *least empowered* will be affected."[16] Why *this* should be of chief concern is not self-evident to outsiders whose concept of equality disallows blatant favoritism. Novices may ask the same question: Why indeed should the "least empowered" (whoever they are) be given special consideration? Isn't this a bit unfair? Yet the inclusion of this clause in the code may trigger curiosity in novice programmers that motivates them to learn why this clause is significant.[17] In other words, outsiders may be bugged, but they can walk away and forget about it. But novices committed to "earning the emblem" will have to wrestle with *how* to implement this concern for the least empowered. How often? How long? To what extent? In what manner? And so on.[18] Those who wrestle with these questions in the context of design have some hope of earning the emblem.

2. Expert Consensus rather than Common Sense

The second contrasting pair that helps us see what it means to read PCOEs heuristically is "expert consensus" versus "common sense."

Recall the discussion about safety factors. Practicing engineers, both new and experienced, refer to a table of Safety Factors as if they were laws etched in stone.

	Safety Factor in Manufacturing
Elevated walkway bolts	2.0
Commercial airplanes	1.5
Military aircraft	1.25
Spring steel in leaf springs	1.2
Cast-iron flywheel	10.0–13.0

FIGURE 4.3 Some Safety Factors[19]

But where did these numbers come from? Certainly not from common sense. Imagine polling the greater society and, after explaining what a flywheel is(!) and reminding them what cast-iron is (the stuff from which Grandma's frying pan and bathtub are made), asking them how many times over a flywheel ought to be safe in comparison to that of an airplane wing. Would the general population guess that cast-iron flywheels ought to be built with a safety factor more than six times greater than that for airplanes!?

We would come closer to values in the table if instead of appealing to the "common sense" of the general public, we polled all engineers. But still not close enough. The safety factors listed in Figure 4.3 are the "common" sense of *those who are on the cutting edge* of engineering practice. Koen refers to the combined skill set of the most experienced, or the expert practitioners, as State of the Art (SOTA). An artifact like a stereo or an automobile is only SOTA to the extent that it embodies the very best skills available. So we will use the more precise definition: SOTA refers to the collective skill set of only the most expert of practitioners.[20] In other words, in the acronym SOTA, the "art" is engineering and its "state" refers to what is considered *best practice* to date. Of course, the "sense," or skilled judgment, of *expert* practitioners may not be very "common," since at any given moment the bulk of engineering practitioners are not yet experts. Nevertheless, the skills that the *experts* exemplify are worth aspiring to. The fact that these skills are worth emulating makes them morally good *for engineers*.

If one reads a professional code of ethics as merely commonsensical, it will be very tempting to set it aside quickly. After all, if the code only amounts to *common* sense, I should be able to re-create it on the spot. This kind of strategy served me well enough in freshman physics. So long as I memorized the key formulas, I had the happy knack of re-creating the applications for the exam. I got so lazy that I only bothered really to read the shaded boxes in each chapter of the textbook. But this strategy backfired miserably when I took psychology. I and my eleven hundred classmates would doze off as the talking head (it was a prerecorded video class in an enormous auditorium) droned on. The textbook was also a snoozer. Everything seemed so obvious, so commonsensical—how could it be otherwise? So, I was pretty shocked by the exam—all multiple choice questions—since each of the wrong answers looked just as reasonable as the right ones! (And since it was a *psych* class, the professors were too savvy to put the right answers in the "C" slot more than one-fourth the time.) I learned that mastering intro psychology would require more than common sense. If I wanted to pass the class, I would have to pay attention to the text and lectures as something more like expert advice than common sense.

What is the point? I am suggesting that professional codes of ethics are as important as safety factors and therefore ought to be *attended to as expert advice* rather than easily stepped over as mere common sense. When push comes to shove, the novice may *not* be able to generate the proper "moral factor" any more than an average person armed only with his or her God-given wits can pull the proper safety factor out of thin air.

3. Covenant rather than Contract

The third way PCOEs ought to be read is as a kind of "covenant" rather than as a contract.

The notion of "contract" has a long, illustrious history in political thought. When the Caesars ruled the world, peace (*pax*) was achieved when a pact (*pactum*)—a treaty or contract—was formed between warring parties. Early modern political philosopher Thomas Hobbes understood "contract" as the logical basis for every modern society. Two observations.[21] First, the contract Hobbes envisioned was the kind that might arise between *actual or virtual strangers* who shared nothing particular in common except the mutual desire for self-preservation. When we walk down a sidewalk, it is logically possible that the next person we pass will lunge at our throats. But we don't *expect* them to. Why not? The same reason they expect us not to lunge at their throats. We may not know the person or have any special reason for trusting him or her, but we are willing to bank on the fact that the stranger, like other ordinary citizens, can be counted on to behave roughly within the terms of societal norms or pay the consequences of going to jail. Granted, genuine friends won't need a contract.[22] Friends treat each other better and trust each other more deeply than is assumed by terms of a contract. That is because we know how each of our friends is likely to behave, and we care for them enough to treat them well for their own sake. But who can be friends with everyone in the nation? So then, what about those whom we do not yet know personally, that is, strangers? Hobbes reasoned that really the only thing one can count on from strangers is that they desire not to suffer or die, just as you and I wish to avoid suffering and death. That mutual desire, he thinks, is the basis for our modern social contract: we agree to preserve the peace because that gives each of us the best chance of surviving without undue pain. So we agree to "get along"—doing things like driving on the right side of the road, even when we'd rather drive on the left—because everyone else agrees to do the same. It's not a bad plan. But it is a plan that assumes that the people involved—strangers, and perhaps even ill-willed strangers—tolerate compromise for the sake of mutual safety and effi-ciency in daily life. Everyone saves time by trusting strangers a little bit.

Second, the sought-for "peace" was not imagined by Hobbes as something substantive or solid, but something wispy and abstract. Peace was a "good" only in the sense that it was the *absence* of something bad. For social contract thinkers like Hobbes, peace is the *absence* of conflict, especially the absence of war. No more substantive account of the common good is offered than a barely tolerable balance of power that may teeter on the brink but does not plummet into civil war.[23] In sum, a "contract" is an arrangement between strangers who might otherwise be hostile.

When we think of engineering codes of ethics as contracts, it is quite natural to think of them as a kind of protection against potentially hostile "outsiders." In other words, codes of ethics are sometimes thought to as-sure touchy *clients* that work will be delivered in a timely fashion, assure suspicious *employers* that profits and trade secrets will stay within compa-ny walls, and assure the technologically ignorant *public* that no harm will come to them (perhaps even when *they* misuse products). In a litigious society in which we sue each other at the drop of a hat, the "peace" that is achieved is merely a legal one; engineers who keep the contract will not be sued.[24] But thinking that the code is aimed at *outsiders* makes nonsense out of this line from the ASME Code of Ethics: "Engineers shall perform services only in the areas of their competence; they shall build their pro-fessional reputation on the merit of their services and shall not compete unfairly with others" (Fundamental Canon #2). Only other *mechanical en-gineers* can spot competence in a mechanical engineer; and "unfair com-petition" can't possibly mean competition with *non*-engineers. This line of the ASME Code seems to be aimed at fellow engineers. As a result, we need an alternative reading strategy to taking the code as a mere contract.

So, what is the alternative? Ethicist William May has suggested that the religious idea of a "covenant" is helpful for understanding the practice of medicine.[25] Maybe the same idea will be helpful for understanding the practice of engineering.

If strangers form contracts, friends form *covenants*. Of course, there are friends and then there are *friends*! In contrast to friendships formed for utility or pleasure, Aristotle described *perfect friends* as those who wished each other well purely for the other's sake.[26] In his mind, the crucial word is "well-wishing." If you desire the well-being[27] of all your neighbors and they desire yours and each other's, then a whole network of well-wishing forms, one that encompasses the whole town (*polis*). This well-being or flourishing is not merely the absence of conflict. Oh no, quite the opposite; in this case flourishing means something positive, something concrete. Granted, you may have to be an *insider* to understand what it is. But at bottom it means having some notion of what human life is for, a *goal* or *end* or *telos* that we pursue in our life together.[28] (Or, in terms of functional definitions, to share a covenant is to share a functional definition for "human being.") When it comes to engineering, the "town" presumed by the professional code of ethics is the network of practicing engineers themselves. Rather than look outside engineering for the other contract parties (i.e., clients, employers, public), the covenantal approach suggests that engineering codes of ethics are best understood as having the force of *covenants formed among amigos*. All engineers, both within a firm and across all firms, form a great community of friends.

A historical example can show us how covenants work among friends. Two millennia prior to *Pax Romana*—the contractual "peace" enforced by the rule of the Caesars—there lived in Egypt a caste of slaves made up of foreigners from Canaan. Through a series of fantastic events in the reign of Pharaoh Rameses II, this band of Hebrews escaped Egypt and was led by their charismatic leader, Moses, to the hinterlands of a country that would one day be theirs. Curiously, this socially backward bunch of former slaves wandered somewhat aimlessly around the desert for an entire generation while they practiced learning how to be friends under the terms of a covenant that had become their own. This covenant became their constitution. It formed them as a distinctive people. It reminded them where they came from. It defined their very form of life. It told them what to do with their pots and pans. It told them to cancel all debts every fifty years and return any land held as collateral back to the original owner. It told them when to work and when to party, whom to have sex with and whom not to have sex with.

This covenant was *highly invasive*; nothing was considered off limits. It was totalizing in scope and seriousness: rebellious children as well as adulterers could be stoned to death for breach of this covenant. But the people shaped by this covenant seemed not to notice any pinch, because the covenant had one overwhelming advantage: *it was an agreement trumping all other considerations that turned strangers into friends.* When the Hebrews said "Shalom!" ("Peace!") to each other, they were not merely wishing for the absence of conflict. They were wishing upon each other the most substantive good possible—the good of true friendship, the good of becoming together the right kind of friends, the kind capable of living the covenant. It was in the sunshine of this friendship that they understood themselves to be the people of God.

In all likelihood, one probably has to be an insider to a covenantal form of life to fully appreciate the fact that achieving such a community is a better, meatier good than the mere absence of conflict. We really do not have an exact replica of this in modern society, although sometimes certain kinds of teamwork come close (for example, a combat unit or a team of medical missionaries). To imagine engineering codes of ethics in terms of *covenant* is to begin to ask questions: "Who is the 'we' that indicates our real friends?" and "What corporate good do we share that can possibly be better than not being sued?"[29]

4. Conversation-Starters rather than a Conversation-Stopper

When I lived in California, the house I owned had an unusual bathroom. My wife, three boys, and I tussled over access to a single bathroom that was seven feet wide and twelve feet long. In order to maintain our sanity, I spent one summer helping redesign the space into two bathrooms. I had a lot of help—a carpenter friend who drew up plans, secured the permits, helped with framing, and lined up rockers; a plumber friend who let me "apprentice" by doing some grunt work in the crawl space; and my dad, a retired mechanical engineer, who donated time and tools (and a couple of ribs—but that's another story) to help me finish. There was one person, however, who was not particularly helpful or easy to work with: the building inspector. My carpenter friend groaned when he heard which inspector the city had assigned to our project. No one seemed to recall his whole name because his initials seemed to sum up his sense of self-importance: "J.C."—as if he thought *he* was the Son of God! There was no budging, no room for negotiation with this guy. The complete building code book for San Bernardino, which he had seemingly committed to memory, was *the law*.

In the case of building codes, a given specification functions as a *conversation-stopper*. If your construction doesn't measure up—conversation over. If your vent stack doesn't hold sixteen vertical feet of water, call back when you get it right. On the other hand, if your construction does meet code, the conversation was also over because J. C. would have signed off on it, and you could move on.

I am suggesting that a professional code of ethics is not happily read as building code: "Thou shalt make the header double wide"—end of discussion. Instead, a given engineering PCOE is *a template for some of the most important conversation centers*. When the ASME Code says, "Engineers shall consider environmental impact and sustainable development," it really means that mechanical engineers must talk long and hard about optimizing sustainability through the design and manufacturing of a given widget.[30] The details of what that will look like in a given case *cannot* be spelled out in advance (as they necessarily must be spelled out in a building code). Rather, those details emerge after much conversation and negotiation. But the code gets us into *the discussions that are worth having*. And in those conversations, designers may discover other topics that have bearing. And so the conversation started by PCOE may quickly and rightly go *beyond* PCOE. But PCOE is the place to begin. It is a conversation-starter.

Consider again the vague wording in the eighth fundamental canon of the ASME Code: "Engineers shall consider environmental impact and sustainable development in the performance of their professional duties." This hardly works as a stipulation of well-defined duties. Rather it is an invitation to conversation, and more specifically an invitation to a conversation of the utmost importance. In this case, the code is helping us see what conversations are worth having first.

5. Prescriptive rather than Proscriptive

In addition to thinking of codes as *emblems*, the *consensus of experts*, *covenants among friends*, and *conversation-starters*, I suggest finally that we think of codes as *prescriptive* rather than *proscriptive*.[31] (To keep these straight, remember that in this case "pro-" means "no," as in "Thou shalt *not.*") Proscriptive statements tend to be fairly specific, enough so that violation is easily recognized. For example, a line from an earlier version of the NSPE Code of Ethics reads as follows: "The engineer will . . . not attempt to attract an engineer from another employer by unfair methods."[32] At some level, "unfair methods" is ambiguous, but surely *some* methods of recruitment (the promise of kickbacks, bribes, or dates with my sister) would be agreed to by all as blatantly underhanded. If we know what "recruiting violations" means when it happens on a collegiate sports team, we get the picture. The code is prohibiting a certain kind of "recruiting violation." In this instance, the prohibition functions like a *stipulation*, namely, an imperative given by an authority the breaking of which makes one culpable and liable to punishment by the authority. Proscriptions in a code of ethics do in fact resemble a building code. As we saw above, if you fail to put in a proper header when framing a doorway, the inspector will make you do it again or put a lien on your house. This sort of sequence makes us worry about reprisals should we happen to "break" a PCOE. To worry in this way shows one is thinking of the PCOE *proscriptively*.

What seems to be *sought* by proscription is a *guarantee* of ethical behavior regardless of whether the individual is a crook or saint at heart. It is called *pro*scription because of its negative form: "Thou shalt *not*." But isn't the mechanism for restricting unjust persons from doing unjust deeds what *laws* are for?[33] If laws succeed, then proscriptive codes are redundant. If laws fail, why would we imagine that prospective codes, with admittedly fewer punitive teeth than laws, will succeed? Whatever PCOEs are, they make for a very poor substitution for laws and government regulations.

In contrast, *prescriptions* are by nature open-ended and difficult to measure. Can one ever be finished with the responsibility to "hold paramount the safety, health and welfare of the public?"[34] That PCOEs cannot be reduced to negative commands illustrates the sheer fluidity of what W. L. King in 1944 called "the unwritten laws of engineering."[35] King acknowledges that engineering is like being in a battle: the engineer is under a strict chain of command. And yet King writes, "of course, there will be times you cannot wait to stand on ceremony and you'll have to go ahead and 'damn the torpedoes.'" King hastens to add, "But you cannot do it with impunity too often."[36] So, the expert has the responsibility to act decisively and even to break the rules, just not "too often." The trouble, of course, is knowing how often is "too often."

The ambiguity King identifies—"Thou shalt follow the chain of command except when it is important to disobey!"—sounds reminiscent of "wicked problems" and "design heuristics," which we met in an earlier chapter. While proscription has a nice black-and-white quality to it, prescription comes only in shades of gray. Consider the following two commands:

Proscription (Stipulation): "Every day thou shalt not eat a quarter-pound stick of butter."

Prescription (Heuristic): "Every day run ten minutes longer than is comfortable."

When we compare the two commands, we see that both appear to aim at health. If I *break* the proscription by eating a stick of butter every day, my health will eventually be jeopardized. Of course, refusing to eat butter daily doesn't force health upon me. After all, I might forego the butter but daily eat a tub of lard or drink a quart of cooking oil. But proscription is easy to measure.

In contrast, it is much tougher to know if I can "check off" the completion of a prescriptive statement because one is never sure one has done it correctly or enough. The worse one's physical endurance, the easier it is to specify when discomfort begins. But the more in shape one becomes, the more difficult it is to detect the onset of fatigue. The really committed runner doesn't even think about fatigue in terms of "discomfort" but rather in terms of challenge.

The important thing to notice about prescription is that *prescription makes for a training regimen that is self-transforming*. Not only is the onset of fatigue delayed the longer one has been in training, but the prescriptive command itself becomes superfluous. The expert runner can safely discard the command because he or she *has internalized it*. All the same, the beginning runner needs a concrete prescriptive command to keep him or her on track.

Once again the ASME Code can illustrate the prescriptive outlook: "Engineers shall continue their professional development throughout their careers and shall provide opportunities for the professional and ethical development of those engineers under their supervision" (Fundamental Canon #3). Once again the wording is vague, not at all easy to check off. But there is also more than a hint of something self-transforming. While new hires have recently graduated and so are sick and tired of schooling, the longer one is in the field, the more one becomes convinced that opportunities for quality "development" are not trials to be endured to please the boss, but chances for genuine gain. The journeyman engineer is self-motivated and therefore eagerly jumps on opportunities for development.

CONCLUSION

In this chapter we've applied the notion of *heuristics* and *design periphery* to professional codes of ethics. I have suggested that PCOEs fall short of their hoped-for power so long as we adopt the wrong reading strategy. But an engineering PCOE is not a uniform, a set of regulations, a contract, a set of building specs, or a set of taboos. Yet codes *can* contribute to (moral) formation of engineering so long as they are approached in the right spirit. That spirit is the spirit of heuristics. When PCOEs are taken as stipulations, ethics gets trimmed down to little more than decision theory (i.e., how to make a tough choice when facing a conundrum). But when PCOEs are seen through the lens of heuristics, ethics swells to include one's entire manner of living. In sum, PCOEs are most helpful when read (1) as a kind of badge of honor (or emblem), (2) as a thumbnail sketch of expert practice, (3) as a covenant formed among friends, (4) as a series of icebreakers that open up vast vistas of deep and significant design conversation, and (5) as a kind of "athletic" training regimen.

DISCUSSION QUESTIONS

1. In 2011, a team of Navy Seals succeeded in doing what ordinary citizens had been unable to do—track down and execute Osama bin Laden. How was Rev. Benke like/unlike a Navy Seal?

2. Explain endnote 14.

3. What are some of the dangers involved in thinking of PCOEs as "common sense"? By way of contrast, what does it mean to read PCOEs "heuristically"?

4. Pick one of the five ways to read heuristically and write a paragraph that explains it to your roommate.

NOTES

1. An earlier version of this chapter was first published as "Professional or Practitioner? What's Missing from the Codes?" in *Teaching Ethics: The Journal of the Society for Ethics across the Curriculum* 3 (2002) 49–66. Used with permission.

2. Merle and Markon, "Ex-Pentagon Official Admits Job Deal."

3. Koen, *Discussion of the Method*, 28.

4. For a quick link to engineering codes of ethics, see the Online Ethics Center's site: http://www.onlineethics.org/Resources/ethcodes/21733 .aspx.

5. The following litany of problems has been described at length in Ladd, "Quest for a Code of Professional Ethics," 130–36.

6. Firmage, *Modern Engineering Practice*, 37.

7. Hughson and Kohn, "Ethics," 132–47.

8. For a list of all Board rulings, see http://www.nspe.org/Ethics/Ethics-Resources/BER/index.html.

9. Wakin, "Seeing Heresy in a Service for Sept. 11."

10. For a more positive example, I know of another Protestant Christian denomination in Dayton, Ohio, that hosted a dinner for the Southern Christian Leadership Conference at which awards were given for local work done in the spirit of Martin Luther King Jr. In attendance were priests, Muslims, Baptists of many different stripes, as well as persons of a variety of colors and genders. In the spirit of welcome, prayers were offered for the nation, the State of Ohio, and the City of Dayton. In contrast to Benke's experience, no heresy trials ensued. We must be careful not to conclude from Benke's experience that all religions spawn intolerance.

11. "A Reaffirmation of the Synod's Position on Close(d) Communion."

12. For a glimpse into the form of life called "military," see Ricks, "Separation Anxiety."

13. "Hosanna-Tabor Evangelical Lutheran Church and School v. E.E.O.C, No. 10-553." Liptak, "Religious Groups Given 'Exception' to Work Bias Law."

14. In the eyes of society, an engineer does not cease to be an engineer when he or she loses membership in Professional Society, but when he or she loses the license to practice (though the two losses are related). But the condition under which one's license is lost is the last step in a divergence from the path taken by excellent practitioners. In other words, *engineers* do not lose their licenses. One who loses the license has already forfeited his or her identity as an engineer long before he or she is stripped of the license!

15. Gotterbarn, "Not All Codes Are Created Equal," 83. Emphasis added.

16. Cited in ibid. Emphasis added.

17. The fact that in this instance the meaning of the code is *not* self-evident may create the sort of dissonance that is a necessary precursor to learning.

18. Aristotle observed that "it is no easy task to be good. For in everything it is no easy task to find the middle . . . any one can get angry—that is easy—or give or spend money; but to do this to the right person, to

the right extent, at the right time, with the right aim, and in the right way, that is not for every one nor is it easy; that is why goodness is both rare and praiseworthy and noble." Aristotle, *Nicomachean Ethics*, ii. ch. 9.7.

19. Koen, *Discussion of the Method*, 67–69.

20. Ibid., 48–57.

21. Hobbes's most important work, *Leviathan*, was published in 1651.

22. Aristotle observed that true friends do not need a judicial system. See Aristotle's *Nicomachean Ethics*, 8.

23. Note that for social contract thinkers, any form of civil unrest is by definition a bad thing, because it disturbs the peace. This is one reason why the civil rights movement was so disturbing to average Americans. Although Dr. Martin Luther King's movement was nonviolent in nature, it was characterized as threatening the peace. When the terms of the social contract are themselves unjust (as were societal norms regarding race prior to 1964), these societal norms ought to be challenged. Notice that this last sentence relies on some notion of justice that cannot be reduced to mere absence of conflict. Prior to 1964, there *was* relative peace—but something was wrong.

24. Steffens et al., "Panel Discussion: Ideas for Better Code." For a less restrained account, see Richards, *Sue the Bastards*.

25. May, "Code, Covenant, Contract, or Philanthropy"; May, *Physician's Covenant*.

26. Aristotle, *Nicomachean Ethics*, 8.

27. Aristotle's term is *eudaimonia*, which is often translated "happiness" but is much deeper. *Eudaimonia* includes happiness, but also personal flourishing, well-being, and excellence in living.

28. See MacIntyre, *After Virtue*; MacIntyre, *Whose Justice? Which Rationality?*.

29. Medical ethics was perhaps the first to realize the importance of thinking in terms of covenant. Although it is beyond the scope of this paper, engineering ethics requires an assist akin to that provided to medical ethics by William May when he argued that medicine needed a goal (an end or *telos*) informed by *religious* sources in order for physicians to transcend the limitations of the metaphors of *technician*,

fighter, and *parent* to which medicine was susceptible. See May, *The Physician's Covenant.*

30. See ASME Code: http://files.asme.org/ASMEORG/Governance/3675.pdf.

31. This distinction was suggested as early as 1975. See comments by N. Balbanian in Steffens et al., "Panel Discussion: Ideas for Better Code."

32. Ibid., 100.

33. Aristotle, *Nichomachean Ethics,* 1144a 12–16.

34. NSPE, Fundamental Canon 1.

35. King, "Unwritten Laws of Engineering: Part 1"; King, "Unwritten Laws of Engineering: Part 2"; King, "Unwritten Laws of Engineering: Part 3." See also Amato, "Unwritten Laws."

36. Cited in Amato, "Unwritten Laws," 28.

5

DESIGN REASONING

HEURISTIC IS A TECHNICAL term that applies both to engineering practice as well as ethics. But it is a very unusual technical term. Instead of having a precise definition, it has a hand-wavy, rule-of-thumb sort of feel: "A heuristic is anything that provides a plausible aid or direction in the solution of a problem but is in the final analysis unjustified, incapable of justification, and potentially falsifiable."[1] Admittedly, this doesn't sound very technical. Heuristics work only most of the time; they are always subject to exceptions; they often conflict with other reliable heuristics; which heuristics apply is always a function of time and place and conditions; and no heuristic can be completely captured in a one-size-fits-all formula. In short, heuristics are inherently and always approximations. This fact means that heuristics require *skilled judgment* on the part of the engineer or ethicist.

The troubling thing is that skilled judgment is not a faculty that can be switched on and off at will. Unlike intelligence, which shows up any time we face a puzzle or problem, skilled judgment cannot be conjured out of thin air. If you don't have it, you don't have it—at least not yet.

The link between heuristics and skilled judgment is part of what is called "practical reasoning." Practical reasoning is the whole enchilada—do practical reasoning well and you will become "ethical," which is to say, a person of good character.[2] Fail at practical reasoning, even if you can defend value claims with the best of them, and you will fail at *life*. What practical reasoning is, how it works, and where we get it is the subject of the present chapter.

The term *practical reasoning* is something of a throwback to ancient philosophy. Aristotle observed that the kind of mental effort we bring to bear on a geometry problem is different from the kind of concentration we employ when figuring out how to settle a dispute between friends. Both of these differ from the kind of mindfulness needed when painting the house. The first kind of mental activity he calls "theoretical," the second kind "practical," and the third kind "productive." Math and logic belonged to theoretical reasoning, which by its nature provides clear-cut answers, but may not be attainable by everyone (theoretical reasoning requires a base level of intelligence). Each of us is born with a genetically prede- termined capacity for theoretical reasoning; not just anyone can learn quantum mechanics. Productive reasoning is more widely accessible. And while some individuals may have a natural "knack" for productive reason- ing, very frequently a "knack" can be captured in the form of a "technique" that can be taught even to young children. Thus it was with lay occupa- tions—butchers, bakers, and candlestick makers. Parents passed on task- specific techniques to the next generation of craftspersons.

In contrast to the limited attainability of theoretical reasoning and the specialization of productive techniques, *everyone* needs to be good at practical reasoning. Practical reasoning is the stuff of relationships, both at the personal level as well as citywide. As far as the ancient Greeks were concerned (we'll take Aristotle as their spokesperson), one needed to do practical reasoning well in order to live successfully each day. Practical reasoning means knowing *how* to be healthy, joyful, and reliable; have good conversations; build and keep friendships; and so on. The whole range of things that go into living well is what Aristotle called "ethics," and each step of this complex business calls for practical reasoning.

In the eyes of many ethicists, the insights of the ancient Greeks sim- ply cannot be improved upon.[3] It is not as though we haven't experimented with alternative accounts of the moral life. But one by one these have fallen by the wayside as unconvincing. For example, twentieth-century moral philosophers have been enamored with "action theory." This strategy sets out to dissect human action into its component parts, in the way that one might disassemble a lawn mower. According to act theorists, human ac- tion can be classified under physics. It shakes out like this: we inhabit a cosmos where stuff happens. We can easily imagine a class that contains everything that happens; this class is {*Events*}. The class {*Events*} seems to have two subclasses: {*happenings*} and {*actions*}. An action differs from a mere happening in that human subjects perform actions, whereas hap- penings simply "happen," with no help from humans. Another way to put it is to say that what makes an event an *action*, rather than a happening, is the addition of human agency. Can the subclass {*actions*} be analyzed further? According to some act theorists, {*actions*} can be subdivided into {*intelligible acts*} and {*unintelligible acts*}. If we chase {*intelligible acts*} a little further down the analytical path, we are told that what makes an action *intelligible* are the reasons *intended* by the agent at the time. In sum, an event is an "action" by virtue of adding *agency*; an act is "intelligible" by the addition of *intention*. It is a natural extension of this line of reasoning that a "moral act" is supposedly further subset of {*intelligible/intentional acts*}. On this view, an intelligible act becomes *moral* by the addition of some sort of "moral ingredient." But alas! What in the world is a "moral ingredient"?

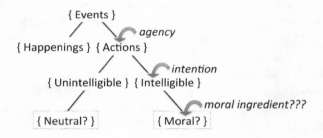

FIGURE 5.1 So-called Action Theory

This line of reasoning has fallen on hard times.[4] The whole picture falls apart because no one has convincingly isolated a "moral ingredient." But hold on a minute. Do we need a so-called action theory for thinking about morality and ethics? Not at all.

Suppose you build a bridge. Your supervisor stops by one day with the following instruction: "Now add the moral ingredient, because we want this to be an ethical bridge!" What would you say? Of course *there is nothing to say*. It is not as though there were some sort of ethical recipe. We can ask the barista what ingredient makes the hot chocolate so tasty ("A dash of cayenne pepper!"). But we cannot go to the shelf and look for a container marked "moral ingredient." There is no such thing as a moral ingredient that turns an ordinary bridge into a "moral" one.

The mistake that the imaginary supervisor makes is in thinking that morality is a special ingredient, one that can be separated from the intelligibility of the whole act and examined in isolation. But if morality is not a special ingredient, how are we to talk about it? This question brings us back to Aristotle and his followers. For Aristotle, "morality" (as well as *talk* about morality, which we call ethics) covers exactly the same region as practical reasoning. Did you catch that? Morality is not a subset of practical reasoning; *morality is identical to practical reasoning. Any act that derives from practical reasoning—whether it is telling a joke or constructing a road—is inherently moral.* Before we can see why this is so, we need an overview of how practical reasoning works.[5] Practical reasoning can be summarized in five points.

1. Every Exercise of Practical Reasoning Terminates in an Action

We are all familiar with how proofs in geometry proceed. One starts out by listing the relevant axioms. Then the axioms are manipulated according to the rules of logic and math. The proof concludes when the last move in the manipulation is the very claim one set out to prove. The Latin flourish at the end, Q.E.D (*quod erat demonstrandum*), is a kind of exclamation point that means "that which was to be demonstrated," or "Ta-da!"

According to Aristotle, the construction of a geometrical proof takes the application of *theoretical* reasoning. In this case of geometry, the reasoning process results in a *proposition*. That is to say, the conclusion of a geometrical proof is a sentence that affirms some factual claim. Not so for practical reasoning. Practical reasoning isn't finished *until an action is undertaken*. Suppose the lawn needs mowing. A practical reasoning argument would proceed this way: "The lawn needs mowing. This mechanical reel mower will do the trick. *To the mower!*" (said while actually commencing to mow the grass). If I pull up short and don't actually commence cutting the grass, my practical reasoning has been aborted. It is *not* enough simply to *say*, "This reel mower will do the trick." That would not yet be an instance of practical reasoning but something deficient, defective, incomplete, stillborn. In order for a line of reasoning to be "practical reasoning," it must generate an action.

2. The Metric of Practical Reasoning Is "Satisfactoriness"

You may be as familiar with logical arguments as you are with proofs in mathematics. If so, you will understand that, as is the case in math, logical arguments terminate in a fact-claiming sentence or proposition called "the conclusion." This is a feature of all forms of theoretical reasoning—the conclusion is a sentence that affirms that something is the case. And you'll also probably remember that the metrics for judging arguments have to do with *logic*. As we recall from chapter 3, what makes for a "good" exercise of theoretical reasoning is whether it is *sound, valid,* and *complete*. A *sound* argument is one for which all the premises are true. To say that an argument of theoretical reasoning is *complete* is to say that one hasn't forgotten any relevant premises. And *validity* has to do with the logical *form* of the argument: is one manipulating the premises according to the rules? Consider:

> Premise 1: Socrates is human.
> Premise 2: All humans are mortal.
> Conclusion: Therefore, Socrates is mortal.

This is a logical argument. Both of the premises are true. And as far as the conclusion is concerned, all the relevant premises are in play. As to formal validity, it can be expressed as an instance of the logical form called *modus ponens*: If some entity (x) has the property of humanity (H_x), then x also has the property of mortality; Socrates is just such an entity (H_s); ergo, Socrates will necessarily die. This is a classic exercise in theoretical reasoning. Using symbolic notation:

$$H_{Socrates}$$
$$H_x \rightarrow M_x$$
$$\therefore M_{Socrates}$$

But now let's look at a line of *practical* reasoning. Suppose I have lost my way while hiking. Night is falling, temperatures are dropping, and a storm is brewing.

> P_1: I need shelter.
> P_2: This sandstone cave is shelter.
> Action: Straightaway, I take shelter in the cave.

Notice that the "conclusion" is not a sentence, but rather an action. This marks one of the differences between theoretical and practical reasoning. But it is not the only difference. As it stands, the above argument is *not* a proper syllogism like the one about Socrates. Its so-called conclusion (i.e., holing up in the cave) cannot be demonstrated in any knockdown sort of way. If we put on thicker spectacles we can ferret out the "logical form." At first blush it looks reasonable enough.

A shelter is needed by a hiker.
If something is a cave, then it is a shelter.
Therefore, a cave is needed.

The formal logic can be symbolized thus:

$$S_{needed}$$
$$C_x \rightarrow S_x$$
$$\therefore C_{needed}$$

But hold on! This is the wrong way around. All arguments of this form are *invalid*. (The error is called *the fallacy of affirming the consequent*. See Figure 3.3.) We can see that it is fishy if we compare it with an obvious example.

P_1: I need shelter.

P_2: If x is a sandstone cave, then x is a shelter.

Action: Straightaway, I take shelter in the cave.

P_1: Susie met an animal.

P_2: If x is an elephant, then x is an animal.

Conclusion: Therefore, Susie met an elephant.

But Susie may have met a dog or cat or platypus. By saying she met an animal, we can't tell in advance what sort it was. But in the practical reasoning argument, we in fact do draw *correct* conclusions about this particular cave as matching what we need. How can we get the right answer using a faulty argument? What is the deal?

The deal is that *practical reasoning arguments are judged by a different metric than theoretical reasoning arguments*. This metric is not worse or of lesser quality. It is simply a metric that fits with practical reasoning. We know that theoretical reasoning arguments are governed by rules of logic. As a result, the theoretical reasoning conclusions are binding; one is *compelled* to assent to the conclusion if the premises are *true* and *complete* and the logical moves are of a *valid* form. But a reliable practical reasoning argument does not carry the same sort of binding clout. It might be a very good idea to hole up in the cave. But I might have instead set up the tent I am carrying in my pack or checked in to the Holiday Inn whose neon sign I can spot in the distance. These are all good solutions to my need for shelter.

The central criterion or metric for practical reasoning is *not* logical necessity. Rather, practical reasoning arguments are governed by the metric called "satisfactoriness."[6] Any course of action that is a *satisfactory* way to fulfill a need—the cave, the tent, the motel—is a "right" answer.

3. Details Change Everything

When it comes to theoretical reasoning, details are incidental. If Socrates is human, and all humans die, then nothing alters the conclusion that he will die too. We can imagine someone interrupting with these comments: "But Socrates was tall!" or "But he was bald!" or "But Socrates had a pug nose!" So what?! These details are of no consequence. Socrates will certainly die. How do we know? Because he was human and all humans eventually die.

In contrast to theoretical reasoning, practical reasoning "syllogisms" make sense, but are not compelling in the same way theoretical reasoning syllogisms are. Suppose you need to get to Chicago for a friend's wedding. You discover that there's a bus that will get you there on time. A satisfactory course of action may very well be: "To the Greyhound!" However, *practical reasoning arguments are susceptible to deal-breaking details* in ways that theoretical reasoning syllogisms are not. Granted, not all details matter or are relevant ("This bus is not yellow!"). But some details may be crucially relevant:

- "Diesel fumes give me severe headaches."

- "The bus driver's union went on a strike this morning."

- "There are no more seats available for this bus."

The addition of these details changes *everything*, because they transform a satisfactory plan into an unsatisfactory one.[7] As they say, it's "back to the drawing board."

The reference to drawing boards reminds us that practical reasoning is a general category that includes engineering design as a special case. Recall the comparison from chapter 2:

- There is no single right answer in *practical reasoning*. There may be entirely wrong answers. But within the range of roughly acceptable responses, each proposed response must be evaluated for its relative satisfactoriness.

- There is no single right answer in *engineering design*. There may be entirely wrong answers. But within the range of roughly acceptable responses, each proposed response must be evaluated for its relative satisfactoriness.

So too:

- There is no single right answer in *ethics*. There may be entirely wrong answers. But within the range of roughly acceptable responses, each proposed response must be evaluated for its relative satisfactoriness.

To say that one satisfactory solution may be preferable to another means that the degree of satisfactoriness is relative to the details of the immediate situation. So, details matter enormously. They matter for practical reasoning, they matter in engineering design, and they matter in ethics. Of course, not every detail is crucially relevant. While "there is a bear in the cave" may change the satisfactoriness of my plan to take shelter there, "there is a moth in the cave" does not. Consequently, we face an important puzzle: How does one know which details matter? There are two answers to this question. The easy answer: "Ask an expert." The more difficult answer: "Undergo a training regimen until your own 'eye for detail' is trained into expertise."

I must be careful not to give a wrong impression. Not all hands-on experience in engineering makes one "experienced." That is a fiction. There are indeed things to be learned in practical crafts like engineering, medicine, and music. But the learning does not simply happen as a result of logging the time. To gain "experience" one must participate in the *right way*—a subject we'll take up in the next two chapters. In the meantime it is enough for us to remember that engineering is one of the practical crafts, and learning to be an "experienced" engineer is as much (if not more so) *practical* as it is theory-based.[8] As we shall see in chapter 10, some of modern engineering's roots extend all the way back to the medieval craft tradition. The age-old crafts—carpentry, stonecutting, bricklaying, and the like—were famous for requiring long years of bodily training through which an apprentice must pass en route to gaining the skills needed for dealing with the many unanticipated challenges.[9] That the title "master craftsman" took years to earn meant that it carried with it a high degree of respect. But today we are impatient with bodily training and look instead for clever shortcuts. Of course, sometimes a shortcut turns out to be a long-term improvement for the practice as a whole. But oftentimes a shortcut is no better than cheap imitation for genuine skill that can only be inculcated the hard way. Despite some variety in the way historians tell the history of engineering in the West, there is widespread agreement that engineering began as a craft.[10] But since the nineteenth century, engineering has been slowly bending to the pressures of consumerism: cheap, fast, standardized, one-size-fits-all, cradle-to-grave, designed obsolescence.[11] If engineers completely succumb to the temptation for shortcuts, both their love of particulars and their eye for details will atrophy. But for now, let's assume that engineering simply is a craft in which master practitioners have the "eye for relevant details" and apprentices have the capacity—and will, with time and mentoring, slowly gain the eye.

To recap, there are two possible ways to determine which details are relevant to a particular design problem: ask an expert or undergo rigorous personal training. The first way to learn the relevant details is to ask an expert. This is fast and pretty reliable. (This method is only as reliable as the "expert" one consults; remember, the one who must rely on an expert may choose the wrong "expert" to rely on.) But reliance on an expert means leaving it to someone else to finish the chain of practical reasoning that we started. In contrast, the second way means *we* finish what we started. I don't mean that one acts in complete isolation. The second way still depends on others to play an important role, at least while we are still learning. So, in a sense, the second way is slow rather than fast. Training is likely to be very time-consuming. Moreover, the second path is fallible—until one improves, he or she may get it wrong more often than not. In some cases, a person may *never* quite learn it. But the fact remains that expertise in engineering *is* successfully passed on from generation to generation.[12] Therefore, one should always be hopeful about the possibility of improving one's own "eye." In that hope, then, let's look at the last two characteristics of practical reasoning.

4. RELEVANT DETAILS COME AS GESTALTS

Gestalt is German for "figure" or "form." It is used as a technical term in psychology for indicating the human ability to see things together as a unified whole. Early in the twentieth century, Joseph Jastrow concocted the now famous duck-rabbit image:

Figure 5.2 Psychologist Joseph Jastrow's "Duck-Rabbit"[13]

As shown, this image is a single figure, not two. We can see it as a duck (facing left) or as a rabbit (facing right), but never both at the same time. Of course, we sometimes experience the gestalt rapidly switching back and forth—now a duck, now a rabbit. But we experience the figure as one thing at a time. Spoken of singly, it makes sense to ask, "Is it a duck?" or "Is it a rabbit?" But it is not intelligible to ask, "What color is the rabbit's bill?" or "How long are the ducks ears?" What it makes sense to talk about depends on which of the two figures one sees at a given moment. Thus we can talk about webbed feet, feathers, and bill when the figure is seen as a duck. And it makes sense to talk about the long ears, soft fur, and wriggly nose when the figure is seen as a rabbit.

The flipping from one aspect to the other is called a gestalt switch. Here is a second example of gestalt perception closer to engineering design. We all remember doodling the Necker cube during third grade.

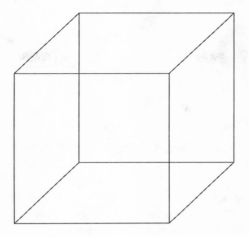

FIGURE 5.3 Necker Cube

You also probably remember the joy that came from doing mental games with the Necker cube—seeing it first as a 3D figure that comes off the page down and to the left, then as one that goes up and to the right. This simple collection of twelve lines cannot be defined as "a collection of twelve lines" because our brains, at least the brains of Westerners, see these lines as a *unit* bundled with *dimensionality*. It is the constellation of *twelve-lines-as-unit* + *dimensionality* that enables us to speak of it as a gestalt.

Back to practical reasoning. When I say that "relevant details come as gestalt," I mean that using practical reasoning requires one to *grasp relevant details as a unified whole* or set. Our ability to perceive patterns that supervene on figures that are distorted or out of context enables us to outperform computers at figure recognition. This is what enables humans to *read* the following CAPTCHA (Completely Automated Public Turing test to tell Computers and Humans Apart) but stumps the computer trying to classify it.[14] Not only can the computer not really read, it never "dawns" on the computer that the pattern of ink dots is, in fact, upside down. What makes the constellation upside down is the fact that it *has significance to us* as a gestalt.

Figure 5.4 Digital CAPTCHA

What makes the collection a unit might be called its *form*. For our purposes, once the details are seen as a set, one is already perceiving the form. So, don't worry about trying to isolate the form.

Perceiving according to a gestalt is more common than you might think. For example, suppose I own a '57 Chevy. In my eagerness to get to the classroom on a cold morning, I pump the accelerator like crazy while cranking the ignition. It doesn't start. I try it again. And again. And again. Disappointed, I get out, slap my forehead, mutter something under my breath, kick the tires, and decide to try it one more time before giving up. Miraculously, the engine springs to life! If I didn't know any better, I might mistakenly suppose that slapping my forehead and kicking the tires *caused* the car to start successfully. After all, these details *correspond* to the fact that, finally, the Chevy starts. But, in fact, they have no *causal* connection with the problem at all. Anyone experienced with mechanical carburetors will diagnose the problem as "flooding." In this case the relevant detail was not slapping or kicking but the *time* that elapsed while I slapped, muttered, and kicked. All the details—"pumping like crazy," "cold engine," and "time passing"—*together* form a gestalt, a picture that means something to a mechanic. The mechanic grabs up these details as a unit and gives the diagnosis with confidence.

The gestalt nature of relevant details in practical reasoning is a feature shared with reasoning in the empirical sciences and engineering design. Strictly speaking, theoretical reasoning does not operate with gestalts as much as it operates with universals abstracted from particulars. Theoretical reasoning does not trouble with concrete particulars or individuals. In order to write about particulars and individuals, we need sensory input about relevant details that together comprise gestalts that complete our reasoning. In other words, the scientist, engineer, and ethicist *need* particulars to do their jobs. A young child can parrot parental advice: "White meat is healthy." But unless the child learns to detect, say, grilled chicken strips as instances of white meat, the child cannot actually practice healthy eating. Principles without particulars do not make for excellence! Parents *hope* the child learns to reason this way:

> P$_1$: White meat is healthy.
> P$_2$: These chicken tenders are white meat.
> Action: "To the McNuggets!"

Notice that recognizing the McNuggets as white meat is not done via theoretical reasoning but by combining sensory data into a gestalt, a recognizable whole.[15] And, like every exercise of practical reasoning, *details matter*: the fact that the McNugget is a fried food may seriously undermine its healthiness, even if it is technically "white meat."

5. GESTALT RECOGNITION REQUIRES BODILY TRAINING

Exercises of practical reasoning terminate in actions that are measured according to "satisfactoriness" in light of an interdependent set, or gestalt, of relevant details. Successful practical reasoning—both success in engineering design and success in moral reasoning—requires repeated bodily engagements with sets of relevant details (i.e., with gestalts). This bodily engagement is a primary means of cultivating the "eye" for spotting relevant details. Cultures use varying metaphors for describing the result of this bodily engagement. In English we say both "She has a good *eye*" as well as "He has a good *ear*." In French the reference is to *le pif* (the nose), which English speakers also sometimes say. In Germany you might hear reference to *Faustregel* (the fist), and in Russia the phrase is measuring "by the fingers."[16] But the connotation is similar in each case—to do practical reasoning well, we must rely on knowledge that is *bodily* in nature.

In general this kind of knowing is called "tacit" because it cannot be put into words.[17] We know what a clarinet sounds like. But we could not describe it so well that a person who has never heard a clarinet could identify the sound after reading our description. That kind of knowledge simply cannot be put into words. Yet we really *do* know what a clarinet sounds like—and even stake our lives on telling the difference between the sound a clarinet makes and the whistle of an oncoming train! ("Hark! Is that a clarinet I hear?" . . . Crunch!)

Acquisition of tacit knowledge figures *very* heavily in successful engineering.[18] For example, the expert practitioner has got to be able to spot calculator errors. The basis for saying, "Wait a minute, that *can't* be right" is tacit knowledge. Tacit knowledge has the disadvantage of being not expressible in words. But tacit knowing has the advantage of being virtually impossible to forget. Who could forget the smell of coffee or how to ride a bicycle? Hands-on experience is the means by which tacit knowledge is cultivated, although a great number of contact hours does not guarantee that experience is converted into tacit knowledge. Yet once tacit knowledge is acquired, it stands forever firm for the reasoner.

When I wanted to turn my Midwestern basement into a family room, I called a structural engineer for advice on what size I-beam could hold up my house so that I could reduce the number of unsightly center posts from four to just two, one at each end of the twenty-five-foot span. Without hesitating, he said, "A ten-inch I-beam." "Are you *sure*?" (After all, it was my house we were talking about!) He responded curtly, "Look, I can show you all the calculations. But trust me, a ten-inch I-beam will do the trick." He was correct. After twenty friends and I hand-over-handed the beam through the basement window, installed it under the center floor joist, and removed the temporary bracing, the house didn't sag. There wasn't so much as a crack in the paint of the first floor walls.

What holds for engineering, in particular, holds for all forms of practical reasoning: Acquisition of *tacit* knowledge figures heavily in successful moral reasoning. As we shall see in chapters 6 and 7, we live most of our moral lives at the level of reflex, not decision. Reliable reflexes are perhaps the most common form that tacit knowing takes. While gut reactions are sometimes equated with the movement of "conscience," in the next section, we'll see why this isn't so.

Let Your Conscience Be Your Guide?

The previous sections provided a five-point overview of how practical reasoning is performed. The metric of a good response is "satisfactoriness." Incidentally, this term must not be confused with "satisficing." Satisficing means doing the bare minimum to get by. Satisficing would be the right label to give the very worst of all the possible satisfactory responses. In design and in moral reasoning, what is sought for is not "satisficing" but rather the closest approximation to the Good, where "Good" refers to the other end of the spectrum, the *best* of all the possible satisfactory responses. We also learned that one small detail can turn a satisfactory response into an unsatisfactory one. The trick, of course, is developing the right kind of sensitivity for picking up on the whole constellation of relevant details and how they impinge on each other. This constellation of details is called a gestalt, and our sensitivity to the gestalt is developed in us as *genuine* knowledge, but frequently as the kind of knowledge that cannot be put into words—that is, bodily or "tacit" knowledge.

Now we are ready to see how practical reasoning can be made easier by the way our bodies are fashioned. In other words, once our bodies are formed the right way—and this will be on purpose rather than by accident (see chapter 6)—then practical reasoning becomes easier.

Recall Aristotle's simple example:

(Implied P_0: Health is good.)
P_1: White meat is healthy.
P_2: *This* [picking up a piece of grilled chicken] is white meat.
Course of action: "tt*Mmpfh ttt chkknn*" ("To the chicken!"—said while chewing.)

We understand by "healthy" that health is something good. And in being "good" it is something we naturally and rightly desire (though we may, of course, debate how to achieve it).

In the simplest examples, there are a couple of ways to go wrong in practical reasoning. Here is a practical reasoning syllogism in its barest bones:

P_0: X is good.
P_1: Y is an instance of X.
P_2: Z is a means to Y.
Course of action: "To the Z!"

We cannot be mistaken about the desirability of good things (Xs). Our bodies are physically fashioned to approve of food, shelter, sleep, and clean air because we need these things to flourish. We are even physically wired to desire friendship, and fortunately we are biologically predisposed to trust others. (The presence of the so-called trust hormone, oxytocin, is evidence that friendship is one of the *physical* necessities of the human animal.) But we can be mistaken about whether some particular thing (Y) is good or not. This is the first way that practical reasoning can go astray. To be mistaken about a Y is a mistake in moving from P_0 to P_1. Of course, we may, through conditioning, be conflicted about P_1. Sometimes we find ourselves wanting X at the same time we fear it. For example, the forming of new friendships is attractive but risky! Yet desire for friendship as a genuine and legitimate human good is built into our physicality, as are the desires for the goods of food, shelter, sleep, and so on. So let us presume P_0 expresses a good we all agree on. Notice that we may still have problems on a case-by-case basis with the Y in P_1. Sure, food is good and health is good. But is this particular food, say, this turkey sandwich, healthier than this steak?[19]

With respect to food choice, we know that the average Joe and Jo may mistake which food is the healthy choice. It is logically possible that we may make mistakes about *moral* Ys too. The possibility of making a mistake is made worse by our cultural confusion about the idea of "conscience." For whatever reason, we today tend to think of "conscience" as an internal faculty that we can count on to shine a light on which Ys are really the morally good ones. Some people imagine the conscience as something they can consult privately, the way one double checks a recipe in a cookbook, expecting to find a black-and-white answer. Somewhere along the line, people have come to think of the conscience as a personal, internal, and "ultimately unarguable private repository of answers" to moral co-nundrums.[20] People also tend to think of the conscience working along the lines of an invisible fence for a dog. The fence is nonexistent as far as the dog is concerned—*until* the dog approaches the border. Then the dog is zapped with increasing amounts of pain the closer it comes to the boundary. When it can take no more, the dog backs away and the zapping ceases.

Granted, when we face a difficult choice, the habit center in our brains, the limbic system, *does* help us make decisions by supplying a bodily aversion to some options (effectively shortening the list of options).[21] But the limbic system must be *trained*, and is always being trained—whether intentionally or accidentally, for the good or for the ill, by self-direction or by directives of those in power over us.[22] Only in the most basic cases can our limbic system be thought automatically to give us "good advice." For example, we are all born with a physical aversion to torturing babies, just as we are born with the natural impulse to help someone in need.[23] But the limbic system cannot be "consulted" like a cookbook or movie times listing. The original notion of conscience (from the Medieval Latin term *conscientia*) refers to our capacity to undertake the entire reasoning process that generates action. It is not something we can reliably consult in advance. In the original sense, a "deliverance of conscience" simply refers to what we've decided to do given all the relevant details and heuristics.

So "conscience," properly speaking, does not give us a handy shortcut preempting the need to think, any more than one can defend one's proposed design to a client by saying, "Of course this is a good design, because I followed my intuition."

If *conscientia* is tied to the whole process of decision-making, and people are capable of making bad decisions as well as good ones, then we can see that *conscientia* is not an infallible moral faculty. In sum, we can go wrong in practical reasoning in the first place by an error with respect to P_1 (e.g., "Is the half-pound butter burger an instance of *white* meat?"). To be properly disposed toward real goods rather than pretenders will take some training. We will return to this training in chapter 7.

A *second* way we can go wrong in practical reasoning involves P_2: can we skillfully concoct the *means* for obtaining the good we seek? Positively, this means taking account of all the relevant details for formulating the plan. Negatively this means avoiding all rabbit trails and wild goose chases. Kicking the tires is not relevant to solving ignition trouble, but a time delay might be relevant (if, in fact, the carburetor is actually flooded). And once again, "attending to all and only relevant details" is a lot harder than it sounds. Consequently, our deliberation over means (P_2) can be mistaken.

In chapter 2 we mentioned the role that "synthetic reasoning" plays in design. Now we can define "synthetic reasoning." The ability to spot the relevant details from the surrounding context and weave it into a plan that most satisfactorily achieves the sought for good is what philosopher Caroline Whitbeck calls "synthetic reasoning."[24] In engineering design, the best designers are those who are able to draw relevant details from the widest context.[25] When architect Maya Lin designs an award-winning house whose roof is curved to blend with the contour of the hilly lot, art critics say she is brilliant. Her decision looks like intuition (or even magic) to the uninitiated. But admiration aside, it is very important to understanding practical reasoning to know that Maya Lin does not simply close her eyes and consult her intuition. Rather, she can and does *defend* her design as "good" by supplying reasons, especially by pointing out all the relevant details (here, the contour of the land), which she has observed through diligent study and subsequently aimed to optimize. The very details upon which she focuses are overlooked by others. Likewise, when Dean Kamen designed a wheelchair that can balance on its back two wheels, it was recognized as "good" in virtue of details that others have perennially overlooked, such as the inestimable value for the paraplegic to be at eye level with her peers.

Moral reasoning is "synthetic" in a way that resembles design and architecture: it is a creative response to all and only relevant details. Seeing the relevant details requires a skillful "eye." However, we can only see what we are *accustomed* to seeing. Consequently, skill in moral reasoning, like skill in design reasoning, will take time, practice, patience, mentoring—in short, "experience" by which we become attuned to all the relevant details. To repeat, becoming "experienced" does not happen automatically, as if sheer number of days, months, and years is all that it takes to improve. (We probably all know people who oddly enough opt to *repeat* former mistakes rather than learn from them.) But becoming "experienced"—becoming someone who has a good eye for spotting relevant details, one who has the tacit knowledge germane to concocting a satisfactory plan—*can* happen. But if it is not automatic, it is wise to look at those conditions under which we are most likely to develop it. In the next chapter, I shall argue that design itself is a formative activity. In chapter 7 we will look at how habituation occurs, so that we learn how to help things along. This discussion comes to a head in chapter 8, in which I argue that the skills of practical reasoning—both in the form of design thinking and moral reasoning—happen best inside a "practice."

DISCUSSION QUESTIONS

1. What are some reasons that "conscience" cannot provide reliable moral guidance? Or, what might you say to someone who claimed his or her design was superior because "I used my intuition"?

2. What is a gestalt? Can you think of any engineering examples to illustrate this concept?

3. List ten examples of tacit knowing from everyday life *not* mentioned in the text.

4. The term *satisficing* means doing the bare minimum to get by. How does the notion of "satisfactoriness" differ from that of satisficing?

5. How might you use the notion of "practical reasoning" to persuade a fellow design team member who belligerently insists that his or her design idea is "the only right way to do it"?

NOTES

1. Koen, *Discussion of the Method*, 28.

2. The etymology of "ethical" is the Greek word for "character" (*ēthos*).

3. See, for example, MacIntyre, *A Short History of Ethics*; MacIntyre, *After Virtue*.

4. For a readable introduction to what goes wrong, see the first chapter of Pinches, *Theology and Action*. The original wound to action theory was inflicted by Elizabeth Anscombe; see Anscombe, "Under a Description."

5. My sketch of practical reasoning is deeply indebted to two sources: Kenny, "Practical Reasoning and Rational Appetite"; McCabe, "Aquinas on Good Sense."

6. The term *satisfactoriness* is Kenny's; see Kenny, "Practical Reasoning and Rational Appetite."

7. Even a device whose implementation is as obvious as the tractor becomes something else in another culture. The American tractor played a critical role in driving collectivization in Soviet Russia, although it did not have this effect on American farming. Remember that an artifact is always an artifact-in-context. Sometimes the context makes the artifact into something quite other than intended. Dalrymple, "The American Tractor Comes to Soviet Agriculture."

8. Crawford, *Shop Class as Soulcraft*.

9. For a fascinating description of the immensely complicated challenge of making wooden hay wagons, especially their wheels, see Sturt, *The Wheelwright's Shop*.

10. Gispen, *New Profession, Old Order*; Layton, *The Revolt of Engineers*; Zussman, *Mechanics of the Middle Class*. Compare Meiskins, "The 'Revolt of the Engineers' Reconsidered."

11. McDonough and Braungart, *Cradle to Cradle*; Staudenmaier, "Perils of Progress Talk."

12. This is why Aristotle urges us to attend to the advice of truly "experienced" persons, even when they cannot "prove" what they are advising, "because experience has given them an eye" by which they see rightly. Aristotle, *Nicomachean Ethics*, vi.11 1143b11–14.

13. This image appeared prior to 1923 and so is considered "public domain"; http://en.wikipedia.org/wiki/File:Duck-Rabbit_illusion.jpg.

14. Eisenberg, "New Puzzles that Tell Humans from Machines."

15. For the more advanced student, this is what Aristotle meant by the enigmatic phrase "ultimate particular." A triangle is an ultimate particular not because it cannot be taken apart into its constitutive pieces, but because when we grasp this figure, $\triangle$, *as* a triangle, we grasp it as a whole. Our grasp of $\triangle$ as a triangle is the simplest act of perception. To break it down further is to make perception more complex. See Aristotle, *Nicomachean Ethics*, 1142a 23–30. See also Dunne, *Back to the Rough Ground*, 296–313.

16. Koen, *Discussion of the Method*, 34.

17. Polanyi, *The Tacit Dimension*.

18. Ferguson, "How Engineers Lose Touch."

19. It turns out that whether the meat is processed is a much bigger factor than whether the meat is white. So, if the turkey sandwich used processed meat, it is more likely to be associated with heart problems and diabetes than the red meat steak! Datz, "Eating Processed Meats, but Not Unprocessed Red Meats, May Raise Risk."

20. For a lucid explanation of conscience, see McCabe, "Aquinas on Good Sense," 421.

21. Damasio, *Descartes' Error*.

22. For an application of Damasio's theory of learning to engineering, see Kallenberg, "Teaching Engineering Ethics by Conceptual Design." We will consider Damasio's theory in more detail in ch. 7.

23. Bloom, "The Moral Life of Babies"; Wade, "We May Be Born with an Urge to Help."

24. See ch. 2.

25. The very widest context may include fields other than engineering. Insight from fields other than engineering into design projects is called "cross domain transfer" and will be considered in ch. 8.

6

DESIGN CAN CHANGE YOUR LIFE

IN THIS CHAPTER WE will look at the practice of design as the means by which engineers might improve themselves in a number of ways. Just as society unblinkingly believes that medical training and practice is likely to make one into a better person, at least eventually, engineering too has the capacity for moral formation. This process is not automatic any more than it is automatic for doctors. So, at some point the budding engineer needs to take an active role by asking, "In what ways can I cooperate? What things should I be doing now in order to be better later? In what manner should I be doing things?" These questions will be much easier to answer if we get a sense of how practical reasoning—especially design work—shapes the way we see and know.

Humans are both like and unlike other animals. Like other animals, our "world" is populated by those things that we pick up on by means of our sensory nervous system. We are pre-wired to detect specific things: we jump at loud noises, we smile back at loving faces, and we run from large fanged carnivores! Some things we are pre-wired to detect; other things we learn to detect, being taught to do so by family members. Yet unlike the animals, our "world" has an added level of significance. Our world is filled with more things than just those things we can sense.[1] Additionally, our world is constituted by all the things we talk about. These things range from the trivial ("What's on TV?") to the monumental ("What will be the long-term biological impact of the subsurface oil clouds off the Louisiana shoreline?"). So long as we talk about these things, they comprise the world we inhabit.

The world we talk about is itself inescapably moral. Why is that? Well, think about the word *moral*. We saw earlier that *moral* describes anything that we do "on purpose." Intentional actions always aim at some good (or evil). These intentional actions range from the trivial (brushing one's teeth) to the monumental (capping a leaking pipeline). Capping the pipeline is certainly more significant than brushing one's teeth. But capping the pipeline is not more moral. Because every intentional action aims at something good (or evil!), all intentional actions are inherently moral. Ethics, then, is conversation about all the things that have bearing on intentional action, especially when that conversation is in service of the quest for the less and less trivial.

Not every intentional action is an attempt to solve a problem. But some intentional actions are geared to problem solving. We are all familiar with the joy of solving a puzzle such as a Sudoku or a tricky integral. And it is tempting to imagine that engineering is comprised of this kind of puzzle solving. But the bulk of an engineer's day is filled with problem solving of a different sort. As we learned in chapter 5, this other kind of reasoning—one always having more than one "right" answer—is called "practical" and involves in every instance the activity of design. While it is certainly true that a relatively small percentage of engineering professionals bear the official title of "Design Engineer," nevertheless, all engineers are designers by virtue of the practical reasoning they constantly and repeatedly employ to devise satisfactory responses to context-dependent problems. In this chapter we want to look at (1) why design sometimes does not admit to shortcuts, and (2) why doing design "by longhand" may change your life. If this is true, then engineers can better themselves in part by engaging in design in the right way.

1. Dimensionless (or Scalar) Similarity

Engineers at the turn of the twentieth century had a special term for the kind of resemblance that a scaled-up version bears to its original: *dimensionless similarity*. They chose this term because the mathematical pattern, the scale, has no units of dimension. In other words, if I measure my garden in feet, the 8' x 11' garden amounts to 88 sq. ft. If I expand it on one side to become 16' x 11', the square footage has doubled to 176 sq. ft. But the scale with respect to area is simply 1:2 because 88 sq. ft./176 sq. ft. = 88 sq. ft./176 sq. ft. The dimensions cancel. If I measure my garden in centimeters (81,741 sq. cm for the original, and 163,428 sq. cm for the expanded version), the scale would be the same. Since the units of dimension drop out, it is called dimensionless similarity. Despite the fancy name, we can see that we already understand the concept of dimensionless similarity.

Since design work often involves sketching out or prototyping solutions, we can learn why some kinds of design are life-changing (and others not) by contrasting kinds of modeling. Below I give eight examples of obeying the command "Now do the same/similar thing." The examples will complete the following table:

Dimensionless Similarity	Dynamical Similarity	
1.	4.	5.
2.		6.
3.		7.
		8.

TABLE 6.1 Models and Similarities

Example #1: Doubling a Garden

Design is ubiquitous. We design flower beds, term papers, vacations, routes around the city, plans for dealing with irate coworkers, strategies for maximizing the food budget, means for nursing sick children, and so on endlessly. One year I planted a vegetable garden. I grew tomatoes, rhubarb, peas, beans, and beets. I designed the arrangement to optimize sunshine according to the various heights of each species. I also aimed at optimizing space, putting the plants close enough to prop each other up but not too close so as to shade or choke each other. The garden was quite small. Suppose next year I want to double it. It is easy to image a plot of land twice the size of this year's and arranged in such a way that its layout is similar to the current one, only larger:

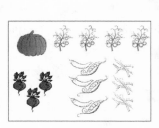 

8 x 11 garden   16 x 11 garden

Figure 6.1 Scalar Proportionality

This expansion of the garden is a kind of design that follows a mathematical pattern; everything has been doubled: twice as many plants, twice as much square footage, twice the harvest. The mathematical pattern is called a "scale." In this case, obviously, the scale with respect to area is 1:2 (the scale with respect to linear dimensions is 1:$\sqrt{2}$). Because this mathematical pattern is in play, even an untrained eye can see that the two gardens bear a special proportional similarity called "congruence."

Not every design expansion is a scale-up affair. Granted, scaling is very common. If I get a 10 percent raise in salary, I am very happy, because this means our food budget increases by 10 percent and that means 10 percent more ice cream! (Perhaps as a result I would thereafter weigh 10 percent more than I do today.) However, it is a mistake to think that designed expansions always follow an arithmetic recipe.

Examples #2 and #3

Consider this common diagram from an elementary geometry book:

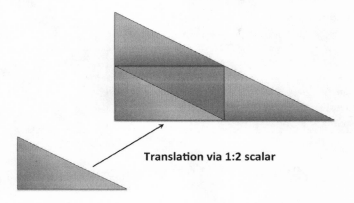

Translation via 1:2 scalar

FIGURE 6.2 Similar Triangles

Geometry texts do not include dimensional units, because they do not need to. You don't need dimensions to convey the idea that the second triangle is n times bigger than the first. In this case, the word *similar* means the angles are the same because the ratio (namely, 1:s) of correlative sides is identical for all three sides. Thus, $s = 2$ and $n = 4$.

The third example can be grasped even by those who flunked geometry. When a jury is given evidence proving fault in a traffic accident, the accident is sometimes reconstructed by means of matchbox-sized cars. This reconstruction is used to show the relative position of the cars before and after the crash. Such courtroom models are truthful representations precisely to the extent they approximate scalar models.[2]

The role that mathematics plays in these first three examples is to make the translation in each case compelling. Because we understand how mathematics drives the translation, we think of this kind of modeling as "theoretical reasoning." In other words, scalar translation is an example of ideal-world thinking. And when the penny drops for the student, and he or she cries, "Oh, I get it!" we say that what the student "gets" is insight into the mathematical regularity behind the scalar translation.

Dimensionless Similarity	Dynamical Similarity		
1. Doubling a garden	4.		5.
2. Similar triangles			6.
3. Courtroom models			7.
			8.
"Oh, I get it!" = Insight of timeless *mathematical regularity*. Conclusion: Theoretical reasoning is at work.			

2. Dynamical (Nonscalar) Similarity

Making a bigger garden and making a bigger triangle are special instances of design. Many times, perhaps more often than not, the designer makes plans from scratch. But in the above examples, design is not from scratch but a special subset of design involving the application of templates. Sometimes the template is a 2D picture. I might have sketched a plan of my garden in the summer so that I remember how to arrange the expanded version come next spring. Then again, maybe not. I can also imagine deciding on the spur of the moment to expand right then. In this case, the current garden itself serves as a template for the expansion and no pictures are used. The use of a template is one kind of modeling.

It should be obvious that templates involve dimensionless similarity. But modeling does not always involve simple translation. Sometimes modeling cannot run along the lines of dimensionless similarity. The rival concept of similarity came to be known as *dynamical similarity*. Seeing dynamical similarity is a constructive act of a human subject, an act that involves a skilled eye. For this reason dynamical similarity cannot be easily drawn (if at all). For the same reason, spotting dynamical similarity is not something that a computer can do. An art expert might be able to make the case that a newly discovered painting must have been painted by, say, Van Gogh by describing how this painting bears family resemblance to others known to be by Van Gogh. But spotting this family resemblance among works of art is a highly skilled activity—again, something a computer cannot do. (This is not because computers are not yet fast enough, but because they are not flesh and blood and therefore cannot think with their bodies like humans do.[3])

Because dynamical similarity is so difficult to describe, the following examples are more complicated. We shall see that they require of human modelers a different sort of reason than theoretical reasoning.

Example #4: Inscribing a Pentagon

Suppose you are presented with the challenge of inscribing a pentagon inside a circle using only a straightedge and compass. You might fiddle around long enough to come up with this nifty solution:

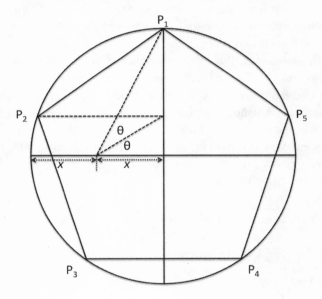

FIGURE 6.3 Inscribed Pentagon

This certainly looks like it works; if eyeballing counts as evidence, we'd say we stumbled upon the correct answer. In fact, someone good with angle bisecting probably can do this every time. After all, there is a kind of recipe involved.

1. Bisect the horizontal radius

2. Bisect the angle made from the midpoint to the apex (also P_1)

3. Mark the point where the nonhorizontal leg of the bisected angle intersects the vertical radius

4. Construct the horizontal parallel

5. Mark the intersection of the horizontal parallel with the circle as pentagon vertex #2 (P_2)

6. Repeat to find P_3, P_4, and P_5

"Fiddling around" until one gets a recipe that works every time is a colloquial way of describing what Aristotle called "productive reasoning." What distinguishes productive reasoning is the presence of a recipe or "technique" that can be taught to others *without* their necessarily grasping *why* the technique works. I suppose a true geometer like Euclid can explain both why the technique works as well as *prove* that each of the interior angles that result is necessarily 108°.[4] Euclid could explain while the youngster cannot. But that doesn't mean the recipe-follower is not engaged in thinking. Some kind of mental process must be involved to remember and faithfully reproduce the technique. For this reason, productive reasoning, while not as sophisticated as theoretical reasoning (and yet not as wide open as practical reasoning), occupies a place in the middle of the chart. What the student "gets" when he or she cries, "Oh, I get it!" is "the hang of it," as when we say, "Now he's got the hang of it!" What is gotten is not insight but a *technique*.

Dimensionless Similarity	*Dynamical Similarity*	
1. Doubling a garden	4. Inscribed pentagon	5.
2. Similar triangles		6.
3. Courtroom models		7.
		8.
"Oh, I get it!" = insight of timeless *mathematical regularity*. Conclusion: Theoretical reasoning is at work.	"Oh, I get it!" = the grasping of a *technique*. Conclusion: Productive reasoning is at work.	

Example #5: Heptacaidecagon (or Heptadecagon[5])

I would imagine that any geometry teacher would be impressed by the student who fiddled his or her way to the technique for constructing pentagons. Now imagine the teacher raising the stakes: "Well done! You've inscribed a regular polygon of five sides. *Now do the same for seventeen sides!*"

We understand, albeit vaguely, what is sought: a regular polygon with seventeen sides whose vertices all touch the circle. But what does the word *same* mean in the command "Do the *same* for seventeen"? As it turns out, the skill of bisecting angles is virtually no help at all. In fact, the "recipe" is so complex that no amount of mere fiddling is likely ever to produce something that a mere fiddler will recognize as part way towards the solution. If the fiddler cannot recognize that she is on the right path, she is likely to give up and try another strategy.

In case your curiosity is piqued, the inscription of a heptacaidecagon looks like this:

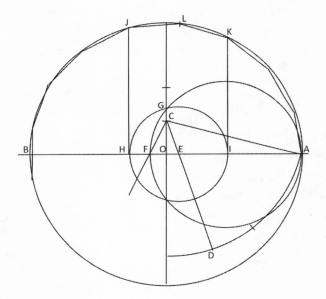

FIGURE 6.4 Inscribing a Heptacaidecagon

Yikes! With effort we would hope be able to follow the recipe well enough to be able to draw the figure. But chances are that many of us would not understand what was going on. The shallowness of our comprehension shows up in this scenario. Here is the drawing recipe, courtesy of Jim Loy's mathematics site:[6]

1. Draw the large circle O.

2. Draw a diameter AB.

3. Draw a diameter perpendicular to that diameter.

4. Bisect one of the radii on this line.

5. Bisect it again, to get point C in the diagram.

6. Draw line AC.

7. With C as a center, draw an arc with radius CA, from A to the vertical diameter in the diagram.

8. Bisect this arc.

9. Bisect it again, to get point D in the diagram.

10. Draw line CD, which then intersects line AB at point E.

11. Draw line CF at 45 degrees to line CE, as in the diagram (so F is on AB).

12. Bisect line AF and draw the circle with AF as its diameter. This circle intersects the vertical diameter of the big circle at a point G.

13. Draw the circle with center E and radius EG. This intersects line AB at H and I.

14. Draw lines perpendicular to AB, at points H and I.

15. These intersect the big circle at J and K.

16. Bisect arc JK, producing point L. J, K, L, and A are vertices of the 17-gon.

17. You can use these points to find the rest of the vertices, and connect them to produce the 17-gon.

If we are merely fiddlers, step 11 is like an item on a grocery list. I might commit a grocery list to memory that includes chili, bananas, green beans, milk, and eggs. If your brain works like mine, I can easily imagine forgetting a given item ("Oops, I forgot to buy bananas.") But memorizing a grocery list does not lend itself to seeing any connections between the items on the list. For example, there is nothing about chili and green beans that help me recall that bananas were the item between them on the list.

Now look at the "grocery list" for the 17-gon. It is easy to imagine forgetting a given step—say, step 11. I might remember steps 1 through 10 and remember how to finish from step 12 to 17. But if I've simply memorized the list, I won't be able to see the connection from step 10 to step 12. This means that I probably would not be able to conjure up the step once I get stymied. Only if I understand that step 11 can *only* be such-and-such, do I really understand what is going on. Otherwise, I'm simply memorizing step 11 by rote.

For this current example as well as examples #6 through #8, the "fiddler" can only begin questing for a solution if he or she already has a fairly high degree of knowledge about what is going on. Along the way, the quest for a solution inevitably requires a kind of *growth on the part of the seeker.* The nature of this growth is more than the accumulation of bits of mere information. It is also more than rote memorization of a mere technique. It is a kind of growth that changes who you are. We learned in chapter 4 to call this kind of reasoning "practical reasoning." What the student "gets" when he or she cries, "Oh, I get it!" is neither insight nor technique but something more elusive, something like know-how. Eventually, this know-how expands into genuine expertise.

Dimensionless Similarity	*Dynamical Similarity*	
1. Doubling a garden	4. Inscribed pentagon	5. Inscribed heptacaidecagon
2. Similar triangles		6.
3. Courtroom models		7.
		8.
"Oh, I get it!" = insight of timeless *mathematical regularity.* Conclusion: Theoretical reasoning is at work.	"Oh, I get it!" = the grasping of a *technique.* Conclusion: Productive reasoning is at work.	"Oh, I get it!" = *expert know-how.* Conclusion: Practical reasoning is at work.

Example #6: The "Peacemaker"

In 1844 a cannon on the deck of the USS *Princeton* was fired in honor of its christening as "The Peacemaker," the largest cannon of its day. The celebration was attended by a number of government and military dignitaries. But things went horribly awry when the cannon itself exploded. The blast sent shrapnel remains of the barrel into the crowd. Five persons of national standing were killed, including two members of then-President John Tyler's Cabinet.[7]

A great deal can be learned from engineering failures.[8] In this case, the failed cannon is a gruesome example of a time when, despite everyone's assumptions, engineering turned out *not* to be a scalar enterprise. Unfortunately, we cannot always predict in advance whether a given call for design is or is not a scalar affair. During the nineteenth century, the size of military cannons steadily increased; each new model was a slightly scaled-up version of its predecessors. Bigger artillery shells meant both a bigger bore and thicker barrel walls so as to channel the explosion safely. The gun on the USS *Princeton* seems to have had all the requisite dimensions. What went undetected, however, was the fact that *time* played a more critical role than wall thickness. How so? The new gun was so big that it required modified manufacturing procedures: the barrel was forged and cooled over a much longer period than smaller cannons. In general, a slow cooling produces malleable rather than brittle metal, generally a good thing when strength is required. However, Lee Pearson explains that "wrought iron is permeated with minute slag particles, is by nature fibrous, and if properly worked has fine grains. If wrought iron is heated to near the melting point for a long time, its grains increase in size, and impurities tend to collect in the grain boundaries, which thus become serious planes of weakness."[9]

Looking back, we can see that the wall strength of each successive cannon was being weakened with each scalar expansion. Meanwhile, the force of the explosion charge was also increasing. In retrospect, we can see what went wrong. While small increases in barrel thickness could still safely contain the force of the larger and larger blasts, at some point the increased blast force would exceed the strength of the weakened wall. This line was crossed with the Peacemaker. Because it took such a long time to manufacture, the barrel was prone to fail wherever there were impurities. We know now that the cannon wall of the Peacemaker had lost nearly *half* its strength.[10]

Dimensionless Similarity	Dynamical Similarity	
1. Doubling a garden	4. Inscribed pentagon	5. Inscribed heptacaidecagon
2. Similar triangles		6. The Peacemaker Cannon
3. Courtroom models		7.
		8.
"Oh I get it!" = insight of timeless *mathematical regularity*. Conclusion: Theoretical reasoning is at work.	"Oh I get it!" = the grasping of a *technique*. Conclusion: Productive reasoning is at work.	"Oh, I get it!" = *expert know-how*. Conclusion: Practical reasoning is at work.

Example #7: The Pénaud Flyer

In 1905, the famous physicist Ludwig Boltzmann published a collection of popular essays. Among them was an encyclopedia article titled "Model."[11] In this article, Boltzmann delineates two sorts of models: *mental models* and *experimental models*.[12] Boltzmann is concerned to warn his readers that mental modeling amounts to giving in to the temptation to oversimplify and idealize. Sometimes engineers and scientists are tempted to idealize because of a metaphysical or religious belief. For example, astronomers once thought that planetary orbits *must* be circular. Why? Because circles are geometrically perfect, and heavenly bodies were likewise perfect, and so heavenly bodies *must* move in perfect circles. As we saw in chapter 1, it is often best to "look and see" whether a model fits the real messy world in which we live. To accommodate the "messy world" requires what Boltzmann calls *experimental models*. Boltzmann is scolding engineers for letting ideals and ideology muddle their design.

For good or ill, engineering students learn mental modeling earlier in their coursework than experimental modeling. But as we have seen already, mental modeling needs to be corrected by tacit mastery of the real messy world we actually inhabit. According to Boltzmann, experimental modeling helps bring about the mastery that can correct mental models.[13]

Each of these two types of modeling—mental and experimental—has its unique attending concept of "similarity." Using terms we have already met, a mental model is *dimensionlessly similar* with the world it models.[14] An experimental model is *dynamically similar* with the world it expresses. We can better appreciate the difference by recalling the story of how airplanes were invented.

Boltzmann warned in the same 1905 article that a toy-scale flying machine might bear its own weight but fail to fly when scaled up.[15] (Remember, if "scale" is the only thing in play, we are talking about *mental* models.) Although Boltzmann wrote three years before the Wright brothers brought manned flight to Europe, the children in France had for some years played with a toy helicopter (really more of a "flying screw") designed by Alphonse Pénaud.[16] (A similar toy can still be purchased today.) The helicopter's rotors generate enough speed for liftoff because of the ingenious rack-and-pinion gear arrangement: the child pulls the foot-long strap (rack gear) quickly, the rotor turns and lifts the toy, keeping it aloft for flights of thirty to forty feet, enough to clear the roof and get stuck in the neighbor's tree. The toy clearly shows that heavier-than-air flight was possible.

Now, if designers were to follow the rule by which I doubled my garden—a.k.a. *dimensionless similarity*—they might scale up the Pénaud flyer by a factor of, say, fifteen. This prototype will look identical to the Pénaud toy. And at fifteen times larger, it will be big enough to house a human pilot. *But it can never fly*, even without the added weight of the pilot. While the strength of each part will have increased in proportion to the cross-section of the members (L^2), the weight has gone up by the *cube* of the linear dimensions (L^3). In other words, the propellers are fifteen times longer and 225 times stronger (because they are both fifteen times wider and fifteen times thicker [in two directions] than the propellers on the toy). But the whole thing *weighs* more than three thousand times (i.e., 15^3) more than the toy! Even if there were an energy source sufficient to pull the strap 15^3 faster than the toy, the thing *still* will not fly. In the first place, if *everything* relevant is scaled up in the replica, air density also should have been increased by the cube of the linear dimension. But since air density has not been scaled up, the large model has to compensate by some combination of vastly increased speed and pitch of the propeller. (A correlative problem faces real helicopters, which at very high altitudes run into a ceiling above which they cannot climb because they cannot get enough lift out of the rarified atmosphere.) Friction also becomes an enemy here—high-speed props do in fact "bend, break or melt." In short, the simple scale, 1:15, will simply *never* produce the kind of similarity needed for manned flight.

So then, no single dimensionless scale or parameter (e.g., 15) can regularize the functional differences that become enormously important when scaling up weight, strength, density, lift, etc. To repeat, the large replica model is *dimensionlessly similar* to the Pénaud flyer, because it is geometrically congruent. But it is *dynamically dissimilar*. For while the toy flies, the big version cannot. In contrast, a real helicopter (which took until the 1940s to perfect) is *dynamically similar* to the Pénaud flyer, but it is *dimensionlessly dissimilar*. In other words, a real helicopter looks nothing like the toy, but it really does fly. And because it does not look anything like the toy, the expansion cannot be easily modeled—either in one's head or on paper—like the expansion of a garden can be drawn.

The point for us is that dynamical similarity functions in quite conceptually different ways than dimensionless similarity. Of course, engineers ordinarily do not stop to consider which concept of "similarity" they employ: as their skills for modeling increase, their use of dynamical similarity completely eclipses concern for dimensionless similitude.

Dimensionless Similarity	Dynamical Similarity	
1. Doubling a garden	4. Inscribed pentagon	5. Inscribed heptacaidecagon
2. Similar triangles		6. The Peacemaker
3. Courtroom models		7. The Pénaud Flyer
		8.
"Oh, I get it!" = insight of timeless *mathematical regularity*. Conclusion: Theoretical reasoning is at work.	"Oh, I get it!" = the grasping of a *technique*. Conclusion: Productive reasoning is at work.	"Oh, I get it!" = *expert know-how*. Conclusion: Practical reasoning is at work.
Mental (or Ideal) Modeling . . . . *Experimental (or Expertise) Modeling*		

Example #8: Projecting Music

Once upon a time there was a young boy who showed promise as a budding engineer by building a working sewing machine out of wood when he was only twelve. He was quite bright for his age, attending school in the Austrian town of Linz at the same time the boy Adolph Hitler was in school. (Hitler was a year behind the others, while our hero, Ludwig, had been advanced a grade.) At the age of nineteen Ludwig enrolled in a PhD program in aeronautical engineering at the University of Manchester in England. The year was 1908, and the Wright brothers had just toured Europe with their flying contraption, piquing everyone's fascination with flying. Ludwig's research was focused on increasing aeronautical lift by improved propeller design and culminated in the design of a jet-assisted propeller.[17] During the summer of 1911, in which his ingenious design was patented in the United Kingdom, he read a book about the philosophy of mathematics by the world-class Cambridge scholar Bertrand Russell and sketched out his own response to a problem posed by Russell. This "sketch" slowly grew into a book. At Russell's invitation, Wittgenstein traveled to Cambridge and worked on his book while studying with Russell. Although Wittgenstein began writing during the summer vacation, he finished the book under much different conditions: while serving as a *Leutnant* for the army back in his home of Austria, during World War I, a war in which he distinguished himself for valor on the front lines, but ended the war as a POW.[18] Surprisingly, the manuscript he lugged around in his backpack survived the war and was published in German, his native language, under the title *Tractatus Logico-Philosophicus*. Soon it was translated and published in English, Russell himself writing the book's introduction. Oddly, perhaps thinking his work in philosophy was complete, Wittgenstein left Cambridge without jumping through the final hoops for his degree and took a job teaching elementary schoolchildren in rural Austria. Meanwhile, the book turned out to be hugely important in the world of philosophy. Several years later, Wittgenstein, the former engineer, finally got around to submitting his book as his "thesis" to the University of Cambridge in order to wrap up his degree requirement. Eager to claim this genius as their own, Cambridge instantly awarded him the Ph.D. and offered him a faculty position![19]

Wittgenstein would teach philosophy at Cambridge for several decades. Surprising to some, everything he taught had about it the aroma of his previous engineering experience. Most notable for our interests here are his use of the ideas of (1) *dynamical similarity* and, as a German-speaking engineer trained in the wake of Boltzmann, (2) *experimental models*.[20] Perhaps a more accurate term for experimental models might be *expertise* models, because the kind of modeling involved is related to all three notions of *experiment*, *experience*, and *expertise*. Wittgenstein shows that he was primarily concerned with experimental (expertise) models and dynamical similarity (rather than mental models and dimensionless similarity) because, like every other bright young engineer of the age, he wanted to solve the problems of manned air flight![21] As we have learned above, he abandoned this career path. But in light of his engineering experience, we can understand the final example.

The last of our eight examples is embedded in a crucial passage in the *Tractatus,* Wittgenstein's "thesis" that explains "dynamical similarity." When it is translated from German, the passage reads this way:

> In the fact that there is a *general rule* by means of which the musician can obtain the symphony out of the score, and that there is *a rule* by which one could reconstruct the symphony from the line on a gramophone record and from this again—by means of the first rule—construct the score, herein lies the *internal similarity* between these things which at first sight seem to be entirely different [i.e., dissimilar]. And that rule is the *law of projection* which projects the symphony into the language of musical notation. It is the rule of translation of *this language into the language* of the gramophone record.[22]

The terms that are ambiguous are "similarity," "projection," and "rule." We will unpack these each in turn.

a. What Sort of Similarity?

We know that as a mechanical engineering grad student, Wittgenstein doodled in his copy of Horace Lamb's textbook on hydrodynamics.[23] But his doodling was important: he consistently inserted dimensions into all the examples and calculations, even if they eventually canceled out. As an engineer (rather than a physicist), Wittgenstein was aware that *dimensions matter for good design*. What holds for middle-sized dry goods might not hold for long-span bridges or cannons (much less for nano-mechanisms). That he relentlessly inserted dimensions shows that he was attuned to the demands of dynamical similarity. What are these demands? Dynamical modeling makes demands upon the modeler: *only the modeler attuned to relevant details of the project is able to make the successful translation from concept to prototype.*

b. What Is "The Law of Projection"?

Some will likely remember the concept of "projection" from descriptive geometry. For example, we know what it means that a pyramid is orthogonally projected onto axis planes (Figure 6.5).

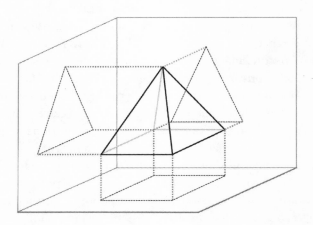

FIGURE 6.5 Orthogonal Projection

We can also draw rays of projection between a polygon and its scalar expansion, in this case between the original garden and its expansion (Figure 6.6).

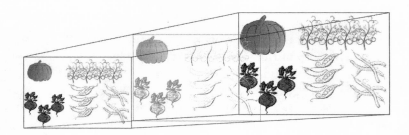

Figure 6.6 Scaling a Garden

Is this the kind of "projection" Wittgenstein is talking about? No. In both these cases, a computer can do the projection. But what Wittgenstein seems to have in mind doesn't seem to be the kind of thing a computer could do.

Think a moment about the examples that Wittgenstein gives. How is a live performance *similar* to the printed sheet music? How is a live performance *similar* to the physical groove in a vinyl record? Surely the relationship of symphonic performance to musical score or again between symphonic performance and groove in the old-fashioned long play (LP) vinyl record are problems much more like the problem of transforming the Pénaud flyer into a real helicopter than doubling a garden plot. Once again the difference is in the sort of modeling involved. In moving from performance to score, and performance to vinyl groove, *the model is varied according to conditions of the problem by means of the skills of the modeler.*[24] This method of projection is not a simple correspondence between archetype and model. Nor is this the sort of translation that can be understood by the average citizen juror. Rather, this method of projection is a function of highly developed experience, savvy, and know-how. That's why we call it expertise modeling. In short, the "projection" of the played symphony onto a previously blank score is *internally related to the actual skill of the particular musician* who is doing the transcription. Or again, if *expertise* rather than mental models is involved, then the "internal similarity"[25] that Wittgenstein refers to does not describe the one-to-one correspondence of dimensionless similarity (as can be traced between my garden and its enlargement). Rather, it refers to *dynamical similarity*. And it is "internal" because assessing the similarity is a skill internal to the conceptual world of the expert modeler. Whether a designer is getting dynamical similarity right cannot be assessed by spectators, because assessing "rightness" for dynamical similarity is a function of human skill. Only *through* the fingers and ears of skilled musicians may the symphony be said to be "similar" to the score. The rest of us have to take the musician's *word* for it. (Taking the word of a skilled expert is what Wittgenstein is alluding to with the mysterious idea of transporting one language into another language.)

c. How Is This Kind of Projection a "Law"?

We see, then, that the kind of projection involved must pass *through* the musician, designer, engineer, etc. Only a living, speaking, hearing, feeling, music-performing musician can read the score and heed the conductor's instructions ("Play as if you are swimming in a vat of melted chocolate!") and turn the score into actual music we can listen to. Only a living, speaking, designing, thinking, model-constructing engineering team can capture the played music in a form that can be replayed. Likewise, only a living, speaking, thinking engineering team can, with a lot of time, effort, experience, and play, transform the Pénaud flyer into a helicopter capable of bearing a human pilot.

How then does Wittgenstein call this projection a "law"? We generally think of laws as universal and unbending. Does "law" in this case refer to such a highly regular pattern that holds whether or not anyone is looking? Not at all. The "law" Wittgenstein is talking about is not so much an objective regularity as a *subjective* one, not so much a descriptive law as a prescriptive one. The law he is talking about is not like the law of gravity but like a traffic law. In the musical example, "law" connotes the fact that musical *convention* is regularized, for the social practice of music is conventional by nature. An individual musician has been progressively trained in her skill by intensive, regular participation in the cooperative practice under the watchful eye of expert mentors over a long course of time. She grows into a particular set of conventions surrounding musical notation and performance. This training amounts to habituation in both tacit and verbal know-how. Skilled musicians both play music well and talk about music well. But again, it takes one to know one: only an expert can vouch for the quality of a given performer.

FIGURE 6.7 Musician Projecting from Heard Music to Score (Transcription)

FIGURE 6.8 Musician Projecting Musical Score into Played Music (Performance)

FIGURE 6.9 Engineer Capturing Played Music Electronically

FIGURE 6.10 Engineer Transforming the Pénaud Flyer into Helicopter[26]

How then is this a "*general* rule"? It may be illuminating to read this phrase as an expression of the regularized *training* that musicians receive. The rule in view, therefore, is not a one-size-fits-all fiat (as in "rules are made to be broken"), but rather an *iterative training regimen,* again akin to the rigors of medical residency or the forming of expert engineers.[27] If the training regimens of doctors and engineers and musical virtuosi are flat-out *grueling,* the kind of life-formation involved indicates that the "rule" in view is best thought of as the heuristics governing the formation of novices—for example, the Rule of St. Benedict. What Wittgenstein seems to have in mind here is the fact that the expertise needed to expertly model is the product of a special kind of whole-body, lifelong training that musicians, monks, doctors, and engineers undergo. If skill is involved in projecting audio performance onto a musical score, a parallel claim can be made regarding the projection of a performance onto a vinyl groove. The projection from performance to vinyl passes *through* the skills, not of the musician this time, but of a team of engineers.[28]

CONCLUSION

In its most sophisticated moments, engineering design involves the construction of models that share "similarity." The comparison of similarity of two things cannot be done in the abstract; the similarity must be realized (made real) by the diligent application of skills by the modelers. This is what we mean by saying that a projection goes *through* the musician, *through* the engineer, *through* the design team. The philosopher-turned-engineer Wittgenstein attended to the participatory nature of this projection when he said, "it is the rule of translation of this language into [that] language." Wittgenstein didn't live in the era of Babblefish or other elaborate computer translators. So we must emphasize that he was *not* talking about word-for-word same-saying. It is very easy to replace the English words "Where is the bathroom?" with "¿Dónde está el baño?" That sentence is so simple that even a computer can do it. But think of the far trickier business of translating lyrics or a poem or even a joke. Comedian Robert Kline once reminisced about attending a family reunion as a small boy. Many of the old people spoke Yiddish. Every now and then the group would burst into laughter. Kline, who didn't speak Yiddish, would beg them to let him in on the joke. But the translated punch line was always anticlimactic. With tears of laughter still in his eyes, the uncle would say, "The gate swings on its hinge! Hahaha!!" Of course, in English this punch line isn't funny at all (except maybe because it is so out of place). Many jokes cannot be translated so smoothly that anyone can "get" them. That's because to "get" a joke requires sensitivity to irony, rhyme, timing, imagery, and verbal allusion—sensitivity that only a native speaker has.

But notice that Wittgenstein didn't say "translation"; he said "*rule of translation*." And the "rule" of translation is a lot like the Rule of St. Benedict—you have to join the community and log many hours, days, weeks, months, even years gaining fluency in the language as an insider. Only when you can bicker with a native like a brother will you then also get his jokes.

There are no shortcuts for the kind of modeling, a.k.a. designing, that necessarily passes *through* the skill set of the design team. This activity of skill building involves both brain and body. To this subject we turn next.

DISCUSSION QUESTIONS

1. Describe the difference between expertise modeling and mental modeling.

2. Compare and contrast dimensionless similarity and dynamical similarity.

3. Explain how Aristotle's three kinds of reasoning map onto two kinds of similarity. Where is the overlap?

4. Explain what the title of the chapter means.

5. Give an additional example for each of the three kinds of reasoning: theoretical, productive, and practical.

NOTES

1. Of course, not everything sensible contributes to an animal's world-of-meaning. The sheep ignores ants, as do we, because ants are not meaningful. But for the sheep, the only things in its world that are meaningful are those it can detect with the five senses. For humans, there is much that populates our world-of-meaning that is *not* detectable by our senses.

2. For courtroom models, the scale need not be precise to be truthful, but only display relative positions.

3. Philosopher John Searle explains this as the difference between semantics and syntax. A computer can spit back the right word (semantics) but cannot *use* concepts the way humans do (syntax) because it has no body. Just as a blind person can truthfully say, "This apple is red" but cannot experience redness, computers may be able to produce correct statements, but arrive at those statements in ways quite unlike humans. See Searle, "The Myth of the Computer."

4. In other words, there doesn't seem to be an obvious way to move from this recipe to the formula for interior angles of regular polygons. We may have learned from a geometry course that for an n-sided regular polygon, Interior Angle = $(180°) \times (n-2)/n$. But we could not have figured this out from the graphical recipe.

5. The current preferred spelling is *heptadecagon*; earlier books sometimes used the spelling *heptacaidecagon*. Since I'm taking cues from Wittgenstein, we'll use his version. For video lessons on how to inscribe a 17-gon, see http://www.youtube.com/watch?v=hDPIT_E-yE0&feature.

6. http://www.jimloy.com/geometry/17-gon.htm. For an impressive animation showing just how complex is constructing a 17-gon, see http://www.youtube.com/watch?v=LBgIWQcC6lM&feature=related.

7. See Pearson, "The 'Princeton' and the 'Peacemaker,'" esp. 169–70.

8. Petroski, *To Engineer Is Human*; Petroski, *Design Paradigms*; Petroski, "Past and Future Failures."

9. Pearson, "The 'Princeton' and the 'Peacemaker,'" 180.

10. See ibid., esp. 169–70.

11. This is an article that Wittgenstein is known to have read. Wilson, "Hertz, Boltzmann and Wittgenstein Reconsidered," 257.

12. Boltzmann, "Model," 219–20.

13. We are quick to insist that we don't want pretty pictures as much as we want devices that actually work. Yet oddly, the attraction of mental modeling is its symmetry and beauty. So, like a pretty picture, a mental model can sometimes serve as its own point. For turn-of-the-century kinematicians, mental modeling was a self-contained language game, like solving a Sudoku, complete with criteria for correctness internal to the game. However, in the education of engineers, mental modeling was merely preparatory for experimental modeling. In contrast to mental models, experimental models achieve *dynamical similarity*

only by means of painstaking hands-on experimentation. Experimental modeling pays close attention to dimensions. Experimental modeling is needed because it is not clear at the outset whether some dimensions thought to be irrelevant turn out later to be of greatest importance.

14. The beauty of mental models involves their "dimensionless parameters." Some of these dimensionless parameters are famous, such as the Mach number and the Reynolds number. Dimensionless parameters are calculated by means of "dimensional analysis." "It is instructive to use the notation to verify that the Reynolds number is dimensionless: one would do so by noting that writing the dimensions for density, velocity, linear dimension, and the inverse of viscosity yields the following 'chain': [M]1 [L]-3 [L]1 [T]-1 [L]1 [M]-1 [L]1 [T]1 which can be rearranged as: [M]1 [M]-1 [L]3 [L]-3 [T]1 [T]-1." Thus dimensions cancel; what remains is a "dimensionless parameter. (See Sterrett, "Physical Pictures," 126.) Sterrett goes on to observe that this notation was widespread and, importantly, used by Horace Lamb in his textbook *Hydrodynamics*—including the copy owned and marked up by the young Wittgenstein. See Spelt and McGuinness, "Marginalia in Wittgenstein's Copy of Lamb's *Hydrodynamics*."

15. Boltzmann explains: "A distinction must be observed between the [mental] models which have been described and those experimental models which present on a small scale a machine that is subsequently to be completed on a larger, so as to afford a trial of its capabilities. Here it must be noted that a mere alteration in dimensions is often sufficient to cause a material alteration in the action, since the various capabilities depend in various ways on the linear dimensions. Thus the weight varies as the cube of the linear dimensions, the surface of any single part and the phenomena that depend on such surfaces are proportionate to the square, while other effects—such as friction, expansion and condition of heat, etc. vary according to other laws. Hence a flying-machine, which when made on a small scale is able to support its own weight, loses its power when its dimensions are increased." Boltzmann, "Model," 219–20.

16. See Sterrett, *Wittgenstein Flies a Kite*. Drawings of Pénaud's can be found in the 1897 edition of *Encyclopedia Britannica* and are reproduced at http://www.uh.edu/engines/epi1129.htm.

17. Fuel was pumped to a tiny reaction chamber at the tip of each propeller blade. Upon reaction, the jet gas would escape the chamber tangential to the rotation of the blade, thus spinning the blade faster. The idea was eventually put into practice years later by Doblhoff in a World War II helicopter and more recently by Fairey's Jet Gyrodyne. McGuinness, *Wittgenstein: A Life*, 68–69. An image of the patent can be viewed online: http://rsnr.royalsocietypublishing.org/content/61/1/39/F1.expansion.html.

18. He was awarded the "Band of the Military Service Medal with Swords" for leadership and repeated acts of bravery. Monk, *Ludwig Wittgenstein*, 154.

19. Monk, *Ludwig Wittgenstein*, 271.

20. For a more technical discussion, see Kallenberg, "Rethinking Fideism through the Lens of Wittgenstein's Engineering Outlook."

    Wittgenstein used the idea of *dimensionless (scalar) similarity* very early on. It shows up in a set of notebooks he kept while writing his "honors thesis." In 1914 Wittgenstein latches on to an everyday example to illustrate dimensionless similarity. A newspaper article detailed a court case in Paris that employed a model of a traffic accident to settle questions of fault. The courtroom model used miniature cars and dolls arranged in such a way as to be "similar" to, or geometrically congruent with, the live scene of the accident. That jurors instinctively comprehend the model as a reliable reproduction of the traffic accident is shown by what they naturally discard as irrelevant details. In other words, this model resembles the crash in all the relevant respects. The model need not correspond with respect to, say, color or temperature or even speed. All that is necessary for dolls and toy cars to "model" what really happened is for them to reflect the relative position and direction of movement of each of the relevant objects. (In Wittgenstein's early jargon, the model need only match the logical or mathematical "multiplicity" of the scene of the crash: "In the [model] there must be exactly as many things distinguishable as there are in the state of affairs which it represents." Wittgenstein, *Tractatus Logico-Philosophicus*.) In their minds, jurors can draw, as it were, dotted lines between the model's relevant features and the corollaries in real life. See Wittgenstein, *Notebooks, 1914–1916*, 29.9.14 p.7e ; von Wright, *Wittgenstein*, 20f.; Wittgenstein, *Philosophische Betrachtungen, Philosophische Bemerkungen*, 2:279.

21. McGuinness, *Wittgenstein: A Life*, 53–72.

22. Wittgenstein, *Tractatus Logico-Philosophicus*, 4.0141.

23. Spelt and McGuinness, "Marginalia in Wittgenstein's Copy of Lamb's *Hydrodynamics*," 131–48.

24. I concede that Wittgenstein's very early book, the *Tractatus*, possesses a serious spirit of generalization, for which I blame the influence of Hertz (and other mental modelers) upon young Wittgenstein, who idolized Hertz. We can see this influence in the passage immediately preceding the one cited where Wittgenstein claims that a "pictorial internal relation" holds between language and the world. In this early passage he envisions a one-to-one isomorphism, which he likens to the parallelism of the Grimms' fairy tale of the "The Golden Lads," that is, "the two youths, their two horses and their lilies" (4.014). See Ackermann, Ackermann, and Hendricks, "Wittgenstein's Fairy Tale." However, in the *Big Typescript*, written a few years later, Wittgenstein surrenders mental modeling and makes explicit his use of "pictorial" as an adverb (rather than "picture") that modifies an instance of skillful modeling. The shift of attention from picture to skill is determinative in Wittgenstein's philosophy. See Wittgenstein, *Philosophical Grammar*, 113. For my discussion of this, see Kallenberg, *Ethics as Grammar*, 101–12.

25. See also the notion of "pictorial internal relation" [*abbildenden internen Beziehung*] in *Tractatus* 4.014.

26. Image of Pénaud flyer is public domain: http://commons.wikimedia.org/wiki/File:Planaphore_skizze_01.jpg. Image of helicopter was obtained through istockphoto.com.

27. For an entertaining account of the way novice engineers become experts, see the biographical account of nineteenth-century engineer John Jervis in Morison, "The Works of John B. Jervis."

28. A whole host of disparate engineers is involved: one team designs the recording equipment and another the playback system (turntable, amplifier, etc.). Other teams manufacture the equipment, while still others—sound engineers, production engineers, and so on—work to skillfully mesh the performance and its recording, and so on.

7

So Be Good for Goodness' Sake!

IN THE LAST CHAPTER, we looked at the way the activity of design shaped the way engineers come to see the world. That they become skilled in making models that actually work is a function of their ever expanding skill set. What it means to "learn" a skill is, among other things, that the skill has staying power in one's life. Once you have learned how to ride a bicycle or throw a football with a spiral, you tend not to forget. Likewise, once engineering skills have been mastered, one tends not to forget them. One may get rusty but never completely forget.

Our ability to effortlessly remember and employ certain skills is not limited to technical skills. Staying power marks other skills of living too. For example, we make long-term friendships on the basis of a host of personal skills and qualities such as constancy, loyalty, and forbearance, but also humor, kindness, generosity (and so on). Taken together, these skills result in the staying power of each person in the friendship. In other words, staying power might be called "moral momentum." How qualities and skills gain moral momentum is the subject of this chapter.

MORAL MOMENTUM

In order to think about moral momentum, let's remind ourselves about the nature of ordinary momentum. Just as ordinary momentum holds promise for storing energy, so too moral momentum holds promise for storing moral resources.

In the face of the global energy crisis, there is an increasing amount of research going into finding better ways of *storing* energy. The sun

147

generates voltage in a PV plate, but only while light shines on it. What are we to do for energy at night? We might opt for battery storage. Joule for joule, batteries aren't a particularly efficient means for storing energy. So, the hunt is on to find better ways to store energy. Some of the "newer" ways of storing energy are also the oldest: mechanical devices. Depressing a car's brake pedal might be used, say, to initiate the coiling of a stiff spring. Energy stored in the spring is later reconverted into linear motion when the light turns green and the spring is allowed to uncoil and reaccelerate the car.

An old means of storing energy is the heavy flywheel. If we revisit Figure 1.1, we can imagine Gear B as the motor input and Gear A as being very heavily weighted, especially out near the teeth.

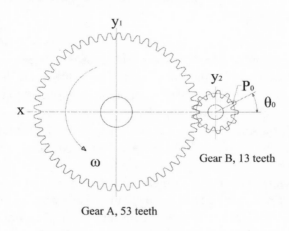

Gear A, 53 teeth

FIGURE 7.1 Angular Velocity ω

As you recall from first-year physics, linear momentum (p) is the product of mass (m) and linear velocity (v). Angular momentum (L) is the rotational analogue; angular momentum is given by the product of rotational inertia (I, a.k.a. moment of inertia) and angular velocity (ω). Increasing Gear A's rotational inertia (I), either by increasing the mass or by shifting the mass away from the axis, will place greater demands on the motor in order to bring Gear A up to top speed. (If the load is very great, a differential transmission may be needed.) But once Gear A reaches top speed, the spinning mass has a strong tendency to keep spinning (i.e., the conservation of angular momentum) and be extremely stable along the axis of rotation (the principle of the gyroscope).

Whether we are thinking of linear or angular momentum, we learned in high school physics that Newton was correct: a body in motion tends to stay in motion. Since momentum is the product of mass and velocity, more massive bodies (e.g., bowling balls >>> ping pong balls) are more difficult to deflect from their paths, as are very speedy bodies (bullets >>> BBs).

On the everyday level, we are also familiar with a kind of *moral* "momentum" associated with relationships. We count on the fact that our friendships today will be pretty much like they were yesterday. That's not to say disaster cannot occur. But when relationships do undergo change, we generally expect the nature of that change to be relatively slow. If a friend confided with you, "This morning, while brushing my teeth, I fell out of love with my fiancé," we would be confused. One might *recognize* in a flash that she no longer loves the fiancé. But reaching the actual state of no longer loving takes time to set in. One doesn't "fall" out of love; love, if it dies, normally dies a slow, gradual death.

The same slow, gradual process applies to falling *in* love. One may be struck, out of the blue, by the *recognition* that so-and-so standing there is infinitely fascinating and is a highly desirable object of a single-minded pursuit. But love itself is like the flywheel—it takes time and energy to get up to full speed. That fact, after all, is what gives love its staying power. We count on love's momentum to carry us through the difficult times that any real friendship undergoes. This is also why breakups are so painful; there is residual love that keeps spinning long after the separation. Only time can help love wind down.

Love is not the only quality that has a kind of momentum to it. Hope also takes time to build up, and then endures. Wittgenstein asks, "Could someone have a feeling of ardent love or hope for the space of one second?"[1] Of course not. Hope isn't fully hope until it begins to have that enduring quality, something lasting much longer than one second.

It turns out that many of the qualities we desire in our friends—love, hope, compassion, generosity, truthfulness, approachability, spontaneity, etc.—*take time to acquire* and once acquired tend to endure. Unfortunately, bad traits—mistrust, pettiness, scheming, self-centeredness, uncaring, etc.—also have staying power. The bumper sticker is correct: "Mean People Suck!" But what the bumper sticker doesn't explain is that the mean person will very likely be nasty tomorrow too. We expect that the "cure" for meanness, if there is one, will take time.

In the last chapter, we saw that what distinguished the engineer from a (mere) draftsperson is that the analogies (or models) that the engineer concocts are more than mere pictures because the modeling, the path from idea to artifact, passes *through* the engineer's real-world skills. Of course, in those examples the skills involved may be largely technical. But as we might expect, skills of communicating and negotiating are also in play for the expert design engineer. Come to think of it, so are other character traits such as honesty and reliability. Engineers acquire these skills, both the technical and the relational ones, by the same means that anyone acquires a skill: by learning them . . . slowly . . . over . . . time.[2] The phenomenon of "momentum" belongs to the nature of how animals learn—whether we are talking about hunting skills or friendship skills or linguistic skills or technical skills. When speaking of the *human* animal, positive skills are sometimes called "virtues" and negative ones "vices." As we shall see, virtues and vices play an important role in practical reasoning. Practical reasoning itself is the mark of being a good engineer, of being moral, and thus of being human.

Neuroscience and Virtuous Habits

Much can be learned about "virtue" by observing those who have been rendered physically incapable of expressing good character. The most famous example is Phineas Gage, the twenty-five-year-old railroad worker who in 1848 survived an explosion that obliterated much of his ability to make and keep friends.

The 1800s were heady times for the railroad industry as track spread all across the nation. The East-West connection was completed with the pounding in of the Golden Spike in 1869. Before that could happen a lot of rock had to be blasted out of the way. That was Gage's job. He oversaw a crew that used a chisel to pound out sequences of holes in which explosive charges would be fitted. Gage oversaw the adding of blasting powder, a fuse, and sand. Then, using his custom-made iron rod, Gage carefully (so as to not cause a spark) tamped the mixture. Gage was so experienced that he could do this job blindfolded—almost.[3]

Gage worked for the Rutland & Burlington line outside Cavendish, Vermont. On this particular day—Wednesday, September 13, 1848— around 4:30 in the afternoon, the powder Gage had been tamping exploded prematurely, sending his 3½-foot, 13¼-pound rod into his cheek and out through the top of his head. It landed some eighty feet away, covered with blood and bits of brain.

Gage did not die! In fact, after being momentarily stunned, he quickly recovered his wits, speaking within a few minutes and walking with little assistance to the cart that carried him—sitting upright—three-quarters of a mile to his lodgings. The first physician on the scene was Dr. Edward H. Williams:

> I first noticed the wound upon the head before I alighted from my carriage, the pulsations of the brain being very distinct. Mr. Gage, during the time I was examining this wound, was relating the manner in which he was injured to the bystanders. I did not believe Mr. Gage's statement at that time, but thought he was deceived. Mr. Gage persisted in saying that the bar went through his head . . . Mr. G. got up and vomited . . . the effort of vomiting pressed out about half a teacupful of the brain, which fell upon the floor . . . [4]

Dr. John Martyn Harlow took over the case about 6:00 p.m. As a military surgeon, Harlow was accustomed to horrific battle injuries. But Gage's behavior was even more impressive than his injuries: "the patient bore his sufferings with the most heroic firmness. He recognized me at once, and said he hoped he was not much hurt. He seemed to be perfectly conscious, but was getting exhausted from the hemorrhage, which was very profuse both externally and internally, the blood finding its way to the stomach, which regularly rejected it as often as every fifteen or twenty minutes. Pulse 60, and regular. His person and the bed on which he was laid were literally one gore of blood."[5]

Clearly Gage was not "all right." Although the rod apparently had been sterilized by the heat of the blast, the injuries required surgical attention and infection eventually set in. The infection resulted in a dangerous swelling in Gage's brain. The procedure to relieve brain swelling left him in a semicomatose state for about ten days (from September 23 to October 3). Hour by hour he was expected to die. On October 7, four days after regaining consciousness, he took his first step. By November he was walking up and down stairs—and all around the town square. By Thanksgiving he was strong enough to travel to his parents' home in New Hampshire. By spring he was ready to start looking for work. Gage was to live another eleven years.

Although his survival was astonishing enough, it was his Dr. Jekyll-Mr. Hyde transformation of character that made him famous. Prior to his accident, Gage was said to be "a responsible, intelligent, and socially well-adapted individual, a favorite with his peers and elders. He had made progress and showed promise."[6] After the accident he was still able-bodied (save the loss of vision in his left eye): "he had no impairment of movement or speech; new learning was intact, and neither memory nor intelligence in the conventional sense had been affected."[7] Gage's *character*, however, had taken a decided turn for the worst. In other words, the damage to Gage's brain meant that overnight he "unlearned" all of his relational sills and was rendered almost entirely unable to relearn them. After recounting Gage's relatively good physical health four years after the accident, Dr. Harlow reports the long-term degradation that had overcome Gage, which prevented his employers from giving him his old job back:

> The equilibrium or balance, so to speak, between his intellectual faculties and his animal propensities, seems to have been destroyed. He is fitful, irreverent, indulging at times in the grossest profanity (which was not previously his custom), manifesting but little deference for his fellows, impatient of restraint or advice when it conflicts with his desires, at times pertinaciously obstinate, yet capricious and vacillating, devising many plans of future operation, which are no sooner arranged than they are abandoned in turn for others appearing more feasible. A child in his intellectual capacity and manifestations, he has the animal passions of a strong man. Previous to his injury, though untrained in the schools, he possessed a well-balanced mind, and was looked upon by those who knew him as a shrewd, smart businessman, very energetic and persistent in executing all his plans of operation. In this regard his mind was radically changed, so decidedly that his friends and acquaintances said he was "no longer Gage."[8]

What is important for our interests, is the way that Gage's character and his practical reasoning were shown to be inseparable. This seems to imply for us that *both character and practical reasoning seem to be tied to our physical bodies.*

Since Gage's lifetime, a handful of similar cases involving brain injury–induced alteration of character have been carefully studied. In each instance an injury to a small region of the brain crippled the patient's ability to do practical reasoning even though the patient's theoretical reasoning was completely intact. You and I, as healthy adults whose theoretical reasoning and practical reasoning work seamlessly together, have difficulty imagining what life would be like after such an injury. In his masterful book *Descartes' Error*, Antonio Damasio details the difficulties of a patient dubbed "Elliot" subsequent to brain surgery that required the removal of both a tumor and damaged tissue from the prefrontal cortex. In contrast to the neocortex (the system that specializes in abstract and theoretical reasoning), which is far more developed in human beings than animals, the prefrontal cortex is comprised of cranial organs that human beings share in common with other mammals. It is located on the underside of the neocortex, roughly on level with the eyes and ears. The prefrontal cortex is closely associated with the "limbic" system and has to do with feeling and reacting.[9] Important for us is the fact that among its other functions, the limbic system specializes in *emotional awareness and practical responses.*[10]

Ordinarily, these two regions cooperate so well that neuroscientists refer to the brain as a "system of systems." In Elliot's case, the system broke down. The surgery on Elliot's prefrontal cortex saved his life but crippled Elliot's emotional awareness and practical response capabilities. Yet Elliot was as smart as ever! His IQ was in the superior range. And after a battery of cognitive tests—including the Wechsler Adult Intelligence Test and the Multilingual Aphasic Exam—Elliot's scores in language, comprehension, memory, logic, and so on, were always in the normal range or above.

On paper, Elliot looked like the sort of person who could reason his way out of a moral dilemma. In point of fact, he could comprehend complex scenarios, list the relevant principles, and even correctly rank competing principles from most important to least important. But listen to how he describes his own disability: "At the end of one session, after he had produced an abundant quantity of options for action, all of which were valid and implementable, Elliot smiled, apparently satisfied with his rich imagination, but added: 'And after all this, I still wouldn't know what to do!'"[11]

After surgery, Elliot lived like one who forever "wouldn't know what to do." Elliot's "decider" was permanently impaired. To cope, Elliot let others decide for him. As a result he soon lost both his job and marriage and was bamboozled out of large sums of money.

Elliot's problem was *not* his theoretical reasoning. Remember, he was as smart as he ever was. His problem was that his practical reasoning, his decision-maker, was broken. What Damasio learned from studying cases like Elliot and Gage was that practical reasoning *requires* "emotional awareness." Without emotional awareness, practical reasoning cannot happen. This strikes us as somewhat counterintuitive. We are often told that the best course of action must be "objective" and "disinterested." But

Elliot excelled at objectivity and disinterest: "he was always controlled, always describing scenes as a dispassionate, uninvolved spectator." Even when recounting his own story, never "was there a sense of his own suffering, even though he was the protagonist."[12] Elliot himself retained factual memory of his life before the tumor. But the things that used to tick him off (or excite him, or sadden him, etc.) no longer generated *any* reaction, either positive or negative.[13]

Elliot's cold-blooded indecision was the result of brain damage to the prefrontal cortex that thereafter prevented him from feeling—or more precisely, *prevented him from being aware of his bodily emotions*. "Bodily emotions" is an odd phrase. But by "bodily emotions," Damasio simply refers to our physical reactions to the environment. When we hear an explosion we jump, our heart rate quickens, our palms sweat, we have "butterflies" in our stomach, and our muscles tremble. This is all good—it is our body preparing itself to act. Interestingly, all these bodily reactions worked just fine for Elliot. What Elliot could not do is *detect* his body's reactions. Where he should have felt nervous (or excited or whatever), *he felt nothing at all*. Elliot's body generated *emotions* (= bodily reactions), but Elliot lacked *feelings* (= awareness of bodily reactions).

The mechanism of Elliot's plight is complicated. Roughly speaking, Elliot's body remembered how to respond to environmental cues. But after surgery removed a part of his prefrontal cortex, Elliot could no longer be aware of the cues his body was sending him. It was precisely this lack of awareness that torpedoed his practical reasoning.

What is interesting for our exploration of ethics is that without bodily cues, Elliot's "chooser" was disengaged, like a gear with no teeth. In some cases Elliot couldn't choose at all. Before being fired, Elliot's job involved (among other duties) sorting of his firm's case files. Granted, a new hire might wonder whether some paperwork might more properly be filed according to the contents of the case than alphabetically by client's name. But Elliot also considered bizarre criteria: should pages be sorted according to the color of the paper? Font size? Whether one-sided or two? Whether bearing a watermark or plain? Whether containing a staple or loose? And so on, *endlessly*! Normal workers simply do not consider such irrelevant criteria. But what makes the odd criteria *irrelevant*? This way of asking the question puts things the wrong way around. The focus of our attention should not be the criteria themselves. Rather, we should wonder how it is that normal workers simply overlook the goofy sorting criteria like paper color or font. The fact that they overlook goofy criteria saves normal workers tons of time. But Damasio wanted to know how it is that workers know not to pay attention to color or font as sorting criteria. They certainly don't mutter to themselves: "Hmm, is paper color important? No; I'll ignore color as a criteria. Is the location of a staple important?" Rather, these goofy metrics *never even cross their minds.*

Damasio explains that our *bodies* are hard at work in proper practical reasoning. The "limbic system" of the brain is not itself a thing, but a system of functionalities that is enmeshed with those of the body. This means that skill in practical reasoning—what we might call wisdom—*requires our brain to be attuned with our body.* This attunement is very complicated because there are multiple systems in the brain and multiple pathways for feedback from the body. For example, the neocortical region—the one most closely associated with theoretical reasoning—is dependent on feedback from the limbic system in the prefrontal region, which in turn is entangled with the rest of the body as well as with signals from the neocortex. Roughly speaking, things get processed this way: (1) the body responds to changes in the environment—say a loud explosion—and alerts the limbic system; (2) the limbic system sends a series of subconscious "directives" back to the body—muscles tense, nostrils flare, pupils dilate, palms sweat, and other things that prepare the body for action; Damasio calls these bodily responses *primary emotions*; (3) the limbic system also becomes aware of the body's nervousness; Damasio calls this awareness of primary emotions *feelings*; (4) the limbic system both passes along to the neocortex the initial sensation (the loud noise) and informs the neocortex of the feelings; the neocortex thus begins explicitly to *wonder* "Hey! What was that noise?" while simultaneously *becoming conscious* of the body's state of nervousness ("Wow! I nearly had a heart attack!").

The communications between the neocortex and the limbic system are not one-way streets. The limbic system also receives images or impressions from the neocortex and will ready the body for action as if the signal came from the body itself. So, for example, if you are watching a really scary movie, your body responds as if it were real: your skin creeps, your palms sweat, you feel butterflies in your stomach, you feel jittery as your heart speeds up (making it hard to fall asleep), and so on.

We don't often notice the instant at which primary emotions are elevated to consciousness. (Remember, they are *never* detected by Elliot). But primary emotions are not the only bodily state we are aware of. Of equal importance is a higher set of mechanisms Damasio labels *secondary emotions*, which constitute the body's habitual response to the brain-body processing of primary emotions. In other words, "we begin experiencing feelings and forming *systematic connections between the categories of objects and situations* [the loud bang, the smell of smoke, etc.], *on the one hand and primary emotions, on the other."*[14] Damasio's point is that secondary emotions cannot be processed by our emotional center (a.k.a. the limbic system) working alone; it takes the entire network of feedback loops between the body and those systems in the brain associated with sensing, thinking, and feeling. We are not always fully aware of these secondary emotions. In other words, while the brain is coping with all sorts of felt data as well as knowledge, theories, and stories it remembers, the limbic subsystem is saving the conscious brain time by *deepening habitual tendencies for certain courses of action.* Networks in the limbic system "automatically and involuntarily respond to signals arising from the processing of the [emotional] images. This prefrontal response comes from dispositional representations that embody knowledge pertaining to how certain types of situations usually have been paired with certain emotional responses, in your individual experience. In other words, it comes from *acquired* rather than *innate* dispositional representations."[15]

Damasio's point is that our tendency to act one way rather than another is often a *disposition that was learned at the level of bodily memory rather than conscious thought.* This does not mean that the subconscious brain peers into the heart of the matter and then chooses rightly—which is how most people assume "intuition" works. *Rather,* practical wisdom is simply *a body that has been trained to remember* the wisest way to act.

Once again Elliot's inability to detect his body's memory helps us understand how things operate with normal persons. He was included in a group given the task of choosing cards from one of three stacks. The stacks had been arranged with predetermined payout rates as well as predetermined penalty cards of varying levels of severity randomly hidden in each stack. Unbeknownst to the players, the stack that had the highest payout rate also held the greatest number of most severe disaster cards that randomly deprived players of their winnings. The other players, normally functioning adults, very quickly learned "to shy away from" the higher payoff stack because they became increasingly nervous toward the stack, *even before they could explain why they felt nervous.*

Note that in this experiment, primary emotions are not in play, as when a child learns from actual bodily pain not to touch a stove. Rather, the bodily emotion of the players results from limbic processing of mental images about winning and losing (even if these images are not processed consciously). In normal adults, nervousness toward the high-risk stack resulted in their shying away from the stack altogether, even before they could explain why they felt an aversion to the high-risk. But not Elliot.

Elliot did not have the capacity to *learn* to fear the high-risk stack because he was unaware of his body's nervousness. While the nervousness of ordinary adults increased with each draw, Elliot's attitude toward the next draw remained the same, as if it were his first. So Elliot's choices were randomly distributed among the stacks, whereas with each subsequent pick ordinary adults found themselves gravitating toward the safer, smaller-gain stacks.

The ability of the body to remember and to learn—and therefore to guide choices—happens by means of what Damasio calls "somatic [bodily] markers": "[S]omatic markers are a special instance of feelings generated from secondary emotions. Those emotions and feelings have been connected, by learning, to predict future outcomes of certain scenarios. When a negative somatic marker is juxtaposed to a particular future outcome the combination functions as an alarm bell. When a positive somatic marker is juxtaposed instead, it becomes a beacon of incentive."[16]

In terminology borrowed from design and heuristics, we might say that somatic markers are *tacit, embodied heuristics* for keeping one's list of options workably short. While Elliot had to wrestle with a seemingly endless list of metrics for sorting files, normal adults had already internalized attitudes toward certain criteria; they never considered paper color or font style. And because normal adults wouldn't even dream of considering them, such criteria seem silly and ridiculous. If Damasio's model holds, we can see that somatic markers play a crucial role in good design as well as moral choices.

If I have summarized Damasio's analysis fairly, four things stand out:[17]

1. The brain does not relate to the body as driver to car. In fact, the term *brain* bewitches us to imagine a unified control center (like the High Priest of Baltia sitting inside the humanoid head in *Men in Black*). In contrast, the brain's ten billion neurons (each of which communicates only to other *nearby* neurons) are organized into overlapping systems. There is no one-to-one correspondence between a given cluster of neurons and a given human function.

2. One system of systems (the limbic system) is entangled with the rest of the body by a combination of neurological and biochemical pathways. A different system of systems (the neocortical) is entangled with the limbic system, and thus more remotely with the body as well. The point is that the neocortical system's links to the body are often, perhaps always, *mediated* by the limbic system.

3. Secondary emotions arising from the limbic system's response to the neocortical awareness of primary emotions are dependent on learned, embodied pathways (in Damasio's language, "somatic markers").[18]

4. Wisdom in practical reasoning (i.e., making good decisions) is crucially dependent upon secondary emotions, which is to say on *felt tendencies* to respond one way rather than another. Importantly, these tendencies or dispositions are felt by our bodies; at the moment we must act, we "feel" something "in our gut" that helps us shy away from what we have formerly learned to be poor choices.

Especially crucial for us is the lesson that we are not born with bodily memory; *we must learn it.* Sometimes our bodies form memories randomly, reinforcing previous fears and prejudice, and wisdom is not the result. (After all, not everyone learns from his or her mistakes.) But the very good news is that *it is possible for bodies to learn wisdom.*

Whew! That may have been more biology than you expected or cared to learn from an engineering ethics book. But biology is another way to compare engineering and ethics. We saw earlier that the concept of "design" is central to both engineering and ethics. Understanding design in engineering helps us understand practical reasoning in ethics. And understanding everyday practical reasoning helps us understand the nature of design decision-making in engineering. We now see that human biology also plays a key role in practical reasoning, whether we're talking about practical reasoning in engineering design or practical reasoning in everyday living. In both cases, "feelings" play a central role. It's not that we must feel euphoric or weepy in order to make good decisions. Rather, one's "nose" or "gut reaction" can be *slowly trained* to assist us in living and designing well. This is not an automatic process (although it seems to come easier to some than to others). But however slowly or quickly the training takes place, *everyone is trainable* in virtue of simply being human. This is good news. Wherever one is on the journey, one can still learn.[19]

Everything You Always Wanted to Know about Virtue, but Were Afraid to Ask

If, as we have seen, our bodies play a crucial role in mental activity like making sound decisions, then it shouldn't surprise us that the whole "living excellently" thing is bodily in nature. The bodily dimension of practical reasoning is a subset of the broader bodily phenomenon called *habituation.* It is this bodily phenomenon that accounts for moral momentum.

The rest of this chapter sketches a quick-and-dirty introduction to the formation of bodily habits called *virtues*.

1. Forming Habits Is Biological

We know that habits are bodily things. As you remember from science films, even pigeons can be "taught" to turn in circles on cue. And flatworms can be conditioned to turn left rather than right in a T-shaped Petri dish by repeatedly injecting saline into the right well. Apparently the ability to form habits is not a reflection of one's IQ. Any living creature with a body can learn. Perhaps a better way to say this is that one's entire body is a memory storage device. Riding a bicycle, throwing a spiral, detecting bacon frying in a pan, dreading the dentist, picking out the sound of a clarinet, tying one's shoes blindfolded, walking upright, and so on, are all examples of knowledge stored in our bodies. If we think about it, the lion's share of our knowledge is stored as bodily memory rather than as "information." (That is why we can't put into words the smell of bacon frying or the sound of a clarinet.)

2. Human Animals Form Habits Intentionally

Fortunately for us, many of our habits are formed without trying. We didn't have to work very hard to learn to dread the dentist! Automatic habit formation is a great time-saving feature of being human. But not all habits happen automatically. Recall the feedback loop between our limbic system (the ventromedial underside of the brain working in tandem with our five senses to process raw bodily emotions as "feelings") and our neocortex (the evolutionarily later top side of the brain, where theoretical reasoning happens). Crudely put, our limbic system "talks" to our neocortex: any list of possible courses of action being deliberated by the neocortex is made more manageable by the bodily attraction we have learned to "feel" toward some options and the repulsion we have learned to feel toward others. (Whether we are *right* to feel these attractions and repulsions is another matter that we'll get to later.) Conversely, our neocortex "talks" to our limbic system. Our reason is able to cognize imaginary threats in a scary movie and our limbic system (not knowing any better) readies the body for fight or flight. The same thing happens when we imagine a future outcome: if we envision not getting hired, our body ends up cooperating, sometimes making us choke during a job interview. But the neocortex can also get involved in a more sophisticated way, namely in *planning the training* of *the limbic system*. One can consciously set up an obstacle course that trains the limbic system to be more useful in the future.

We are born with a number of natural inclinations, such as pain avoidance. We conclude that anyone who *pursues* pain is emotionally disturbed. But what if the pain is endured for the prospect of some hoped-for good? While there may be exceptional individuals, average people don't *naturally* run marathons or kill other humans (in battle). Yet average people can be *trained* to do both.[20] Initially, our bodies put up quite a fuss, because we are inclined to avoid exhaustion and to help rather than hurt others.[21] But our neocortex can anticipate our bodily reluctance and devise a training regimen that will eventually produce in us a different set of dispositions, which is to say a different set of bodily habits—ones that will assist the marathoner or the soldier.[22]

3. A Person's "Character" Can Be Read Off His or Her Habits

We sometimes think that "character" is something inside our skin. In fact, character is very public. As we travel through a day, we leave in our wake a trail of deeds from which onlookers decide what sort of person we are. If I regularly say mean things, people will call me "mean." It is no use trying to say, "But that's not who I really am in my heart of hearts." Because what I really am has already been shown by what I regularly do: I'm mean. Of course, any deed requires full description. And if my meanness is the result of extenuating circumstances, then we are tempted to reclassify my actions as something other than simple meanness. But the point is this: when an external act is truly described, it simultaneously reveals who I really am.

Let's say you do something positive, like an act of kindness. There are a couple of ways that one can be kind. A kind deed can be done (1) for the right reasons or (2) for the wrong reasons. Doing a kind deed for the sake of impressing onlookers cheapens the quality of the deed. On the other hand, the deed could be done for right reasons (for example, "She was in need," or "I care about him"). If you do a kind deed for right reasons, we can learn something further about your character by watching how your friends respond.

On the one hand, your friends may be unsurprised. That would mean that your friends have grown to expect this sort of deed coming from you. They cannot have formed this expectation unless they'd seen you act kindly *many* times before. This would be a good thing: you simply *are* just the sort of person who would act kindly. On the other hand, your friends may be surprised by your kindness. That doesn't mean the deed is less noble or that you must have some hidden, nefarious agenda. No, you'd still be doing the right thing for right reasons. But the surprise of your friends tells us that this deed doesn't quite fit what they've come to expect from you. In other words, the act of kindness, sad to say, is "out of character." Now, if from now on you repeatedly did kind deeds, your friends would revise their expectations about you. By the same token, you would have begun to change your character.

In sum, character involves bodies acting in discernible ways repeatedly over time. We can visualize this with the following diagram.

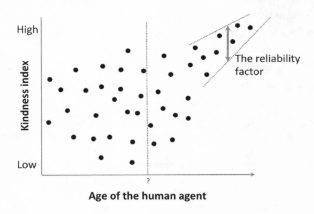

FIGURE 7.2 Integrity as the Solidifying of Character over Time

We don't have any numbers to work with, but qualitatively speaking, we can imagine our actions as being measurable in terms of being better or worse examples of what it means to be generous, truthful, brave, kind, joyful, etc. If we stick with the kindness example, it is easy to imagine that early in a child's life, the relative kindness of the child's actions would be all over the map, though not exceedingly kind or excessively cruel. A three-year-old sitting quietly in a circle listening to story time turns and punches her neighbor square in the face! Whatever was going through the three-year-old's mind, we cannot call her act "vicious"—not at the age of three. As a youngster, her actions are still likely to be somewhat randomly distributed. As her brain and body mature, however, so do her capacities for good and evil.

At some point, one's character begins to become more distinct. To the right of the vertical dotted line, the data points begin to converge. The convergence of these data points is a good thing, making easier the formation of increasingly solid friendships. After all, friendships develop more quickly between persons of settled character. (My wife banks on the fact that I'll be today pretty much like I was yesterday; I don't tell myself while shaving, "I think that just for today I'll become an ax murderer!") And most of us act more or less "within character." The more we can be counted on to act within character—the tighter the data points—the greater our "reliability" factor.

We can imagine redoing this fanciful thought experiment for every possible character trait—courage, faithfulness, honesty, peaceability, self-discipline, patience, etc. Together, all of the graphs can be thought of as constituting a qualitative "map" of one's character.

A person of "high" or "good" character is often said to have "integrity." In addition to being truthful, "integrity" also means that one's life is of *a piece, unified, well integrated*. It means that the person can be counted on to act in the same good manner as they always do. In terms of Figure 7.2, the "data" for our imaginary person displays these four features:

a.   A sufficient number of data points to establish a discernible pattern. (The inactive person doesn't leave much data to work with.)

b.   The data points are "tightly packed," or at least clustered closely enough to display a pattern.

c.   The trajectory of the data points (where the data appears to be moving into the future) seems to be holding steady and, even better, moving in a positive direction (i.e., up to the right).

d.   We rightly expect that the overall pattern or constellation of data will begin to resemble other familiar examples. Philosopher Alasdair MacIntyre observes that we can navigate through the social world only because we can read character types of the people around us. ("So-and-so reminds me of Snidely Whiplash; therefore, I don't trust him.") We make these comparisons by means of exemplar stories, both positive and negative, that we carry in our heads (e.g., "Honest Abe").[23] It is against these stories that we rate ourselves and others rate us. If real-life persons exemplify patterns akin to stories we read about, then it would be highly significant if the distribution of data looks more like Hitler's map rather than Mother Teresa's!

Again, this is an abstract analogy; we have no numerical data. Yet the point is plausible: virtually all of one's "data points" are viewable by one's friends and family; one's character is always publicly accessible!

4. Doing Well and Being Good

Grandmother: "How have you been?"

You: "I'm good."

Grandmother: "Mind your grammar! You should say 'I'm doing well'."

You: "Yeah . . . That too!"

Strictly speaking (which is something we almost never do), the word *well* is an adverb that describes the *manner* in which something is done or exists. Its counterpart, *good*, is an adjective that describes the quality of a thing or person. To say, "I'm good" literally means, "I have good character" or "I'm a good person." To say, "I've been doing well" includes the idea that "I've been doing quality work." (If all we really mean to say is "I'm healthy," a compromise might be to say, "I'm fine.")

The terms *good* and *well* are related. In the case of self-transforming practices such as medicine or engineering, one cannot do well without also being good (at least to some extent). Think about it. A mean, evil doctor would not inspire trust from patients. No trust, no disclosure of symptoms; no disclosure, no diagnosis; no diagnosis, poor doctor. Conversely, no one can be fully good unless he or she is also doing or living well. The good person who doesn't *do* anything in particular all day long will, over time, degenerate into a soft, lazy, undisciplined, and direction-less person. It is because of the interrelatedness of *well* and *good* that these practices are "varsity sports," in the sense that those who regularly and skillfully perform well see a lot of "playing time," while those who don't do well "ride the bench."

So what virtuous habits do engineers, in particular, need in order to do engineering well? Engineers flourish as they develop two kinds of habits. One set of habits has to do with reasoning. The other set of habits has to do with characteristic ways of relating to other people.

If you had to guess what it takes to earn a "varsity letter" in engineering, you'd probably first think of rational habits or virtues of clear thinking. As we saw in chapter 6, there are several kinds of thinking. When the limits of a system are well known, engineers are involved in engineering science, which is to say the application of science to well-structured problems: How long will it take to fill a distillation column? What is the position of a gear train at time t_i? What is the load on column C? What is the total impedance of this circuit? The kind of reasoning involved in engineering science is sometimes called "theoretical." To do it well, one needs familiarity with "fundamental principles" (e.g., "wholes are greater than parts") and theorems (e.g., $V = I \times R$). But one also needs to be skillful at recognizing *which* principles or theorems apply *now*, under *these* conditions, as well as how to make the logical moves that combine principles, theorems, and data to get answers. When the limits of a system are less well known (or even unknowable), the kind of reasoning called for is "practical reasoning." Designing, building, maintaining, and repairing actual physical artifacts, infrastructures, and other systems are activities that some engineers are better at than others. The best players are able to couple the most relevant heuristics with tacit awareness ("feel" or "eye" or "nose") of how best to apply them. Tacit awareness is a kind of bodily knowledge, like the bodily know-how of keeping your balance on a bicycle. Tacit knowledge is also habitual in the sense that the more one does it, the harder it is to forget how.

Medieval philosophers had special vocabulary for practical reasoning virtues. Correct knowledge of relevant heuristics was called *synderesis*. Those possessing synderesis knew *which goods* should be maximized under *these* conditions. (Is safety *always* more important than affordability? Should reliability be maximized so that an artifact that has a cultural life span of only two years nevertheless be built to last for a hundred?) Those with expert *know-how* in getting from A to B—from a broken machine to a repaired machine, from a blueprint to a prototype, etc.—were said to possess *phronesis* (Latin, *prudentia*). Roughly put, synderesis helps you recognize which contingent goods are best to maximize, and phronesis helps you plot the best means for getting there.[24] And, as we have seen, engineering ethics is much more like practical reasoning than theoretical reasoning, and so good engineering requires *both* of the habits internal to practical reasoning, namely, synderesis and phronesis. We do well to get clearer on these terms.

No one is born with *habits* of practical reasoning and theoretical reasoning. We are merely born with the capacity for acquiring these habits. Left to their own devices, children would be at a loss for determining the best path for building these habits. Luckily, children are born into families with parents who guide their education from the very first day. Eventually parents are joined by teachers and coaches who apply curricula that give students chances to form rational habits—initially, habits of theoretical reasoning. As students grow older, they are also given more and more chances to form practical reasoning by participation in practical activities of fields like engineering. These chances to learn include lab work, fieldwork, shop work, drafting work, shadowing, co-oping, internships, and so on. With repetition and guidance, skillful habits—habits of "doing well"—begin to sprout and grow.

5. The Problem of Moral Entropy

To be a good engineer requires one to "do well." In order to "do well" one must have skills, else what one does will be done poorly. But what about the other set of habits, the habits of "being good"? In addition to virtues of skill, it is hard to deny that *virtues of character* are also needed in engineering.

Imagine that you own a respectable engineering firm. Imagine also that the firm is still small enough that you personally must make a new hire. All else being equal, it is obvious that you'll hire the hard worker over the lazy one, the honest one over the deceitful one, the one who is peaceable rather than short-tempered, tidy over sloppy, and so on. Now look at the list: hardworking, honest, peaceable, tidy—the traits you would look for in a new hire are virtually the same as those traits that make for an excellent person.

If this list is so obvious, how is it that bogus engineers and bad persons ever get hired in the first place? One answer may be that the bogus engineer doesn't start out as bogus. Perhaps he or she *becomes* that way. But that only pushes the problem back one step. Recall the example from chapter 3, a forty-four-year-old software engineer working at a lucrative firm in Silicon Valley who was brought up on charges of attempting to sell fighter pilot training software to the Chinese Navy. He was convicted of two felonies: economic espionage and exporting controlled military technologies.[25] If engineering truly is a morally formative practice, why did engineering practice fail to guide this wayward person into the path of excellence?

While the list of desirable qualities may be obvious, the simple truth is (1) that we are not born with these traits, and (2) *acquiring* them is never straightforward or easy. Remember, we live in the messy world, and it is not easy to stay on track. The engineer-turned-philosopher Wittgenstein poignantly observed: "No one *can* speak the truth; if he has still not mastered himself. He *cannot* speak it;—but not because he is not clever enough yet. The truth can be spoken only by someone who is already *at home* in it; not by someone who still lives in falsehood and reaches out from falsehood towards truth on just one occasion."[26]

As we saw earlier, being truly honest involves a history of being honest so many times in a row that no one is even slightly surprised when you tell the truth. If becoming good is a journey, it makes sense that along the way we are likely both to face obstacles and to encounter helpers.

There is a very old and perplexing debate about the odds of whether one who *acts* the part of the good person will in fact make real moral progress. Will such a one really form lasting moral habits such that it is easy to be good? Or is the actor forever stuck at the level of faking it?[27] Keep in mind, the stakes are high: if I am currently a cad who desires to mend my ways but finds it impossible, the only kind of employer who will hire me is the obtuse person who can't detect my faulty character. And if this firm's human resources department is so obtuse, then this particular firm is likely *filled* with all the fakers that more discerning firms refused to hire. In the long run this would be an unpleasant place to work. While the optimistic side of the debate says moral progress is simply a matter of pulling up one's socks and forming good habits, the skeptical side observes that formation of new habits can't help but begin as the desire to win others' praise (impress the girlfriend, reel in the boyfriend, wow the boss, etc.). The skeptic goes on to observe that this desire is tainted because it is self-serving. In the mode of self-service, one is not likely to practice virtue for the sake of the virtue itself because the "new habits" are *self-serving* to the core. By stark contrast, real virtues are *self-forgetful* to the core. So, concludes the skeptic, the new habits are really vices in disguise; perhaps splendid vices, but vices nonetheless.

Still, even the skeptic concedes that genuine formation does happen under one set of conditions: childhood. Something about the state of children makes them morally malleable. At one level, the child wants to pull the cat's tail, but at another level, it learns that this will have bad consequences or disappoint Mom, etc. With repetition, the child undergoes a *natural* transference of desires: the desire to avoid painful consequences that follow from tail-pulling (whether physical punishment or emotional rebuke) slowly becomes transformed into the *loss of desire to do the bad thing*. Ethicist Jennifer Herdt suggests that part of what makes this process natural for children, but not for adults, may be the fact that children are unable to comprehend consequences as an effect of their actions (something adults can't help noticing). Rather, children simply grow to associate unpleasantness with tail-pulling.[28] As we saw above, unpleasantness is an emotion that gets routed through the child's limbic system. That routing is a mechanism that shortens the child's list of options for what to do next. At the emotional level the child *learns* to *want* not to pull the tail and so (eventually) doesn't even notice opportunities to pull the tail. That bears repeating: *The child learns to want not to pull the tail and so doesn't even notice opportunities to pull the tail.* Unfortunately, this doesn't work so well for adults, whose ability to scheme and rationalize short-circuits the way new desires might otherwise be internalized.

Trying to settle the age-old debate of whether playacting produces real virtue would take us too far afield. But the fact that this debate may never be settled doesn't need to stymie our enthusiasm for the virtues. We can find enough hopefulness to go on in the outlook of both Jesus, the prophet from Nazareth, and Hippocrates, the father of medicine. Jesus said that whoever wanted to become a naturalized citizen of his heavenly empire must do so by becoming "as a child." Matthew's Gospel brings out the hopefulness of Jesus' words, "Truly I tell you, unless you change and become like children, you will never enter the kingdom of heaven."[29] How is that hopeful? Well, by most accounts, Jesus is not the sort of person to tempt us with the impossible. He must have thought that "change and become like children" was something actually achievable for adults. The term for "child" is *paidos*, a cognate to the Greek term for "schooling" (*paideia*). The idea seems to be that the unformed-yet-formable character of children may possibly be recaptured by adults. This is good news indeed! *The unformed-yet-formable character of children may possibly be recaptured by adults.* This possibility is borne out by the ancient school of medicine that Hippocrates reported.

We largely remember Hippocrates for the famous oath taken by physicians when they graduated from ancient med school. But Hippocrates wrote a number of other essays describing how physicians were educated in sixth-century BCE Athens. Important for us is the fact that when a master physician took on a new student, the new student was adopted into the physician's family (apparently regardless of the student's age, though most novices were young). Unlike the first day of med school today, this was not merely a ceremony. Rather, the novices swore allegiance to their new siblings and to care for their new "father" in old age, just as the "father" tacitly pledged to train up the novice until *all* the skills of medicine became second-nature reflexes. These students literally became children of their master. Two more points. In taking the oath, the novice was promising not only to be a good physician; the novice was also promising to become a good mentor of the next generation.[30] (The "next generation" would be the current master's future "grandchildren" in the practice.) Second, the sought-for skills included more than technical prowess. In the eyes of ancient physicians, technical expertise and good moral character are two sides of one coin:

> Medicine possesses all the qualities that make for wisdom: disinterestedness, shamefastness, modesty, reserve, sound opinion, judgment, quiet, pugnacity, purity, sententious speech, knowledge of the things good and necessary for life, selling of that which cleanses, freedom from superstition, pre[-eminent][31] excellence divine. What [physicians] have, they have in opposition to intemperance, vulgarity, greed, concupiscence, robbery, shamelessness. This is knowledge of one's income, use of what conduces to friendship, the way and manner to be adopted toward one's children [i.e., the next generation of novices] and money.[32]

In short, Hippocrates presumed medicine to be a morally formative practice. And so we think today. It is my argument that all the social practices—not just medicine but also engineering, music, architecture, painting, farming, carpentry, etc.—are morally formative. We'll look more closely at this in the next chapter. For the present let us proceed on the assumption that training of novices in a practice is a little like training up children: in the transformation of desires there is genuine moral formation. That said, we come to the crux of the problem: moral formation is not automatic. It is not straightforward. It is not easy. No formula covers all the cases. In fact, one is more apt to fail than to succeed. These facts indicate a kind of *moral entropy* at work in the lives of human adults.

The idea that moral entropy opposes character development does not come as much of a surprise. Our language contains a huge variety of ways to describe moral lapses, which it would not contain if moral lapses were rare. Think of lying. One can lie, deceive, prevaricate, trick, snooker, spin, exaggerate, embellish, posture, fudge . . . Now think of all the other kinds of failings that mark human society: greed, gluttony, laziness, pride, jealousy, selfishness, inconstancy, and so on, each of which has its own dozen or so descriptions. In fact, the relative ease with which we repeat bad deeds is why we say bad habits are something we *fall* into. By contrast no one "falls into" a good habit!

So moral entropy is undeniably a problem. What can be done? Nothing—at least not by us as lone individuals. If moral entropy is to be offset, it will come as a gift offered to us by others.

6. Virtues Are Socially Assisted

Aristotle once stated the obvious: "it is no easy task to be good." He continues,

> For in everything it is no easy task to find the middle, e.g., to find the middle of the circle is not for everyone but for him who knows; so, too, any one can get angry—that is easy—or give or spend money; but to do this to the right person, to the right extent, at the right time, with the right aim, and in the right way, *that* is not for every one, nor is it easy; that is why goodness is both rare and laudable and noble.[33]

The difficulty, Aristotle writes, is that doing the right thing in the right way demands three things of the doer: "in the first place he or she must have knowledge, secondly choose the acts, and choose them for their own sakes, and thirdly the agent's actions must proceed from a firm and unchangeable character."[34] So difficult are these three demands that Aristotle said it would take a certain amount of "luck" to get on the right path and then stay there. Another word for "moral luck" is *grace* or *gift.*

A religious account of "moral luck" helpfully observes that there are multiple sources from which grace pours into the life of the one humble enough to admit need and receive help. One of the most important sources of grace for developing virtues is *friendship.*

Moral entropy feels like a kind of gravity that pulls us down. Or, to change the metaphor, moral entropy is like a natural current continually pulling us "downstream." Grace, then, is like a good stiff breeze that enables us to sail against the current. Often, progress feels like a standstill, where one's progress upstream is exactly matched by the speed of the current in the other direction. Still, we are lucky for any breath of wind that helps offset moral entropy.

Medieval theologians argued that it made sense to trace all gifts back to a Giver, namely, God. Some ancient pagan philosophers and poets agreed in part, admitting that so surrounded are we by the divine breath or "Spirit" (*wind* and *spirit* and *breath* are the same word in Greek as well as Hebrew) that "in this One we live and move and have our being."[35] Other ancient thinkers were more uncertain about the God hypothesis. But they still insisted that no man or woman is really "self-made." The skillfully lived life requires recognition and humble acceptance of those goods that are by nature *gifts* that come to us not by our doing.[36]

There are countless "graces" or "gifts": nurturing parents, bodily health, sunshine and rain for crops, books for reading (and the ability to read), a stable government, shelter from bad weather, *ad infinitum*. Yet, as just mentioned, one of the most important gifts of grace is *friendship*. In particular, there are at least three ways that friendship is home to virtue building. All three have to do with the gracious or gift-like nature of friendship: (1) the spirit of giving found in parental examples or mentors, (2) the esprit de corps found among like-minded others on the same journey, and (3) those creative geniuses found among expert practitioners.

a. Exemplars

Morally formative crafts, like engineering and medicine, today still resemble in important ways the clan-based guilds from which they evolved, particularly in the role played by "parental" models or mentors. Like "Mom," mentors on the job are marked by the "spirit" of self-sacrificial giving. The term "spirit of giving" is familiar to many as designating the Christmas holiday season (thus we all give more to charities in December than any other month). But the true mentor has a spirit of giving that isn't seasonal but lasts all year long. Like a good parent, the mentor is one who takes particular interest in the novice's progress and well-being. It is a kind of "friendship," though not a friendship between equals. Precisely because the novice is not on par with the mentor, the mentor takes care to teach the novice "the ropes." Learning the ropes can be tedious, if not downright painful. The novice may be assigned seemingly menial tasks to do, redo, and *re*-redo while never quite seeing the point.[37] Perhaps only much later, when the novice gains more expertise, will he or she able to look back and see the value in the tedious repetition. Before the novice sees properly, he or she may even resent the mentor for assigning such "stupid and boring" jobs. We see then that mentoring can be a pretty thankless task, because typically only those who have "graduated" are grateful.

In an ideal world—and never forget that we live in the messy one—every senior practitioner is a patient, self-giving mentor. Unfortunately, this doesn't hold true. In fact, mentorship programs instigated by managers are sometimes resented by both senior engineers and their charges. And, truth be told, logging years of work for a firm does not automatically make for expertise, much less produce genuine mentors whose hearts are in it. Moral entropy is an ever-present undertow even for mentors; engineers with two decades of experience but the heart of a trifler inevitably wind up farther *down*stream. So, whatever "mentorship program" the firm you work for has in place, it is wise always to be on the lookout for unofficial mentors, namely, seasoned practitioners who are marked by a spirit of giving. Once you've sniffed out one, try to keep him or her in your sights and learn whatever you can—even if you have to be clandestine in your observations. (A friend of mine, who is VP of engineering for a local engineering firm, calls this "stealth mentoring.")

b. Esprit de Corps

A second kind of friendship that makes for progress in the formation of virtuous habits is the "juice" that comes from training together with like-minded others. We know that rabid sports fans are sometimes said to have "team spirit." But the real spirit of the team is shared by the *players*. This is called esprit de corps, spirit of the "corps" (as in the Marine Corps).

It is pretty obvious that not every team achieves esprit de corps. Sometimes triflers, cheats, loafers, and nasties drive a team into the toxic zone. "Toxic" here signifies the poisonous fallout from unresolved tensions that, if unchecked, will become irreversible. The toxic group smells, almost like rotting flesh, because the humanity of the group and its members is morally decomposing. Sometimes, though not always, toxicity can be offset by human heroes who act as catalysts for goodness. To be specific, catalysts for goodness are those persons who work extra hard, play to win yet play unselfishly, speak encouragingly, and are themselves coachable. When there is a critical mass of this sort of player, the team begins to "click." In physics, you'll remember that "clicking" is more technically called *resonance*. In the social sciences, it is called *synergy*. Resonance or synergy is a kind of grace under which *the whole becomes more than the sum of the parts*; there is something extra that seems to show up out of the blue, for free, as it were. Once you've experienced synergy or esprit de corps, you hope to meet it again in every group you are a part of, from athletic teams to design teams. Sadly, a lone individual is powerless to generate resonance. The best the lone individual can do is *be* a good friend and so *forge* good friendships—and hope friendship catches on until synergy is achieved.

In addition to the magic of synergy, good friendships are grace-filled in a second way as well: good character is somewhat contagious.[38] We must recognize that not everyone is blessed with a warm and nurturing family. Even so, most of us are able to recognize blatant goodness when we meet it in other persons. We all prefer friends who are kind, loyal, generous, optimistic, good-humored, and so on. The simple fact that we reflexively spot these traits as "good" often triggers in us the urge to reciprocate and imitate the good qualities. (Thus the common Hollywood plotline of the ruffian refined by rubbing elbows with the kindhearted lover.) At first, the attempts to imitate the good qualities of the hoped-for friend may be feeble and clumsy. But as long as we have the good friend close at hand, we profit from witnessing his or her living example of how we ought to behave, especially if we want to win the good person as a true friend.

Clearly this is a fragile enterprise. No one is perfect. So, even a "good" person can only take so much disappointment from a hoped-for friend before moving on. For her part, the friend, being only human, can make progress only so fast. As a result, sometimes budding friendships break down. Still, having plenty of good persons nearby as a source of potential friendship is a genuine gift that can help offset the down drag of moral entropy.

The third way friendship with like-minded others is a gift can be seen in the amazing way that a group marked by the right sort of friendship is to some extent *self-repairing*. Since we live in a messy world rather than the ideal one, injury happens. There are moral lapses and incidents of meanness. Offenses are real and each one tears at the tissue of the group. However, sometimes *forgiveness* is freely offered and the tissue of the group heals.

We must be clear about what is at stake in the offer of forgiveness. If a child's baseball inadvertently breaks my car window, and I "forgive" that child, I am volunteering to bear the expense of the offense: I repair the broken window without holding a grudge or keeping score. I simply absorb the cost (including the inconvenience) so that there is no leftover cost. Once the window is repaired, all is well. The case of the broken window is simplistic—no people were injured, no feelings were hurt, no miscommunication occurred; in short, no significant cost is incurred apart from the price of a pane of glass. And after the repairs, things are back to normal: the "offense" was not intentional but accidental, and the offender was merely a child. Things may get nastier when adults are involved, as adults may inflict *intentional* wounds, thereby damaging emotions and reputations as well as windows. Still, the broken window illustrates the concept of cost-bearing that is at the heart of forgiveness. Of course, it is much easier to generously bear the cost of injuries inflicted by other adults (say, your coworkers) if the injuries are rare and if the offender shows real remorse.[39] Nevertheless, part of the synergy of a healthy group is the willingness to bear the injuries inflicted by members with poorer character and who may not even be able to see their speech habits and acts as offensive.

Not every offense comes from direct action motivated by meanness. The healthy group forgives those offenses that also come from a member's *inaction*, perhaps because he or she is timid or fainthearted.[40] In a design course I once co-taught, four teams competed for money that could be won or lost over a series of ten design exercises. While the money was not real, the amount accumulated did have a direct impact on one's course grade. So, everyone was highly motivated to win. One particular team had a lot of horsepower. But one of its members was a serious "glass-half-empty" sort of guy who shot down every idea and refused to work on prototyping ideas he thought were stupid. Another teammate was so mad at him that she couldn't think straight, essentially taking her out of the loop. Their winnings plummeted. But the remaining two were exceptionally generous and hardworking. They cared enough to talk it out as a team. Since the problem was not one of mean intentions (the offender couldn't even detect that he was a problem!) but one of poor relational skills, the two generous ones laid down some ground rules for design conversations. Their next project was still dismal, but better. Then they began winning and ended the course with the highest team earnings. Another group in this same class was not so lucky. The same "killjoy, can't-do" attitude of two teammates crippled group interaction. In this case the remaining two were unable to be catalysts for repair-through-forgiveness. That group finished dead last.

The good news in all this is the *possibility* of group self-repair. One biblical author advises an ancient community with this recipe for group health: "Flee from strong urges" that are fueled by nothing more than youthful hormones, because these detract from the functioning of any group. No design team can survive individual members who constantly cave in to greed or lust or pride. The antidote, says St. Paul, is twofold: Flee *and pursue*. "Flee from strong urges and pursue justice, faith, love and peace with those who call on the Lord from cleansed hearts."[41] Notice that the key to this antidote is that the "pursuit" St. Paul speaks of is a *team* effort: one pursues along with others. Notice, also, that the best teammates may not necessarily be those who are morally perfect (no such person exists), but rather those who "call on the Lord from *cleansed* hearts." One who "calls on the Lord" is someone who recognizes genuine need and is not too proud to ask for help. One who "calls . . . from a cleansed heart" remembers what it is like to have fallen, but has since gotten back up. In other words, people who remember themselves as having previously given offense make for sympathetic friends. Sympathetic friends are ones who can help us understand that our goal is not perfection, per se, but *progress*. And progress is unencumbered when we embrace this truth about ourselves: we are *imperfect but may be forgiven*.[42] Admitting one's own failings and accepting forgiveness is a mark of humility. *Forgiven* offenders make good teammates because they realize the value and healing power of the gift called forgiveness.

c. Creative Genius

Human beings need the gift of moral luck, a.k.a. "grace," because moral entropy is as real in the social sphere as physical entropy is in the physical realm. I have argued that two kinds of friendship are repositories of grace. We come, then, to a third kind of friendship that serves as a conduit of grace. In addition to a spirit of giving shown by mentors and the esprit de corps shared by like-minded pursuers of excellence, there is the rarer gift of "creative genius." In the world of the arts, artists are said to be inspired by their "Muse" or "genie."[43] (Here the word *inspire* has the sense of "breathe into" [Latin, *in + spirare*].) A creative genius, then, has something of the breath of the gods/God in them. We cannot build a theology on the etymology of words like *inspire*. Nevertheless, it seems clear enough that while the rest of us mere mortals struggle against the drag of moral entropy, a creative genius blows in like a breath of fresh air. Despite the fact that creative geniuses may be tortured persons,[44] the rest of us experience an enormous sense of gratitude for their gifts.

Creative geniuses are "friends" in the sense that financial donors to the orchestra are "friends" of the arts. I don't mean that the cello player gets together for coffee with a donor or that the violinist has the donors over for dinner! Yet the donors are "friends" because they are benefactors (*bene* + *facio*)—they "do good" for the orchestra as a whole. Ben Franklin was this kind of "friend" when he declined a very lucrative patent for his invention of the lightning rod, insisting instead that it be a gift to humanity.[45]

It is in this sense that creative geniuses may give to the practice as a whole. In fields like engineering and medicine, creative geniuses are not so much outside-the-box lone rangers as they are persons who combine technical expertise with the ability to see the world in morally insightful ways. I'm thinking here of MIT's Amy Smith and the University of Dayton's Margie Pinnell, both of whom have shown how clean-burning cookstoves can be built from indigenous materials resulting in the vastly improved respiratory health of children under five in developing nations.[46] Or consider designer Dean Kamen, whose design of the Segway seems to have been motivated by the desire to construct wheel chairs capable of balancing on two wheels, enabling paraplegics to climbs curbs or even stairs unassisted![47] Kamen has since gone on to design artificial limbs for amputees.[48]

But Smith, Pinnell, and Kamen are not isolated examples as benefactors of engineering.[49] Recently, Emily Pilloton has cataloged one hundred designs that empower the world's most powerless people.[50] The designers behind all these designs are an enormous gift to the practice as a whole because they remind us what engineering is *for*. They join the vast host of past experts—from Kettering to Watt, from Edison to Steinmetz—who set the standards for expertise *and* supply models of generosity for novices to emulate.

In this section we've seen that the down drag of moral entropy may be countered, at least in part, by moral luck, a.k.a. *grace*. We know that input of energy from outside a physical system enables that system to offset physical entropy. Sunshine provides the energy such that the earth's system does not run down. What I am suggesting is the existence of an analogous situation in the social world. You may have read William Holden's chilling tale *Lord of the Flies*, in which schoolchildren marooned on a desert island survive physically but, lacking adult supervision, degenerate to a state of all-out war among themselves. This is moral entropy at its worst. But what counters social chaos is the inflow of moral energy, grace, or luck. One of the most accessible and widespread gifts is that of friendship. When novices are in the process of developing good habits (both the moral kind and the technical kind), they greatly benefit from the assistance of self-giving mentors, like-minded teammates, and the field's creative geniuses.

In this chapter we have considered the moral life as one of virtue acquisition, which is to say, one of building good habits. Keep in mind that good *character* (*kalos ēthos* for Aristotle, spelled with a long *e*) in the end comes down to good *habits* (*kalos ĕthos*, with a short *e*). And although forming good habits is trickier than falling into bad habits, there is cause for some hope to be found within the practice itself. Chapter 8 describes how the very nature of engineering-as-practice can be harnessed to resist moral entropy. While this hope is real, it is not all that we need. Chapter 9 examines the phenomenon of cross-domain transfer. There we will explore how non-engineering sources may make real contributions to good design and the building of good people.

We are at last in a position to understand the definition of virtue. *Virtues are skilled reflexes for living well formed by habit with others in a practice under the tutelage of a mentor.* Some have said that this definition comes very close to the nature of athletics. For example, it takes time to build virtues, just like it takes time to build muscles. If a burglar is breaking into the house, it is too late to begin lifting weights! One would need to have begun weightlifting long before one hopes to repel a burglar by muscle power. So, too, with virtues. If you need courage immediately, it is too late to *begin* building courage. But if you may need courage someday (or generosity, or perseverance), why not begin building it today?

One might wonder: "Might not virtue be especially comparable to endurance sports?" Virtue does involve a kind of endurance, like that of a long-distance runner. And if we are lucky, virtue will be as addictive as long runs seem to be for distance runners. I confess that I loved the long training runs far more than I liked competing in any of the marathons I ran. That's because I loved the sheer loneliness of the long training runs. When I had a chance, I just slapped on my shoes and bolted out the door for an hour or two, sometimes even longer. (Okay, perhaps I have a lower than usual IQ!) I didn't need anything from anybody; I felt completely free. But in contrast with distance running, virtue acquisition is decidedly a *team sport*. In the next chapter we'll look more closely at the nature of engineering as a social enterprise called a "practice," and how the nature of engineering as a practice contributes to the formation of good character.

DISCUSSION QUESTIONS

1. Explain the difference between *prudentia* and *synderesis*.

2. Why is it better for your friends to be unsurprised by your doing of a kind deed?

3. The example of sailing upstream is meant to be an analogy of what? How does the analogy work? To what extent do you think the analogy succeeds? Fails?

4. How would you explain the moral significance of the following sentence to your roommate who has not read this chapter: "If a burglar is breaking into your house, it is too late to start lifting weights."

5. Think of someone in your past who mentored you. Write a letter thanking them and telling them why their mentoring was important for your growth as a person. (Actually mailing the letter is optional, but encouraged!)

NOTES

1. Wittgenstein, *Philosophical Investigations*, §583.

2. Sometimes fully developed skills begin as "knacks." Having a knack doesn't save one the trouble of having to learn; it simply gives one confidence that one *can* learn more.

3. The doctor who later treated Gage surmised by the trajectory of the tamping rod through Gage's head that Gage had been distracted by men behind him so that he was looking over his right shoulder at the moment of the blast.

4. The case notes and correspondence of Drs. Williams and Harlow (and of others) was collected by Dr. Henry J. Bigelow and published in July 1850 by *The American Journal of Medical Sciences*. Facsimiles of the Gage papers comprise Appendix A of Macmillan, *Odd Kind of Fame*, 391–441. Quotation from Harlow's original report is contained in Bigelow's article (ibid., 394). The Macmillan book is widely regarded as the definitive work on Phineas Gage, around whom something of a mythology has developed.

5. Cited in ibid., 395.

6. Summarized by Damasio et al., "Return of Phineas Gage," 1102.

7. Ibid.

8. Harlow's report (titled "Recovery after Severe Injury to the Head") to the Fellows of the Massachusetts Medical Society was published on June 3, 1868. A facsimile has been included in Macmillan, *Odd Kind of Fame*, 403–22. Quotation from ibid., 414–15.

9. For a helpful introduction, see the online version of Rand S. Swenson's *Review of Clinical and Functional Neuroscience*, a site maintained by Dartmouth Medical School: http://www.dartmouth.edu/~rswenson/NeuroSci/index.html. The limbic system is featured in ch. 9: http://www.dartmouth.edu/~rswenson/NeuroSci/chapter_9.html.

10. Neuroscience is not my field. So, I am indebted to writers like Damasio who have packaged recent research into an accessible form, and for good friends like Dr. David Wright who checked my facts and made sure my neuroscience was on the level. Of course, there are risks with such simplification. But the main point for this present chapter is that practical reasoning is inescapably *bodily* in nature. I have summarized the import of Damasio's work for engineering ethics elsewhere. See Kallenberg, "Teaching Engineering Ethics by Conceptual Design."

11. Damasio, *Descartes' Error*, 49.

12. Ibid., 44.

13. Ibid., 45.

14. Ibid., 134.

15. Ibid., 136.

16. Ibid., 174.

17. See Kallenberg, "Teaching Engineering Ethics by Conceptual Design."

18. Damasio, *Descartes' Error*, 165–222.

19. Of course, it may be bad news as well. After all, it is easier to learn bad habits than develop good ones. (Why else do we say that bad habits are things we "fall" into?!) We never achieve stasis; we are always climbing or descending.

20. Not all battle training is successful. There is a horrifyingly high rate of emotional and/or psychological breakdown reported among combat veterans who have returned home after seeing front line action. Even while on the front line soldiers may "snap," meaning their training failed to steady them against the horrors of war. The My Lai Massacre

in South Vietnam (March 16, 1968) is perhaps the most famous example from U.S. history. The killing spree in March 2012 is one of the most recent. See Shah and Bowley, "U.S. Sergeant Is Said to Kill 16 Civilians in Afghanistan."

21. On our natural reticence to kill, see Bloom, "The Moral Life of Babies"; Grossman, *On Killing*. Grossman observes that in World War II only 15 to 20 percent of front line soldiers actually fired their weapons!

22. Church historians report that in the early years of Christianity, some believers went off to live in caves, depriving themselves of sleep and of sunshine, mixing ashes with their food, even inflicting on themselves extreme pain. Today they would be classified as religious nuts and locked up for their own protection. But in fact, their behavior was entirely rational. These stories come from an era when being a Christian was illegal. Roman emperors tried to quash the movement by torturing believers into denying their beliefs. In this light, we can understand that the "nut cases" were simply adopting a training regimen in order to prepare themselves for being tortured, just as marathoners learn to endure the pain of muscles that are digesting themselves for fuel. As a result of their toughness, the imprisoned Christians were not broken, but their jailers *were*, and *would-be executioners* converted to Christianity! See Tilley, "The Ascetic Body and the (Un)Making of the World of the Martyr."

23. It is important to realize that the exercise in graphing someone's character is entirely mythical. The sort of skill we employ to assess moral character is not a geometric skill but the *ability to read stories*. See MacIntyre, *After Virtue*, esp. 204–25.

24. There are parallel virtues in theoretical reasoning. Knowledge of Fundamental Principles is called the habit of *intellectus*; skills of theoretical reasoning was called, among other things, *ratio*. In point of honesty, it is not entirely accurate to say *phronesis* is simply about the *means* and *synderesis* is about the end, because some means are ends in themselves. See McDowell, "The Role of *Eudaimonia* in Aristotle's Ethics."

25. Associated Press, "Engineer Becomes First Sentenced under Economic Espionage Act."

26. Wittgenstein, *Culture and Value*, 35e.

27. For an outstanding retelling of this age-old debate, see Herdt, *Putting on Virtue.*

28. Ibid., ch. one.

29. Matthew 18:3.

30. The novice pledges "to impart instruction, written, oral, and practical, to my own sons, the sons of my teacher, and to indentured pupils who have taken the physicians oath, but to nobody else." Hippocrates, "The Oath," 299.

31. "Preexcellence" or "pre-excellence" is an uncommon word that means absolute superiority or preeminent excellence.

32. Hippocrates, "Decorum," §5, 287.

33. Aristotle, *Nicomachean Ethics*, bk. II.9.

34. Ibid., bk. II.4.

35. Acts 17:28. St. Paul cites the Greek philosophical poem *Phaenomena* by Aratus.

36. For discussion of this theme in works as diverse as Horace and Simone Weil, see Phillips, *Religion and the Hermeneutics of Contemplation.*

37. French artisans of the last century had a phrase for describing the sore muscles that the teenaged apprentices complained of: "It is the craft entering their bodies!" This phrase noticed by philosopher Simone Weil. Weil, "Love of God and Affliction," 131–32.

38. Having the right sort of friends is something every parent prays for their children, as you will one day pray for your own children, for legitimate fear of the proverb "bad company corrupt good morals." 1 Cor 15:33. For an illuminating illustration of corrupting peer pressure at work in the corporate world, see Rorty, "How to Harden Your Heart."

39. Note: There is a difference between *remorse* and *regret*. Regret is simply being sorry that things turned out the way they did, while remorse is admission that things turned out the way they did because of one's own personal failings. Everybody regrets unhappy consequences, but few have genuine remorse.

40. Thus the wisdom of St. Paul's advice to shore up things in a manner that fits the individual case: "Admonish the unruly, encourage the fainthearted, help (i.e., train) the weak, be patient with all" (1 Thess

5:14). If you can figure out which case is which, you will make for an excellent leader.

41. Paul's second letter to a pastor named Timothy, 2 Timothy 2:22.

42. Forgiven by others and by God; this double forgiveness is really two sides of one coin. See, for example, Matt 18:15–35.

43. The Muses were lesser Greek gods of the arts. The idea of "genie" comes from ancient Rome. Roman citizens were required to burn incense to the divine spirit of the Roman emperor called "the genius of Caesar."

44. For example, Leo Tolstoy experienced crushing depression for two years before he became the literary genius we now recognize him to be. See Drury, "Madness and Religion."

45. Allen, *Artifice and Design*, 115. Likewise John Jervis offered his cutting-edge design of railroad carriages free of charge. See Morison, "The Works of John B. Jervis."

46. See, for example, Kennedy, "Necessity Is the Mother of Invention"; "Margie Pinnell, an Ethos of Service."

47. This technology was prototyped by Kamen's company DEKA (http://www.dekaresearch.com/ibot.shtml) and later developed by Independence Technologies, through which it entered the market as the iBot. For informational videos, see http://www.ibotnow.com/function.html.

48. For an entertaining interview with Dean Kamen, see this clip from *The Colbert Report*: http://www.colbertnation.com/the-colbert-report-videos/269864/april-05-2010/dean-kamen.

49. See the growing list of participants of organizations such as Engineering for Change: https://www.engineeringforchange.org/home or Engineers without Borders <http://www.ewb-usa.org/>.

50. Pilloton and Chochinov, *Design Revolution*. See also Stohr and Sinclair, *Design Like You Give a Damn*; Smith, *Design for the Other 90 Percent*.

8

DESIGN AS A SOCIAL PRACTICE

IN THE SPRING OF 2010, a social media company in Seattle (Social Strata, Inc.) offered to their workers unlimited vacations. Not only did Social Strata offer vacation time without any restrictions whatsoever, they made it clear that they were offering unlimited *paid* vacations.[1] And this company is not the only one in recent months to do so!

The logic of the "unlimited paid vacation movement" seems to be that challenging work is sometimes so meaningful that it can be "addictive" in the best sense of that term. Employees not only enjoy what they do, they find themselves highly, highly motivated to sacrifice—both in terms of time and energy—for the joy of keeping on working. So, Social Strata and others are not really in danger of going bankrupt when employees take advantage of the new policy. Quite to the contrary, they expect profits to rise, because their employees will be both jazzed and well rested.

What is it about the nature of these jobs that inspires such loyalty and labor from the workers? What is it about the nature of these jobs that employees, becoming hooked, inspire such complete trust from their bosses? This isn't a game of merely exchanging favors: "Give me more vacation and I'll work harder." Rather, the workers inspire trust *because they have already become trusted as dedicated workers*. In fact, the very nature of the job has somehow helped them become increasingly trustworthy the longer they work there. Something about the nature of the work is *morally formative*. I am willing to bet that engineering, under the best conditions anyway, is one of these morally formative vocations. We will label morally formative occupations with a philosophically technical term: *Practice*. Before we can unpack the five marks of a Practice, let's remind ourselves of something we learned in chapter 1, namely, the huge role that design language plays in the formation of engineering practitioners. It is language that makes the difference between Og-the-caveman and the modern engineer.

DESIGNING A "SIGNIFICANT" WORLD

Ethics and design are cousins. To engage in either requires us to participate in practical reasoning. And skills in both ethics and design are cultivated as we build fluency in a language. On the one hand, at the core of design is design *discourse*. Remember that according to MIT professor Louis Bucciarelli, designers share a world, a world that they *talk* about. In fact, any given design team may talk in ways that are entirely unique to the team.[2] On the other hand, moral agents also share a *world-of-things-that-they-talk-about*. They talk perhaps *least frequently* about whether X is right or Y is wrong. However, they very frequently talk about a *host* of non-engineering things like happiness, friendship, milkshakes, commitments, sports, cars, marriage, divorce, sickness, weather, suffering, officemates who are greedy, jealous, lazy, mean, arrogant, the purpose of living, the nature of love, of beauty, of truth, and so on.[3] These complex but very ordinary conversations constitute "communication," a term from the Latin *co-munus*, meaning "a shared world." To share a world is to communicate about it. If you and I occupy different worlds, it is not because my surroundings and possessions are different than yours, but because you and I happen to *talk* about different things and therefore inhabit different modes of discourse. Each of us talks with friends, with coworkers, with classmates, with neighbors, in such places as the gym, church, at parties. The kind of "world" we inhabit at any given moment is reflected in *what we talk about*.

Now, let's be honest: language is not a favorite topic among engineers. I remember as a small boy that my dad (a mechanical engineer) had to give a speech in front of a large audience. He was clearly nervous. Talking was *not* his strong suit. He was good at mechanical design, not giving speeches.

But when MIT professor Bucciarelli or Austrian-born engineer Wittgenstein talks about "language," they don't simply mean giving speeches or writing papers. In fact, in the case of engineers, words themselves are only a small part of engineering "language." Physicist Richard Feynman (perhaps best known among engineers as the hero investigator of the Space Shuttle Challenger disaster) once told this story:

One time, we were discussing something—we must have been eleven or twelve at the time—and I said, "But thinking is nothing but talking to yourself."

"Oh, yeah?" Bennie said. "Do you know the crazy shape of the crankshaft in a car?"

"Yeah, what of it?"

"Good. Now tell me: how did you describe it when you were talking to yourself?"

So I learned from Bennie that thoughts can be visual as well as verbal.[4]

Feynman's point is that engineers think in pictures. Of course, they often *talk* in pictures too. Perhaps you've seen them hunched over a table furiously passing sketches back and forth—"What about this?" "Okay, but then this happens . . ."—accompanied by more sketching. Sketching is a crucial part of communication for engineers. So when Bucciarelli refers to "design discourse" and Wittgenstein talks about "fluency," they mean sketches as well as words.

But wait, there's more. *Sketching* is not the only nonverbal language that engineers must master. They also communicate by building *mock-ups and prototypes* and by giving live *demonstrations* that *combine objects and gestures*. When they do deign to talk, their speech is often sprinkled with *heuristics* ("You'd better clamp that before drilling!") and *verbal pictures* borrowed from other conversations ("It fits snugly but not too tight, like piston and cylinder.")

Keeping in mind that engineering "language" includes all these nonverbal "dialects" as well as the verbal ones, close attention to how language works reveals surprising insights about excellence in both design and daily life.

The Messy World Is a Linguistic World

What makes us human? Ancient thinkers gave quite different answers than those we might hear today. Theologian and bishop St. Augustine (d. 430 CE), for example, spoke of immaterial souls housed in material bodies. All dogs don't go to heaven because no canine has that kind of soul. But, according to Augustine, human beings do have souls. Ergo, we all survive the death of our bodies. He borrowed this "dualism" (i.e., we are composed of two fundamental parts, material body + immaterial soul) from the secular philosopher Plato. Body-soul dualism has a long and distinguished history. And it has its advocates even today. But it is important to see that dualists have assumed the key question about what makes us human is primarily concerned with *stuff* (what philosophers call "ontology"): What kind of *stuff* are human beings? More particularly, how many *stuff-parts* have human beings got—one, two, maybe more?

Philosopher and theologian Herbert McCabe thinks that the dualists are asking the wrong question. So, he answers a different question than the one posed; what it means to be human is not something that can be *counted*. Rather, *homo sapiens* are "human" by virtue of the fact of their distinctive manner of existing. Whatever "stuff" comprises human beings, it is clear that we are the *linguistic* animal (68).[5] Here the word *linguistic* is not the name of a property, like gorillas are strong, cheetahs are fast, and humans are talkers. Rather, the word indicates a *distinct mode or manner of existing or living*. This mode of being is "new" in the sense that it emerged out of the evolutionarily older animal mode of existing. But it is also "new" in the sense that it cannot be comprehended by the level of existence that preceded it. There is a sense in which we *can* understand animals where they cannot understand us. ("Blah, blah, blah, *Fido*, blah, blah, blah," hears the dog![6]) While both humans and animals act *for* a reason, only humans can be said to *have* a reason.

The phrase "mode of being" is McCabe's way of referring to diverse kinds of "world." By "world" McCabe means not something already out there to which we subjects accustom ourselves, such as when we buy thicker coats when living in Canada. To use "world" in the already-out-there sense is to speak in strictly empirical language. But that is not what McCabe means. Rather, the kind of "worlds" he is talking about are the worlds that are *made*.[7] Not "made" like artifacts are made, but "made" as in "made sense of." Perhaps this is an unusual use of "world." We usually think of "world" as stuff that surrounds us, like the desk I stubbed my toe on or the sun that tans my skin from ninety-three million miles away. But there is a limit to thinking of "world" in terms of brute surroundings. Even engineers must confess that we cannot ever get to "bare reality" that underlies our interactions of "stubbing" and "being warmed."[8] MIT professor Bucciarelli confesses,

> I am a realist. I believe that there is a material world apart from me (and you). But I also suspect that we can never know its true essences, ". . . the bare reality itself." We see "shadows on the wall of our cave," "now through a glass darkly," but never "the thing in itself." We do fairly well, though, constructing general

theories framed with mathematical rigor and working up phe-
nomenological laws linking cause to effect—as well as thinking
up cause and effect—and these suffice, at least for a while, to
explain the workings of "bare reality." They suffice in that they
provide a set of coherent, socially valued and useful stories—ex-
planations that enable us to *make sense of* the world around us
in quite general terms and to *remake the world to our liking* in
many particular ways.[9]

The closest we can come to "bare reality" is our activity of interact-
ing with our surroundings. In other words, human *activity* is even more
fundamental than the surroundings themselves for our knowing. For all
practical purposes, world-as-human-activity is good enough, because human activity is all we need in order to be able to talk.

Human interactions with their surroundings cannot help being colored by our perception of significances, of things that are *meaningful to us.*
Something analogous happens for other animal species. Animal subjects
inhabit one kind of world. Dogs see in shades of gray, and so "color" is not
significant or even intelligible to dogs. But "color" means something to
human beings, thus we talk about beautiful sunsets and brilliant autumn
leaves. Our human "world," therefore, is composed of things and topics
that are significant to us as human subjects. So "world" is short for "world-
as-experienced" or "world of meanings" or "world of significances."[10]

The tricky part to keep in mind is that we understand something of
the animal world of meanings, since we are animals ourselves. Obviously,
living things exist in a different mode than nonliving things. Things that
are alive "experience" their surroundings, and seem to do so in a holistic
way. For the cheetah, the "world" is something that can be run through
(clearly not true for the rock!). Moreover, we say that the cheetah as a unit
is fast. But notice: we *don't* say, "Its legs are fast." In other words, speed is
the property of the whole animal. If the cheetah injures a paw, the pain
in the paw is experienced by the whole animal; we say, "The cheetah is in
pain" (not "The paw is in pain."). So, one kind of world is the animal world.
*A "world" is the sum total of things that are significant or meaningful to the
animal as a whole organism.*[11]

The range of things that count as "significant" or "meaningful" to
a given animal are (1) conducted to the animal through its sensory ap-
paratus and (2) for which the animal's nervous system is "wired" (by a
combination of genetics and parental conditioning) to respond. If a wolf
walks within range of a sheep's senses, the presence of a wolf is taken up
into the sheep's nervous system via its senses, and the sheep responds to

the wolf as a meaningful part of its world. Bodily senses, then, are avenues of response to an environment and therefore determine the shape of this animal's "world."[12] A sheep has a *sense-shaped world*. It has no world other than what it is able to detect by means of its senses. And of course not everything theoretically detectable by its senses is significant to the animal. In escaping its notice, such things are not *in* the animal's world. My dog never notices butterflies, but will stop, back up, and detour around bumblebees. There are no butterflies in the world of Angie the dog, but there are bumblebees. For my dog, bees are significant, butterflies are not.

A given collection of significances, which is to say the "world" for the sheep or bee or dog, "becomes the clothing of the animal and in a way, the extension of its body . . . almost like another skin."[13] We typically think that the skin is the outer limit of "me." But McCabe is saying skin is only the outer limit of one's *tactile* world. Other senses, like hearing and sight, extend the radius of the world even further. So, if the "world" is what is detected by the animal, then the whole collection of significances—including the sighting of a waterfowl that makes the dog point or the scent of a rival canine on the wind—constitutes Angie the dog's world.

Animals "communicate," but only after a fashion. McCabe explains that for animals, communication is nothing other than "actively sharing a common life" (73).[14] This is only to say that a pair of dogs, who share the same sensory capacities, will take up meaning from the environment in virtually identical ways. Thus they share a world: *co-munus*, co-world. The thing to keep in mind about animal communication is that it is *not* the sharing of *information*. This is difficult for us to understand. Although it looks to us as if they are conveying information, that is just our anthropomorphic projection on animal behavior. Members of the pre-linguistic world simply react to stimuli—as an animal, a human will squint at bright lights, my dog barks at the mailman rattling the mailbox, and bees laden with pollen dance in the presence of their fellows. The bee that dances *as if* to show the others where the pollen is, is no more (and no less) sharing information with its fellow bees than when it shares their lives in other ways (73). Think about the last example. The bee's dance is a genetically determined response; *its fellows are wired to respond to the scout's dance in the same way they respond to the flower itself*. In other words, bees do not *decode* the dance of their fellow and subsequently draw a cognitive map of the location of pollen before flying out to find it. Rather they respond instinctively and mechanically to the wiggles and turns of the dancing bee.

(For this reason they never get lost or make a wrong turn, like I do when I'm following someone else's directions.)

Like the animals, humans occupy a world shared among all those with human bodies. Our senses play an obvious role. Imagine I encounter a flock of sheep while out running (this actually happened to me in the hills of Southern California). Imagine also that I encounter a bear. (This also happened, but on a different run.) If I see the same bear that the sheep see, my body will take up the sensations of the bear (sight and sound, etc.) into my neurological hardware much like the sheep does. And our animal limbic systems respond: nostrils flare, eyes widen, muscles tense for action. Of course, hormones and genetics may play a part in the style of one's reaction. But on this occasion, both my style and that of the sheep would be for flight rather than fight. Both the sheep and I share a visceral reaction to the danger signified by the bear.[15]

So far, so good? *Now for something completely different.*

Beyond the animal level of existing, humans also occupy an expanded (or meta-) "world." To repeat: our human world is, of course, undeniably sensory—but only in part. Because it is partially sensory, we share some significances with other animals. Both my dog and I run for cover when an unexpected cloudburst catches us by surprise. Yet, in addition to that which is meaningful via the sensory conduit, humans have a *linguistic* conduit that animals lack. Human communication simply *transcends* animal communication, although in both cases "communication" is *not* fundamentally the transfer of messages but *the sharing of life.*[16] Perhaps unfortunately, the "world" we share as humans is simply inconceivable to the animals. Whatever can be talked about has the possibility of constituting a given human's "world." Of course, humans *do* share information. But we also say many, many things that are *not* informational; we say things that cannot be judged either true or false (like an informational sentence can): we give orders, speculate about an event, form a hypothesis, invent a story, tell a story, playact, sing a jingle, make up a joke, tell a joke, ask for something, thank, curse, greet, pray, and so on.[17] All these innumerable ways of talking constitute the human world we share.

The emergence of talking on the evolutionary stage constitutes a new level of existing: "With the appearance of language we come, in evolution, to one of those radical changes. . . . a change in which we do not merely see something new but have a new way of seeing; in which something is produced which could not be envisioned in the old terms and which changes our whole way of envisaging what has gone before" (75).

This is the emergence of non-reductive capacities.[18] The newness is so radical that it is properly "revolutionary" in that, like Edwin Abbot's *Flatland*, it involves a higher dimension that cannot be adequately described in terms of lower ones.[19]

In this higher mode of being, "the central point is that with the linguistic animal [a.k.a. human beings] *the media of communication are created by the animal itself*" (76). Not only do we create messages, we (together) made up the language for expressing messages. For dogs and bees, the media of communication are determined by what kind of body the animal has; the means of communication are hardwired into the animal (both the means genetically inherited and those acquired by nurture). No animal can innovate novel ways of sharing the world, of *co-munus*. McCabe quotes Nobel Prize-winning zoologist Conrad Lorenz in this respect: "the automatic and even mechanical character of these signals [bird calls] becomes strikingly apparent and reveals them as entirely different from human words" (cited 79). So, animals are born with built-in systems of communication, "whereas for children the entry into a language is a personal matter, a matter of their own biography" (79). A bluebird cannot learn to moo with cows, but I might have very well been raised to speak Romanian rather than English.

In short, we humans are able to tweak and invent our very *means* of communication, whereas animals are stuck with whatever built-in system they are born with.

McCabe compares and contrasts human language with animal communication in three ways: *nature, history,* and *biography*. The first aspect is one that typifies other mammals as well as humans. By *nature* McCabe means the physical aspect of learning a language by immersion into a particular physical form of life. Chimps and wolves, but neither frogs nor turtles, are socialized into family communication. To learn a new language at the natural level, human beings, like wolf cubs, must become a "tuning fork" and resonate with the rhythms of the host pack, whether in Beijing or the Bronx (79–80).

By *history*, McCabe means the fact that a speaker joins a language *already in play*. Before I was born, English was being spoken by the community into which I was born. The language I pick up is a product of that community-over-time. Since language is an evolutionarily new way of being in the world, it makes sense to ask not only "*What* do you eat?"—a question appropriate for asking any animal—but also the meta-level question, "What does eating *mean in your community*?" (84). Always keep in mind that in contrast to animal behavior, human language involves an emergent property that is evolutionarily new: a new way of seeing and being. My dog and I may share bread; but I experience the bread in ways that transcend what the dog can understand. For both of us, the bread is food (we both salivate and chew). But for me, the bread is meaningful in other ways as well. I can ask numerous questions about the bread that mean nothing to the dog. The bread is significant to the dog only as food. But for me as a human the bread may be significant in other ways, for example, as a trigger to the childhood memory of my mom baking rye bread, or of present-day consecration of the eucharistic host, and so on. (Think of what "last meal" means to the inmate on death row as compared to what it means to Christians celebrating Maundy Thursday before Easter.)

What makes our mode of being, our manner of existence, a *human* one is not as body-soul dualists envision it. Our bodies are not shells that house a little tiny person at a control center in the head. I am *not* a lone homunculus who uses words as public pictures of private thoughts like the High Priest of Baltia uses his humanoid host to convey information. No, my world is not inside, but outside. My world is not private, but social. *My world is shared with others.* What we call "concepts" are nothing like experiences of some little person inside my head. Rather, what we call concepts "are simply skills in the use of words" with others (86). McCabe's account nimbly steps over body-soul dualism: "Instead of saying that I have a private mind and a public body, a mind for having concepts in and a body for saying and hearing words, I say that I have a body that is able to be with other bodies not merely by physical contact but by linguistic communication. Having a soul is just being able to communicate; having a mind is being able to communicate linguistically" (86).

If it is the historical community that "inhabits" the language, then the community inhabits the world-of-significances too. As individuals, each of us joins a "world" that has been talked into existence long before we were born. "Meanings, then, belong first of all to the language, to the community who live by this language; the individual learns these meanings, acquires these concepts, by entering into the language, the culture or history of [this] community" (87). This means that as far as I, as an individual, am concerned, many meanings have a "quasi-objective" status, because they exist prior to my birth and independent of my will. No strictly private language is possible, nor can one change meanings on a whim any more than one can alter the temperature of a piece of metal by telepathy. The quasi-objective character of meanings is crucial to morality. Morality answers the "what" question: *what* is right (or wrong)? Being able to answer the "what" question correctly indicates that one has the ability to keep playing the game with everyone else.[20] *"Moral values are objective in the same way as meanings and, indeed, are the meanings of behavior"* (89, emphasis added). (A certain arrangement of pieces on a board is "objectively" a checkmate, but only for those who inhabit the world of chess playing. The term *objective* can only be relative to a given world-of-significance.)

By the third facet, *biography*, McCabe has in mind the fact that we all live at the intersection of multiple overlapping communities, some of which are subsets of other larger ones. You are simultaneously a member of a family, a neighborhood, a school, and perhaps a congregation, but also (in the near future) an engineering firm. Just as *history* indicates that a human joins in the speaking of a language that has been going on for a long time, so, too, each sub-community has its own dialect in which the subject not only shares but also contributes to the ongoing evolution of the dialects in which they live. Human creativity is such that "no traditional interpretation of the world is final; [we reach] always beyond the language [that humans have] created, towards a future which, just because its language does not yet exist, can be only dimly perceived. This means that every language is in the end provisional, or at least can be seen [someday] by hindsight to have been provisional" (90).

For McCabe, *biography* is simply the *history* of the sub-communities. *Biography* is not an individual's private story but rather *the individual's story as the intersection of several sub-communities*. We are never the sole authors when it comes to our own story, but coauthors at the mercy of others who write in the book of our life.[21]

We can see how McCabe's model of humans as linguistic animals fits with our understanding of design. *Design is one of the things that can happen when my body communicates with other bodies.* A world is shared by a group, and sometimes the group encounters a problem. The longer it takes to seek out a satisfactory solution, the more a dialect emerges that enables them more effectively to talk together about proposed solutions. To recall Bucciarelli's words, designers share an "object world" and the dialect that emerges is our "design discourse."[22]

How does all this relate to ethics? Just as for animals, the human body is intrinsically communicative, capable of sharing a "world" with similar bodies. Moreover, "all behavior is in some sense linguistic" not only in the sense that human activity is always potentially the sharing of a world, but also in that human activity can play a role in communicating with another human body. "We call a [person's] activity [his or her] 'behavior' when it plays a part in [his or her] communication with others. A piece of human behavior is not simply an action that gets something *done*, it also has meaning, it gets something *said*" (90–91). The activity of speaking a sentence is not on a different level than the activity of voluntarily mowing my neighbor's lawn when she is ill. Both are *behaviors* that communicate, that are inherently communicative.[23]

Sometimes, but not always, an act is meaningful because of close connection with outcomes: "It is because of the effect on you of having a knife stuck into you that my act of knifing you has the meaning that it has" (92). Other times the meaning of an act is context dependent: being struck in rebuke versus being tackled in a football game. In the first case the child will cry. In the second instance the child will laugh—even if the tackle is physically more forceful than the swat.

In chapter 3 I gave a provisional definition of "ethics" as answering the "why" question: *why* is ABC right (or wrong)? But here is a more nuanced definition: "*Ethics is just the study of human behavior in so far as it is a piece of communication, in so far as it says something or fails to say something*" (92, emphasis added). Hmm, that's not very satisfying. What is McCabe getting at? The human language is never the language of mere facts (as if the language of human behavior was the language of the physicist[24]). Rather, human talking is a conversation about significances, about meanings, about the things that matter most.

According to McCabe, learning ethics is akin to taking a literature course. A good teacher of literary criticism enables students more deeply to enjoy a piece of literature—say, a poem—by teaching them how to respond more sensitively, that is, "*by entering more deeply into [the poem's] significance.*" McCabe says that something similar holds for ethics: "*Now the purpose of ethics is similarly to enable us to enjoy life more by responding to it more sensitively, by entering into the significance of human action.*"[25] (For this reason, when it comes to learning ethics, novelists often offer us more help than do philosophers![26] The analogy holds in another sense: neither ethics nor literary analysis comes to an end. There is always something more that can be said.[27])

The same sort of comparison might be made between ethics and music appreciation, or ethics and carpentry, or ethics and . . . In other words, ethics can be compared to any discipline that helps a student enjoy a field more fully by entering more deeply into the significance of the subject matter. Important for our purposes is the fact that the list of enjoyment-expanding enterprises includes engineering, most obviously engineering *design*. *Design is formative to the extent that doing design work under the watchful eye of a mentor sensitizes the novice to things that matter most.*

If ethics involves gaining attentiveness to meaning and significance, ethics is not a "level" of analysis. (Much less is it an isolated design criterion.) Rather, the conversation called "ethics" *permeates all of living and talking.* Here is the upshot: *Ethics simply is the ongoing quest for the less trivial.*[28] For McCabe, if we follow this "less and less trivial" toward its asymptote, we may realize that it points to God.

McCabe's analysis may seem pretty abstract. It is important for us, however, because it not only fits our best scientific understanding of human evolution, it also gives an account of how we can be animals whose concerns include but also transcend bodily concerns. We are bodies whose behaviors are aimed at the Good and bodies whose behaviors are communicative. All our intentional bodily action is part of sharing a world (*co-munus*, co-world). Remember, we're not talking about the world-as-inert-cosmos, but a world comprised of topics that are significant to us and therefore worth talking about. On the one hand, we share many topics of significance with the animals: food, shelter, sleep, etc. On the other hand, because we are gregarious animals, the sharing of a world contributes to the making of friends.

For the rest of this chapter, we need to get clear on the role that one special kind of "friendship" formed within one special kind of sub-community plays in cultivating sensitivities to those things that are significant to a good engineer. This is the world of "practitioners." This sub-community may be smaller than a regional language group (for example, the funny way Minnesotans speak). But it is not as small as a single design team. The "world" in question is the world of all engineering practitioners. Such a community is broad enough to have a rich language at play at any given moment.[29] It is equally important to note that such a community exists *through time.* It may be difficult to settle whether contemporary engineers trace their roots to Ancient Greece or Rome or whether they have their origins rather in the sixth or the ninth or the seventeenth century CE.[30] The point is that what I am here calling "practitioners" of engineering were striving to take the craft to the next level decades—even *centuries*—before you or I even contemplated getting into the game.

FIVE MARKS OF A "PRACTICE"

The technical term *Practice* is borrowed from political philosophy.[31] It involves a slightly different way of slicing the pie than the notion of "Profession," although there is some overlap. "Professional" has to do with the way society regards engineers, for example, whether they pay them highly, entrust them with large-scale projects, and grant them the right to self-governance (by means of a professional code of ethics). But the notion of "Practice" has much more to do with the character of the enterprise *as understood from within*. (Admittedly, outsiders to a Practice will often misunderstand the Practice—and in misconstruing it, sometimes blame practitioners for things that practitioners have nothing to do with or demand that they do the impossible.) While it is hoped that every professional is a genuine practitioner, it is sometimes the case that a fully developed practitioner is not granted recognition as a "professional." Such was the case with American engineers in the eighteenth century. Highly skilled practitioners, with geniuses among their number, had to *claw* their way to respectability during the late nineteenth and early twentieth centuries.[32] And even today, engineers do not command the same level of awe and respect (not to mention the salary) that society seems happy to grant doctors and lawyers.

Mark #1: C3—Coherent, Complex, and Cooperative

Many human activities are coherent. "Coherent" just means that the activity *aims* at something. Coherent actions span a wide spectrum, from the trivial to the monumental. In taking a shower after mowing the lawn, I am aiming to get clean. Showering is an intentional act and therefore qualifies as "coherent." In building a durable bridge that can withstand spring flooding in a remote corner of Ethiopia (whose town became known simply as Sebara Dildiy, literally, "broken bridge"), Ken Frantz also acted intentionally.[33] Obviously, Frantz's bridge is more monumental than my shower. Yet both actions are intentional.

A word of caution: It is easy to get the idea that everything we do is intentional. But that isn't quite right, because many actions that we perform go unnoticed. If my chin tickles just now, I scratch it absentmindedly. Scratching an itch is one of those behaviors that my dog does too. Here's the point: if an action is absent-minded and animalistic, it is an *animal* act—in particular, "an act of *homo sapiens*." As an animal act it has zero moral content. But in sharp contrast to animal acts (argues medieval theologian St. Thomas Aquinas), if an action has even a speck of intentionality of which we are conscious, then it falls into a different class. Intentional actions are "*human* acts." *Every human act is a moral act.* A human act may be trivial (taking a shower) or monumental (building a mercy bridge), but both the trivial and the monumental intentionally aim at something good. It is the "aiming at something good" that gives them an unavoidable moral quality. In other words, it is morally good to take a shower when you are dirty. But obviously, ethicists don't debate this, because it is so trivial.

To say an act is "human" is to distinguish moral acts from merely absent-minded or animalistic reflexes. When my dog rushes to the food bowl when I set it down, she is acting *for* a reason. But this is not a reason she can spell out. Animals act *for* a reason, but only humans can also be said to *have* a reason. Said differently, only humans act intentionally. The second c-word is *complex*; Practices are complex. This further narrows the range of actions that constitute a "Practice" from "all intentional actions" to "all intentional actions *that require effort*." As I write this sentence, the growling in my stomach reminds me that I haven't yet eaten breakfast. In a moment I'll seek out a bowl of cereal. (Hmm . . . I think I'll also add a few fresh-picked raspberries from the bush.) Eating cereal is an intentional action that aims at some good (nourishment), and therefore it is a moral act. But it is not complex. My children were feeding themselves cereal since before they could walk. It is not a tough task. But now consider playing the piano. On the surface it looks as straightforward as eating Cheerios.

- Put each Cheerio into the face-hole, chew, swallow.
- Plunk each note in sequence as printed on the score.

But of course the instructions are deceiving. Playing piano is complex because it is difficult to master. It takes extended concentration and effort to begin even to play poorly. The good news is that complex tasks are those at which we can improve over time. No one drastically "improves" in their eating of Cheerios. But with effort, concentration, and repetition, one may get to the point of obeying the command to "plunk each note in sequence as printed on the score."

The third c-word, *cooperative*, narrows the range of coherent, complex actions even further. Some coherent and complex acts can be done, roughly speaking, "alone." But many cannot.

Michael Davis observes that the English word *engineer* is French in origin and dates from the time when France boasted a standing army of three hundred thousand. The *corps du génie* were those in charge of operating the engines of warcraft; their officers (*officeurs du génie*) did similar sorts of research and underwent similar sorts of training as today's engineers.[34] But unique to this corps in the history of warcraft was the fact that maintaining and operating the "engines of war" took an enormous amount of cooperation. (Think of the size of a trebuchet.) Davis's point is well taken. Whether erecting a skyscraper, collating a million lines of machine code, constructing a bridge, or building a dam, engineering by its very nature is a cooperative enterprise. As such, engineering joins a long list of human activities that aim at *goods that can only be achieved together*, when each team member excels at his or her distinctive role. Thus, not only engineers but also quarterbacks, surgeons, politicians, and rock stars succeed only when the team succeeds.

The clever student may see that one kind of cooperation—the very best kind, in fact—involves *friends*. To say that the Practice is cooperative by its very nature means that it is possible, even likely, that one can form good friends inside the Practice. And if friendship is a conduit of grace (or "moral luck," if you prefer), then Practices, because they are by nature cooperative, have within themselves resources for combating moral entropy.

Mark #2: Internal Goods

It is the coherence, complexity, and cooperation of the enterprise that make victory sweet. Players will tell you—whether they play baseball, volleyball, football, or soccer—that victory is sweetest when everything "clicked." Sometimes a game is won in spite of the performance of a team. Conversely, sometimes a team loses despite their having played excellently. And a loss, while painful, is not quite so devastating when players know that, scoreboard aside, everything clicked.

What I've called "clicking" is a *good internal to the Practice*. Only a certain sort of player is able to savor the internal goods, namely, only a *skillful* player (a.k.a. a virtuous one). These goods are not a zero-sum game, or winner takes all. Rather, internal goods are shared without diminishment among all practitioners. In this regard, internal goods can be compared to victory for a sports team: the team enjoys the victory together. (The illustration is imperfect, because the losing team may also experience internal goods despite the loss.)

Recall the definition of virtue from the last chapter: "*Virtues are skilled reflexes for living well formed by habit with others in a Practice under the tutelage of a mentor.*" This definition is paraphrased from Aristotle.[35] But the paraphrase leaves out what Aristotle said about joy. The greatest joy of playing excellent soccer together is . . . playing soccer together well. The greatest joy in playing music together well is simply to have played music well. The band or the choir or the orchestra tastes joys the audience cannot know.

The centrality of joy for virtue is why philosopher Anthony Kenny reminds us that the practitioner cannot be said to have mastered the virtues until he or she *enjoys* doing what is right.[36] The mark of true virtue is not so much obedience as it is *joy*. As a practitioner becomes virtuous within a Practice—both technically virtuous and morally skillful—he or she will thoroughly enjoy the Practice *for its own sake*. That is why a Practice is so "addictive." Physicians sometimes neglect other legitimate goods—getting a good night's sleep, cultivating a healthy marriage, raising emotionally healthy children, etc.—because the Practice itself is so rewarding. Non-practitioners shake their heads and accuse such practitioners of "going overboard." But perhaps outsiders level these accusations because they've never tasted similar joys. I'm not saying neglect is permissible for the doctor, only that it is understandable. One has to be an insider to understand just how marvelous are the goods internal to a Practice.

Mark #3: State of the Art Is Embodied in Living Experts

Players—"addicts" who can't stop drinking more and more at the well of internal goods—can't help making progress in their individual skill sets. Those who have been at it the longest—and who have been both playful and lucky, both diligent and graced—evolve into *masters* of the Practice. It is their *manner* of execution that everyone else wants to resemble. In fact, everyone else *ought* to imitate their excellence—a.k.a. their skills and character, their virtue—because these premier players *embody* the highest form the Practice can take at this moment.

Another way to put this point is to say that the current standards of the Practice reside in the fingers of the masters. Think of the Practice called tennis. Is there a rule for how high one ought to throw the ball when serving? No. Is there a standard exemplar? Yes—Andy Roddick. Whatever else his weaknesses were before he retired, the mechanics of his power serve ought to be emulated because it was the best in the world (155 mph).

Of course, outsiders will have their share of the benefits of excellent Practice. But outsiders are likely to mislocate *where* the excellence really lies. For example, it is common for salespersons to boast, "This home theater system is state of the art!" Does the current state of engineering really reside in its artifacts? Those who are inside the Practice know better: "State of the art" refers to the *human skill set* needed to design and manufacture a high-quality home theater system.[37] The home theater system will eventually break. But the state of the art called engineering keeps getting better and better.

Novices aspire to these skills. Where they really reside is in the experts—not in the rule book, not in the PCOE, not in the artifacts, but in the experts themselves. How *ought* an engineer to behave? The answer to that question is always to be found by pointing to living experts: "copy her, imitate him!"

Mark #4: Requires and Develops Virtue

In chapter 1 we saw that we live and practice engineering in a messy world. While models of theoretical reasoning are extremely helpful, having the tacit sense for the limits of such models is even more helpful (e.g., being able to spot when a calculator display can't be right[38]). In a very real way the skilled reflexes of master practitioners serve as a hedge to protect against the gung-ho spirit of young players who initially see the world with a clear-cut, black-and-white, answer-in-the-back-of-the-book sort of optimism. So, without the tacit skill set of the masters, the Practice would run aground. Conversely, without the gung-ho optimism of the new generation, the Practice would soon simply die as one by one the masters retire. Fortunately, human bodies are the sorts of things that can be trained. Thus do the masters become the mentors of the next generation.[39] In time, new generations of master practitioners are formed. The incoming crop goes through the (sometimes painful!) training paces by which the Practice "enters their bodies."[40] Novices become apprentices, who become journeymen, who become masters as they learn both the know-what and the know-how of the Practice.[41]

To say the same thing differently, a Practice is dually characterized as the sort of enterprise that *both requires and develops the skills and character, a.k.a. the virtues,* on which the Practice's level of excellence depends.[42]

Mark #5: Evolves over Time

Imagine a group of thoroughly urbanized accountants shipwrecked on a deserted island. In order to make a go of survival, a list of important tasks (hunting, finding water, building signal fires) is drawn up and assigned randomly to the survivors, each of whom does his or her level best. Despite an equally devastating lack of training for each task, it may turn out that some of the marooned accountants discover they possess latent talent for the assigned task. Those who display a knack for hunting will quickly be acknowledged for their prowess, and their judgment will naturally be relied upon more than those lacking natural ability in hunting.

As a first approximation, we might think of a Practice as the voluntary association of those who share a knack for some task. However, if "knack" is all this community of survivors has going for it, then the manner in which hunting (etc.) is practiced by another group on another island, or by a future generation on this same island, "would be in all respects haphazard."[43] In other words, should those with the special knack fall ill or die, the community would be at the mercy of the Fates to grace them with another knack-endowed one, for a knack, by definition, dies with its possessor. But unlike the deserted islanders, novices in a Practice can be expected to *grow* toward excellence, not on the basis of knack but on the basis of the *latent potential to be trained*. Apprentices grow into journeymen who may then develop into expert practitioners. Thus what may be a knack in the first-generation leader becomes transformed into know-how and skilled judgment in the second generation as their experience matures into genuine practical wisdom. Once a Practice has gotten going, thereafter no one starts from scratch. All novices join the enterprise midstream, as it were, adopting the methods, research, and discoveries of their forebears, who are in many ways authoritative—at least provisionally so (until said novice makes enough progress to pass judgment on former things). Not to acknowledge this authority is deeply dangerous.[44] Likewise, honor is not reserved for rugged individuals who attempt to achieve excellence on their own steam. Rather, genuine honor is bestowed by experts of one generation upon up-and-coming journeymen of the next generation in recognition both of their "fit" with the current Practice and their potential to "go on."[45] Such an award could never be "people's choice" because only the masters know what they are talking about when picking an award winner.

The idea that novices must learn to "go on in the same way" does not mean that they are expected to slavishly follow protocol. They may need to do that at first, of course. After all, anything worth doing is worth doing . . . badly, that is, until one can learn how to do it better. But divine grace leaves a trace in the fact that the old skills of former generations are carried by newbies into new contexts and can morph into brand new skills. In other words, as novices mature into masters, they may actually raise the bar of excellence. Because Practices are cooperative, breakthroughs are shared by all and improvements are accumulated over time. Thus the final mark of a Practice is simply that a genuine Practice *evolves over time*. A hundred years ago, physicians treated high fevers by "bleeding" their patients. Today they use Ibuprofen. Before Louis Pasteur discovered microbes, doctors actually fought duels over whether "balsam of Peru" was better than "tar oil" for treating infected wounds![46] Today doctors use antibiotics. What medicine (or engineering) will be like in a hundred years from now is anyone's guess. But because medicine (like engineering) is a Practice, we can be sure that it will be better than it is today.

CONCLUSION

We live in the age of Twitter. Yet not everything that is worth talking about—family, engineering, health, music, God—can be conducted in 140-character bursts. One could not employ Twitter to do engineering design or engineering ethics any more than one could try a court case or discuss philosophy by means of smoke signals! Consequently, the path to engineering excellence goes through the construction zone of language fluency: the excellent engineer is the one who can deliberate (talk well) with others. I'm not making this stuff up. Engineering firms say that the top two skills they want to see more of in newly minted engineering graduates are (1) the ability to communicate clearly and (2) the ability to work well on a team.[47]

The first part of this chapter tried to instill the hope that learning skills of deliberation and discourse, although difficult, is not impossible, because *talking* is central to what it means to be human. As one learns to speak a new "language," one finds him or herself entering a new "world." It is a world of new meanings and significances. Five of those new significances that make for an engineer's world distinguish what it means to call engineering a "Practice."

Just as important, these same five marks also show how engineering is a morally formative Practice. How so? Because these five marks constitute a functional definition of a Practice, and as we know, a functional definition tells us how the thing *ought* to be.

Remember the wristwatch. We know how a watch ought to behave simply by knowing what it is for (its "functional definition"). A wristwatch is for keeping time, and therefore a good wristwatch is one that keeps time well. Or, a wristwatch ought to be accurate. And, a wildly inaccurate watch we rightly declare to be a bad watch.[48] Similarly, the marks of a Practice help us get a little clearer on what sort of thing "engineering" is and what engineering is *for*. Obviously, engineering is *for* building cool stuff. But it is also *for* developing a new generation of practitioners. Therefore, a firm in which mentoring doesn't happen is, in this one respect, a *bad* firm. It is also the nature of engineering that standards of excellence (i.e., those skills called "state of the art") are embodied in the expert practitioners. This too gives an angle for thinking about ethics in engineering. For those inside a Practice, moral decisions are not so much sorted out by consulting a rule book as they are by answering the question, *"WWE$_p$D?"*—*"What would the expert practitioner do?"*

These five marks constitute another set of touchstones for moral reflection in engineering. As a Practice, engineering has a kind of built-in gyroscope for staying on track, morally speaking.[49] Some think that this internal gyroscope is a sufficient condition for morality, which is to say, some think that the gyroscope is all that a Practice needs to stay on track. In the next chapter we will explore the phenomenon of cross-domain transfer in order to suggest that Practices may be made even more excellent in the presence of a catalyst that comes from *outside* the Practice.

Discussion Questions

1. Apply the five marks of a Practice to one of your favorite hobbies in order to explain whether your hobby is or is not a Practice.

2. Give an example of a communication shortcut that you have observed among engineers at work. The shortcut might be a made-up word, a use of pictures or sketches in place of words, etc.

3. The idea of "internal goods" does not mean simply that one experiences good feelings on the inside (where else would one feel them?). Rather, the term *internal* means "internal to the Practice." It could also be called a good that emerges *among* practitioners at work. Pick a Practice and list one of the goods that practitioners share.

4. NOVA once aired a program called *Dogs Decoded* that featured an Australian Shepherd with a vocabulary of over three hundred objects; the dog could retrieve them by name or even by sketch. What else would need to be true of this dog in order for McCabe to say that it has language?

5. McCabe's favorite philosopher, the former engineer Wittgenstein, once quipped, "If a lion could talk, we could not understand him." Use McCabe's notion of "world" to explain.

NOTES

1. Ludden, "Unlimited Vacation Time Not a Dream for Some."

2. Bucciarelli, "Between Thought and Object in Engineering Design"; Bucciarelli, "Designing, Like Language, Is a Social Process."

3. Pinckaers, *Sources of Christian Ethics*, 14–45.

4. Cited in Ferguson, *Engineering and the Mind's Eye*, 41.

5. Of McCabe's many wonderful books, the one from which I have drawn most heavily for this section is *Law, Love and Language* (hereafter cited parenthetically).

6. Granted, dogs, chimps, dolphins (and so on) have rudimentary symbolic skills. But language is not merely nor primarily the ability to manipulate signs. Read on.

7. Goodman, *Ways of Worldmaking*.

8. Critical realists call "stubbing" and "being warmed" phenomena, data that reflect human *experiences* with the world rather than data about the world per se.

9. Bucciarelli, "Knowing That, and Knowing How," 43. Emphasis added.

10. For a helpful introduction to this notion of constructivism, see Goodman, *Ways of Worldmaking*.

11. In McCabe's words, "Each animal is the center of a world, it is an area of sensuous [sensory] activity that constitute a world from the environment." McCabe, *Law, Love and Language*, 72–73.

12. Ibid., 71.

13. Ibid., 74.

14. Parenthetical references are all to ibid.

15. For example, human animals are wired for trust. This is to say that what Wittgenstein would call a primitive reaction (children are born with instinctive trust) has a biological basis—oxytocin, dubbed the

trust hormone. See Hertzberg, "On the Attitude of Trust"; Spiegel, "When the 'Trust Hormone' Is Out of Balance."

16. McCabe, *Law, Love and Language*, 74. There is a growing body of research that among all animals, only dogs come close to sharing the human form of life and so share rudimentary language with humans. Koko the gorilla may learn to string sytmbols together, but chimps cannot fathom the notion of pointing. Dogs not only understand pointing, they will respond even when humans point with their eyes. Moreover, some breeds of dog are able to learn not only names of objects, but also to fetch a thing after being shown a two-dimensional picture of it. This is the beginning of symbology. See the Nova program *Dogs Decoded*, which first aired on PBS stations in the fall of 2010.

17. The list can obviously be extended indefinitely! Wittgenstein, *Philosophical Investigations*, §23.

18. An example of a non-reductive property happens in the shift from physics to chemistry. Some chemicals have mirror image isomers called stereoisomers. This property means that one version is inert while the other one is able to serve, say, as an enzyme. But stereoisomerism requires three-dimensionality, something that atoms lack. So, stereoisomerism is a non-reductive property—a property that cannot be explained at the level of atoms.

19. Abbott's fantasy envisions trying to explain a sphere to inhabits of a two-dimensional world! See Abbot, *Flatland*. There is a similar sort of failure of explanation that happens in scientific revolutions: quantum physics can encompass classical mechanics as a limiting case. But classical mechanics cannot account for the quantum world. Kuhn, *The Structure of Scientific Revolutions*. Similarly, in the political realm, McCabe points out that a genuine political revolution "is never intelligible in terms of the society that precedes it." McCabe, *Law, Love and Language*, 30.

20. Moral relativism is avoided by the conviction that God is a member of the linguistic community.

21. The observation is often attributed to MacIntyre; see MacIntyre, *After Virtue*.

22. Discussed in various places. See Bucciarelli, *Designing Engineers*; Bucciarelli, "Between Thought and Object in Engineering Design."; Bucciarelli, *Engineering Philosophy*.

23. However, nonverbal behaviors do not communicate as visual words (say, like gestures or like charades). The communication is not at that level of specificity. Every act is not a gesture such that we are always "talking" without words.

24. McCabe dismisses the "Is-Ought fallacy" from the start: ethicists are wrong to worry whether it is possible to move from statements of fact to statements of value or of obligation. The "Is-Ought fallacy," also known as "the naturalistic fallacy," is simply beside the point because communicative behaviors already have built-in values; all communicative behaviors involve things that matter. See McCabe, *Law, Love and Language*, 93.

25. Ibid., 95. McCabe goes on to deal with two objections to the analogy that ethics is like literary criticism: isn't *enjoy* the wrong word? Isn't it both too trivial and suggestive of the spectator stance? No. In the first place, see *eudaimonia*. In the second place, enjoyment of literature, like life, requires self-involvement and participation.

26. Ibid., 103. See also Diamond, "Martha Nussbaum and the Need for Novels."

27. So, it is wrongheaded to think that technical moral vocabulary somehow locks down conversation. In many ways, to say something is "good" is simply irrelevant; McCabe, *Law, Love and Language*, 97.

28. "[E]thics is the quest of less and less trivial modes of human relatedness" (ibid., 99). What makes a behavior evil, on McCabe's linguistic model of being human, is not simply that it has catastrophic effects but that "its meaning fades relatively soon when we try to take it seriously. The life of the evil man has meaning only at a fairly superficial level. It is entirely unsurprising that Hitler's table-talk should have been so *boring* (even if his public speeches were so charismatic). Bad, cheap behavior devalues the structures of human meaning in the way that bad cheap prose devalues the language" (ibid., 101).

29. In a sense, the language of "engineering" is spoken across national boundaries. The fact that IEEE is an international society is indicative that American-born engineers have siblings in the Practice who are Iranian-born just as German engineers have siblings who are

Chinese-born. The fraternity of engineering knows no national boundaries.

30. Lynn White thinks sixth century; David Noble points instead to Joachim Fiore in the ninth century; Michael Davis thinks seventeenth-century France. For comparison, see Davis, *Thinking Like an Engineer*; Noble, *The Religion of Technology*; White, "Technology, Western."

31. By "Practice" is meant "any coherent and complex form of socially established cooperative human activity through which goods internal to that form of activity are realized in the course of trying to achieve those standards of excellence which are appropriate to, and partially definitive of, that form of activity, with the result that human powers to achieve excellence, and human conceptions of the ends and goods involved, are systematically extended." MacIntyre, *After Virtue*, 187.

32. This "clawing" constituted something of a "revolt." Layton, *The Revolt of Engineers*.

33. Glick, "Building Bridges of Hope."

34. Davis, *Thinking Like an Engineer*, 9–11.

35. For example, "Hence also it is no easy task to be good. For in every-thing it is no easy task to find the middle. . . . any one can get an-gry—that is easy—or give or spend money; but to do this to the right person, to the right extent, at the right time, with the right aim, and in the right way, *that* is not for every one, nor is it easy; that is why good-ness is both rare and praiseworthy and noble." Aristotle, *Nicomachean Ethics*, ii.9.

36. Kenny, *Brief History of Western Philosophy*, 66.

37. Koen, *Discussion of the Method*, 41–57.

38. Ferguson, "How Engineers Lose Touch."

39. The *Journal of Science and Engineering Ethics* devoted an entire issue to mentoring. See vol. 7, no. 4, December 2001.

40. The phrase is reported by philosopher Simone Weil, who overheard aged craftsmen respond to the complaints of aching muscles by a new apprentice that "it's the trade entering his body!" Weil, "Love of God and Affliction," 131–32.

41. See Ferguson, *Engineering and the Mind's Eye*; Vincenti, *What Engineers Know and How They Know It*.

42. This is badly put. Excellence doesn't depend on the virtues, it is constituted by the virtues. To think that virtues are the means to excellence
tempts us to think excellence is one thing and virtue another. Virtue
and excellence are two sides of the same coin. This temptation (called
instrumentalism) must be outgrown. See Herdt, *Putting on Virtue*, 34.

43. This insight comes from Hippocrates,s writing on the nature of medical Practice in ancient Greece.

44. Hippocrates writes, "But anyone who, casting aside and rejecting all
these [lessons of the masters], attempts to conduct research in any
other way or often another fashion, and asserts that he has found out
anything, is and has been the victim of deception." Hippocrates, "Ancient Medicine," II.8–12, p. 15.

45. Today the bestowal of intra-communal honor is carried on by organizations such as the Honor Medical Society (Alpha Omega Alpha, est.
1902). Significantly, not all awards conveyed by AOA carry a monetary prize. That honor does not reduce to external rewards without
great remainder is reflected in the words of AOA's founder, William
Webster Root: "It is the duty of members to foster the scientific and
philosophical features of the medical profession, to look beyond self
to the welfare of the profession and of the public, to cultivate social
mindedness, as well as individualistic attitude toward responsibilities,
to show respect for colleagues, especially for elders and teachers, to
foster research and in all ways to ennoble the profession of medicine
and advance it in public opinion. It is equally a duty to avoid that
which is unworthy, including the commercial spirit and all practices
injurious to the welfare of patients, the public, or the profession."
Cited in http://www.alphaomegaalpha.org/AOAmain/History.htm.

46. Verghese, *Cutting for Stone*, 118.

47. For example, Thomas K. Grose, a contributing editor for the journal
Prism, published by the American Society for Engineering Education,
argues that today's graduates lack what they simply must have: "Today's engineering students must be able to communicate well, work
in teams, and take societal concerns into account." Grose, "Opening
a New Book."

48. In the older lingo, the property that makes something maximize its
functionality is its virtue. Thus Aristotle defines virtue as "excellency

of function." The virtue of a racehorse is *speed*, that of a thief is *stealth*, and that of a wristwatch is *accuracy*.

49. This is a gyroscope rather than a compass. Do you see why?

9

CROSS-DOMAIN TRANSFER
AND DESIGN

CROSS-DOMAIN TRANSFER IS A special kind of modeling. Recall from chapter 6 that "dynamical" modeling requires *tacit* skills, which is to say skills that can be trained for but never quite spelled out in words. So, the musician who judges *this* recording to be the same as *that* sheet music does so by means of tacit musical skills, not only the ability to read complicated sheet music but also to *hear* intervals, *feel* rhythms, and so on. Likewise, the engineering team that successfully scales up the child's toy helicopter (the Pénaud flyer) will have succeeded not because they simply multiplied all the dimensions by some proportionality constant. Rather, the *function* of the toy passes *through* the tacit skills of the design team in order to become the *function* of the full-size chopper.

At least some of the tacit skills necessary for "dynamical" modeling are the product of long hours of direct, physical engagement with the practice.[1] As a result of this long-term, intensive engagement, two things happen. First, engineers develop new languages. Master engineer Walter Vincenti notes that designers who puzzled over the optimization problem for airfoils not only became fluent in a vast number of wing shapes, but they also became able to converse about shapes using only their model numbers! In other words, these engineers would employ each NACA four-digit airfoil designation as if it were a word in the language of wind flow.[2] We understand how this happens by recalling what we read in chapter 8 about Herbert McCabe's account of language. Unlike other animals whose communication skills are hardwired into their biology, human beings are able continually to create and re-create the very *means* of communication. Likewise, MIT's Louis Bucciarelli observes that inventing new means of communication commonly happens within any design team that has had to live with a problem for a long time.

Second, direct hands-on participation in a practice cultivates the kind of knowledge that cannot be translated in terms understandable by the uninitiated. Of course, discussing airfoils by means of their NACA numbers is itself a kind of tacit skill.[3] But we must keep in mind that an engineer's hard-won skills are not shortcuts for an analytic process that could be flowcharted for just *anyone* to follow. Rather, tacit skills are simply indescribable. (No one can describe to a blind person what seeing the color red is like, because color recognition is tacit knowledge.) In the 1950s, after eight years of hands-on experimentation, Richard Whitcomb devised a way for airplanes to exceed Mach 1. What made the difference for him was not how quickly he could solve Bernoulli's equation. His work was running far ahead of the theoretical frameworks available. Rather, what made the difference was the eight long years he spent in the wind tunnel. As one observer put it, "Whitcomb was a guy who just had a sense of intuition about these kinds of aerodynamics problems. He sort of *feels* what the air wants to do."[4] Whitcomb's breakthrough was a by-product of the *feel* he had developed for the quirky behavior of wind wrapping around asymmetrical shapes like hands and wings.[5] His "feel" was developed during years of searching for a practical solution to a particularly tough design problem. In other words, it was his engineering research that led him to the hands-on exposure, and the hands-on exposure solved his problem.[6] This is all good. Yet, in addition to breakthroughs that are part of design research, sometimes a breakthrough comes from an entirely different arena of life, one that won't be happening *inside* the walls of whatever firm you end up working for. Some solutions come from the outside.

Any time an insight or tacit skill from an unrelated field informs satisfactory design in another field, it is called cross-domain transfer (CDT). In the simplest case, CDT looks like "change of aspect." Recall the duck-rabbit diagram from chapter 5. If your friend simply cannot see the duck in the diagram, continuing to stare at the diagram may not be helpful. There is nothing in the diagram that *compels* one to see it as a duck. Nevertheless, if you give your friend a sack of duck food and send her packing to the nearest duck pond to feed ducks all afternoon, something amazing happens. The next time your friend sees the diagram, the chances are far, far better that your friend will blurt out, "Oh! It's a *duck*!"[7] What makes the difference is the friend's recent and increased familiarity with ducks. An improved ability to read the duck-rabbit diagram comes from having spent the afternoon observing and feeding ducks. Something similar happened to the four Cambridge students who solved a unique mathematical problem that has become known as "Squaring the Square."[8] How they solved it will illuminate another dimension of ethical reasoning.

Cross-Domain Transfer from Circuits to Geometry

The problem was to make a perfectly square quilt by sewing together squares of fabric, each of which is of a unique size. The four Cambridge students had played around with the problem long enough to know it could be solved for a special kind of *rectangle*, one that was almost, but not quite, square (say, 352 x 354).

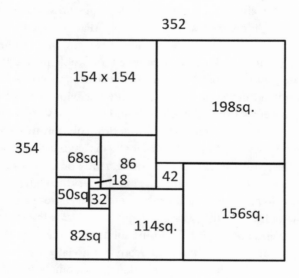

Figure 9.1 Squaring a "Perfect" Rectangle

They hoped something analogous could be concocted for squaring a square. In other words, they tried to use *geometry* to solve the problem for the rectangle. And they *assumed* the solution for the square would come from doing similar *geometry*. But the skill set for forming this analogy eluded them *until they stopped doing geometry!* It happened like this. They had begun to play around with describing the perfect rectangle solution in *non*-geometrical ways. One student, named Smith, was familiar enough with circuits that he proposed thinking about the area of each dissected square as the rate of flow of electrons in a network, which is governed by Kirkhoff's Law. Kirkhoff's Law says that the current between any two points must be the same no matter the pathway taken.

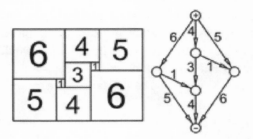

FIGURE 9.2 Smith's CDT Insight[9]

This is easiest to see by further simplifying the example. We can see below that 6 + 5 = 4 + 3 + 4. Obviously this is *not* geometry, since no two sides of a triangle add up to the third side. The "triangle" only represents two different pathways of current flow. It was this non-geometrical relationship that enabled the students to set up their geometry problem in an entirely new way.

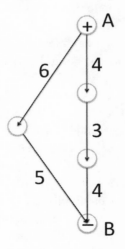

Figure 9.3 Kirkhoff's Law

BY DESIGN

Of course, actually solving for the squared square still takes some doing. But the point for us is this: the key that unlocked the solution came from *outside* geometry.

Who would have thought that Kirkhoff's Law would lead to a solution to an unsolved puzzle in planar geometry! Even more puzzling: who would have thought diagramming Figure 9.1 as a circuit was even worth playing around with! Not me, because circuits are not second nature for me. But nearsightedness isn't just my problem alone; the idea was unlikely to occur to *anyone* unfamiliar with circuits. Not only would we, the unfamiliar ones, never dream of making such a comparison, we would likely oppose a teammate's suggestion to do so as stupid, random, and a waste of time.

One practical lesson to be learned from this tale is that designers ought always to entertain the possibility that no matter how harebrained and implausible a proposal for solving a problem strikes us, *we could be wrong*. This is not to say that every strategy is advisable until proven wrong. But it is true that being convinced of one's own "rightness" can slam the door too early on possibly valuable avenues for design. Consequently, we need to approach design conversations with openness, humility, and willingness to listen and learn. (Of course, not every rabbit trail can be pursued. These two poles form another design heuristic: *Allocate resources to a strategy as long as the cost of not knowing exceeds the cost of finding out.*[10])

There is a second lesson to be learned from this story—namely, that one's fluency in practices *other than engineering* can make one a better engineer. Figure 9.1 was like the duck-rabbit to Smith. He initially saw it under the aspect of geometry. But unlike his peers, he *also* could see it under the aspect of circuits, something he was apparently very familiar with. This is not to say that everyone familiar with circuits would instinctively see a given "perfect rectangle" as a kind of circuit diagram. If that were true, squaring the square might have been solved long ago. However, seeing the problem under the aspect of circuits was instructive for Smith. We say that Smith's familiarity with circuits was a *necessary* though not a *sufficient* condition for CDT.[11] In other words, for Smith, familiarity with circuits wasn't all he needed, but in this case, it turned out to be one of the key ingredients for cross-domain transfer to happen.

Some may argue that the solution to squaring the square should be called the work of a genius. Someone is labeled a "genius" when his or her contribution to the field changes the field because it has widespread, even universal, significance. Thus we call Einstein a genius not because his IQ was above average, but rather because $E = mc^2$ changed *everything*. Then again it might be that Smith is not a genius per se, but only looks like a genius because CDT led to a new breakthrough. Both geniuses and occasions when CDT helped inform genius-like breakthroughs in design are relatively rare. Vincenti has shown that opportunities for "radical" breakthrough designs are relatively infrequent.[12] If we survey the full range of design problems, the most common kind of design amounts to low-level tweaks of existing solutions (A_3). Because they are tweaks, the level of constraint is high. For example, every year new cars are designed. But the new models really do not differ drastically from last year's models. The designers who work on these cars have to pay close attention to fitting in with well-known boundary conditions. Even odd vehicles like the Tango or the Puma are still relatively conservative: passengers still ride on platforms supported by wheels in contact with asphalt. Only very rarely are designers given the chance and freedom to do radical design (A_1).

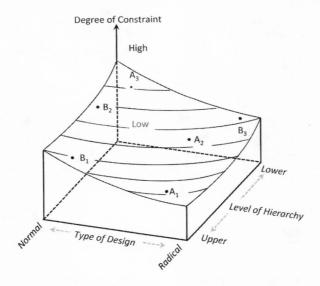

FIGURE 9.4 Vincenti's **"Degree of Technical Constraint as a Function of Design Type and Level of Hierarchy"**[13]

In other words, most design problems have tight technical constraints that prevent designers from proposing designs of monumental significance. This seems to suggest that CDT is rarely needed. Nevertheless,

I shall argue that radical design isn't the only time CDT is useful. A more common form of CDT happens for "local geniuses." In contrast to the genius, whose innovation has universal application and significance, a *local genius* is someone who *habitually makes the just-right contribution for a local context and is able to do so because of a life well lived and a Practice (like engineering) well executed over time.*[14] I claim that CDT may strike out of the blue for the person aspiring to be a local genius. The imminence of CDT is more plausible when we realize that the unrelated field from which the crucial tacit skill is imported (like Smith's familiarity with circuits) can be anything from poetry to painting, from bicycling to baking. In the following sections, I will give some examples and then argue that religion—in particular, the narratives and practices of Christianity—may produce CDT for engineering.

CROSS-DOMAIN TRANSFER FROM BIOLOGY
TO ARCHITECTURE

Transfer from one scientific domain to another does not surprise us. After all, both geometry and electrical engineering involve mathematics. Slightly further afield might be crossover between architecture and biology. For example, architect William McDonnough calls for a change in paradigm from *buildings as structures* to *buildings as living things*. We all understand that buildings consume energy, water, and emit greenhouse gasses just as animals do. To be specific, buildings consume 40 percent of the world's energy and emit 50 percent of the world's greenhouse gasses, and waste untold amounts of potable water.[15] In light of these data, McDonnough gives idea after idea for improving building design.

> For example, in a conventional [building], the opening and closing of truck docks constantly leaks in uncomfortably hot or cold air. A pressurized system keeps undesirable air at bay rather than having to cool or heat it to restore the status quo. And excess heat generated by air compressors (which lose 80 percent of the energy they use as "waste" heat), welders, and other equipment could easily be captured and consolidated for use. . . . It turns what is generally a waste and thermal liability into a working asset. If you combined such a system with a grass roof to insulate the structure and protect it from heat gain in the summer, wind loss in the winter, and the wear and tear of

daylight, you'd be treating the building as an aerodynamic event ... a machine that's *alive*.[16]

Granted, McDonnough and his coauthor, Michael Braungart, are visionaries. But the point we need to see is that improved design results from a Gestalt switch; rather than seeing buildings as structures we live in, we do well to see buildings as machines that are themselves alive. What triggered the Gestalt switch did not come from within architecture but from outside, from the field of biology. This trigger is another instance of CDT.

CROSS-DOMAIN TRANSFER FROM NONSCIENTIFIC FIELDS TO ENGINEERING

It doesn't take much imagination to realize that the "domain" involved in CDT might very well be a nontechnical, nonscientific, nonmathematical field. One famous study of the lives of two hundred famous researchers showed that "the most scientifically imaginative scientists ... were almost always artists, poets, musicians, and/or writers."[17] In this light we can understand the recent claim made by Yale's computer scientist David Gerlernter that even *art* can be a source for CDT:

> Art education is crucial to the nation's technological and scientific well-being. Not because ignorance of Velazquez (say) makes a person incapable of doing physics; because studying Velazquez sharpens the sense of beauty, which in turn helps guide physicists toward the truth. Art study to a scientist or engineer is like jogging to a boxer. It is no replacement for mathematics or assiduous punching-bag smashing, but it develops a faculty that is crucial to success.[18]

FIGURE 9.5 *Cristo de San Plácido* by Diego Velázquez[19]

Mathematician, philosopher, and novelist Alexander Solzhenitsyn makes a similar claim. The context for Solzhenitsyn's science career was Stalin's Russia (beginning after the October Revolution of 1917). It is from Solzhenitsyn that the world first learned the story of Pyotr Palchinsky, an expert engineer who was highly critical of Stalin's "gigantomania" engineering undertakings. Palchinsky criticized Stalin's projects because they were both highly impractical and brutally inhumane. In the course of one such project, the White Sea Canal, workers died at the rate of ten thousand per month. When it was "finished" some twenty months later, it had cost the lives of two hundred thousand conscripted laborers. Sadly, the whole thing was ill-conceived. During summer months, there was only enough water in the canal for flat-bottomed barges. (Solzhenitsyn reports that decades after Stalin fell from power, he was able to visit his homeland and spend a day observing the White Sea Canal. During the eight hours he watched, only *two* flat-bottomed barges passed, both loaded with timber and going in opposite directions![20]) For his complaint that Soviet engineering was ignoring the human factor, Palchinsky was summarily executed. As Solzhenitsyn fills in details from his own days as a Gulag prisoner, Palchinsky was only one of *many* to die. In fact, Stalin imprisoned, exiled, or killed nearly an entire generation of engineers, mathematicians, and scientists. Executing the engineers was even more boneheaded than the crazy projects themselves. If the engineers are exiled, who will build the future? As Ingrid Soudek explains, by the 1930s "it became very urgent for the Soviet government to recruit its own engineers, people who would not be influenced by the past, who would be completely loyal to the government, and who would not try to think for themselves."[21]

In his massive two-volume, 1300-page *Gulag Archipelago*, Solzhenitsyn chronicles the qualitative difference he observed between the humanist engineers of the older generation and the new generation of mere technicians. Some of the older generation were simply waiting to die. Others were forced to teach technical classes to the "new" generation. Solzhenitsyn found the "new" generation "to be sadly lacking when compared to the older generation, both in 'the breadth of their technical education' and 'in their artistic sensitivity and love for their work.'"[22] The source of their incompetence? The new generation of engineers "lacked a well-rounded education and exposure to different ideas, which lack gave them 'tunnel-vision' and allowed them to justify or ignore infractions against basic human rights."[23] In short, the new crop of pseudo-engineers suffered from "tunnel vision" that resulted from a narrow and lopsided education.

In order to replace the technical expertise that was lost when Stalin executed or imprisoned Palchinsky's generation, a whole new breed had to be educated from scratch. Of course, Stalin didn't want more Palchinskys. He wanted people who would be slavishly devoted to Soviet ideology. Therefore, responsibility for educating the new breed was yanked out of the hands of the Ministry of Education and given instead to the *industrial* sector of government. Not surprisingly, courses having anything to do with social justice went out the window, along with virtually every other humanities course. In fact, only three non-engineering courses would survive Stalin's makeover: (1) Political Economy (a.k.a. Marxism 101), (2) Dialectical Materialism (a.k.a. Marxism 102), and (3) The History of the Communist Party (a.k.a. Marxism 103). In place of general humanities education, technical coursework was drastically expanded. But rather than producing engineers with more technical breadth, the abovementioned courses produced technicians with more and more narrow specialization. This became the Soviet way.

Loren Graham reports that the Commissariat of Heavy Industry insisted on such extreme specialization that there was an engineer for oil-based paints and a different engineering specialization for those who worked with non-oil-based paints! Even as late as 1960, when Graham first traveled to the Soviet Union to conduct research for his book on Palchinsky, he reported meeting a young female engineer and asking what kind of engineer she was: "'A ball-bearing engineer for paper mills' was the reply. I responded, 'Oh you must be a mechanical engineer.' She rejoined, 'No, I am a ball-bearing engineer for paper mills.' Incredulous, I countered, 'Surely you do not have a degree in "ball bearings for paper mills."' She assured me that she did indeed have such a degree."[24]

Please do not misunderstand the lesson we are to learn from all this. I am not claiming that technical training or specialization are evils. Rather, they are only evil insofar as they displace something more important in one's education. Solzhenitsyn lamented the flimsy-mindedness and spineless ideological compliance of the new breed. One contributing factor to their being such poor engineers apparently was their poverty in general humanities knowledge and dreadful lack of exposure to non-engineering practices. In other words, they could do plug and chug theoretical problem solving with the best of them. They were adept at "transom window" engineering, where engineers are cloistered in institutions with no outside contact except for project specs they received from Stalin through the transom window above the closed and locked front door.[25] These mere technicians seemed genuinely happy behind these "closed" doors. After all, problem solving *is* fun. But their "happiness" was shallow. Admittedly, thinking about social ramifications is difficult and messy. But what real joy can come out of a designer who is too slavishly submissive to question whether a requested project is even a legitimately worthwhile idea? In stark contrast to these "wet noodle" engineers, the humanist engineers like Palchinsky, who dot the pages of *The Gulag Archipelago* and were immortalized in Solzhenitsyn's novel *The First Circle*, were excellent engineers precisely because they were able to think *outside* the bounds of technical coursework.

> I had grown up among engineers, and I could remember engineers of the twenties very well indeed: their open, shining intellects, their free and gentle humor, their agility and breadth of thought, the ease with which they shifted from one engineering field to another, and, for that matter, from technological to social concerns and art. Then, too, they personified good manners and delicacy of taste; well-bred speech that flowed evenly and was free of uncultured words; one of them might play a musical instrument, another dabbles in painting; and their faces always bore a spiritual imprint.[26]

Solzhenitsyn lamented the loss of the old breed. And the dreadful quality of Stalinist engineering projects undertaken by the new breed—such as the still glowing Chernobyl power plant—shows that mere technicians simply cannot replace real engineers who are broadly educated.

CROSS-DOMAIN TRANSFER FROM NARRATIVE TO ENGINEERING

For the rest of this chapter, I want to suggest ways in which one arena in particular can inform the manner in which engineers approach design. The arena I have in mind is not poetry writing nor pastry baking nor portrait painting, but the more widely accessible art of thinking by means of *stories*.[27] To cite one poignant example, Christian ethicist William May has shown how the various attitudes taken over the years by engineering toward the environment can be aptly expressed by classic stories such as *Beowulf* ("slay the dragon") or St. Francis ("befriend the wolf"). Other authors have reflected on the outlook depicted by Mary Shelley's *Frankenstein*. But I want to focus our reflections on one story in particular. The range of this story is so culturally pervasive that we often think we know what it is about, when in fact we may have forgotten many of the particulars. I have in mind the story of a one-time itinerant preacher from Nazareth, an unimportant town, a backwater of the Roman Empire. The preacher's given name was Jesus. Later followers referred to him also as "the Christ" (or in Hebrew, *hamashiach*, "the Messiah"). And he figures prominently in all manner of moral norms today. Since it is the details that make all the difference in design and CDT, an overview of the particularities of Jesus' life and times is worth the trouble.

WWJD: WHAT WOULD JESUS DRIVE?

In 2002, a number of the religiously faithful, concerned with the impact of the auto industry on the environment, posed a question that became in some circles a national campaign: "What Would Jesus Drive?"[28]

The question seems straightforward enough. We imagine Jesus with his laptop surfing www.cars.com. We know that a nearly infinite range of choices wouldn't pose any difficulty to the Divine Mind. In narrowing his options, Jesus simply applies (divine) metrics to the field of choices. Presumably, Jesus is not interested in color or seat warmers, although—so the argument goes—he *would* care about fuel economy and renewable materials.[29]

What goes uncontested is the assumption that some of Jesus' choices are supposedly obvious—maybe a Prius, but certainly *not* a Hummer! Yet what reasons have we to think that we all *simply know* what Jesus would drive? Do we really know Jesus well enough to predict his car selection? Do we even know what Jesus looked like? Well, how do we think he looked? Sandaled itinerant preacher in Palestine around the turn of the first millennium—right? Eggshell-colored bathrobe and a beard? Perhaps a halo if you look real close? Blue eyes—no, green (or brown?). Truth be told, we don't even know what he *looked* like much less what he would drive. If the original Jesus drove a Prius to the airport, he'd probably be detained by security simply for *looking* like a terrorist! (To cite the Bellamy Brothers' lyrics: "Jesus is coming, and boy is he pissed!") Some have even pictured Jesus in terrorist fashion, holding a machine gun or a battle-axe. Other artists depict him in the opposite way, as "Buddy Jesus." So which portrayal reflects the *real* Jesus? If we can't come to agreement on Jesus' physical features, can we assume everyone shares a correct understanding of Jesus' *character*?

We may never know what Jesus looked like physically, but we *can* know something of what his *character* looked like. Remember from chapter 7 that "character" is a technical term in ethics, naming "the pattern of habitual actions over time." By looking at the pattern of Jesus' habitual actions, we can get clearer on what *sort* of person he was. Of course, there can't be an exhaustive account, any more than a biography of you or me could ever be truly exhaustive. (The writer of John's Gospel tells us that a complete account of Jesus would take more books than the world could hold.[30]) So, we'll have to approach this problem from a different tack. I will recap three episodes from Jesus' life that are typical enough to reveal his character in ways that suggest heuristics for ethics and design. In the next chapter I'll try to show that Christ-followers retain a clear enough memory of this character throughout the centuries so that when engineering begins to take root in western Europe, it takes on a cast that is decidedly *Christomorphic*, which is to say, it looks like Christ.

JESUS IN THE CONTEXT OF FIRST-CENTURY PALESTINE

In an earlier chapter we saw the difference between reading a professional code of ethics (PCOE) as a *contract* between strangers and reading it as a *covenant*. We call an agreement a contract when we are striking a deal with a *stranger*, someone whose word I cannot count on simply because I don't know his or her character. Under these conditions, it makes good sense to have a legal protection device—a contract. By contrast, a *covenant* is the kind of agreement that *friends* form with each other. The example used in chapter 4 to illustrate "covenant" was taken from Jewish history.

More than a millennium and a half before Christ, the twelve great-grandchildren of Abraham moved their families to Egypt to escape famine in Mesopotamia. They grew in number and "prospered" as the working class of Egyptian society. In short, they were slaves. After four hundred years this by then enormous group of slaves—following their charismatic leader, Moses—miraculously escaped their Egyptian taskmasters and fled into the wilderness northeast of the Sinai Peninsula. For forty years they wandered around the wilderness as they practiced living according to the terms of a (divinely given) covenant in order to become at last a people, a culture, a nation.

Like any nation, this one had a checkered history. After Moses died, they moved east out of the wilderness. Under the military leadership of Joshua, Moses's right-hand man, they incrementally took possession of the land between the Dead Sea and the Mediterranean Sea. Their unity and military might reached its zenith under the king simply known as David (ca. 1000 BCE). This ancient nation's wealth and renown reached a maximum during the rule of David's son Solomon. But after Solomon died, the kingdom fractured into north and south, and for the next several centuries the number of wise rulers could just about be counted on one hand. Unskilled and selfish rulers emptied the twin kingdoms (called "Israel" in the north, "Judah" in the south) of all their wealth, power, and renown. Beset by enemies on every border, the nation virtually popped out of existence for the better part of five centuries. That is to say, around the time Homer was writing the *Iliad* and the *Odyssey* over in Greece, the northern kingdom (Israel) was conquered by the Assyrians from the north (722 BCE). About the time Socrates was debating Gorgias in Athens, the southern kingdom (Judah, whose capital was Jerusalem) fell to the Babylonians (587 BCE). The bulk of the survivors were deported five hundred miles to the east (just shy of present-day Baghdad in Iraq). The walls around the former mountain fortress of Jerusalem were leveled. And Solomon's world-famous temple was looted and ruined.[31]

For centuries the only thing that changed for the regions formerly called "Israel" and "Judah" was the nationality of the foreign ruler.

Tyrannical control changed hands from Babylon to Persia to Greece to Rome. Somewhere along the way, a replacement temple was constructed and the capital city's wall repaired well enough for Jerusalem to be inhabited.[32] During this Second Temple period, the people were no longer referred to by the language they spoke (that is, as Hebrews), but for their religious practice: Jews who practiced Judaism.

Although the people had ceased to be a nation, the Jews remained a *people* precisely because they *never* surrendered the covenant. The original covenant, formed when Moses still led them, continued to bind them together in fierce loyalty to one another. Of course, it is one thing to practice a covenant when you are the reigning superpower in the region, as they were under King David. When your enemies are at bay and far away, the covenant could double as a national constitution. But by the dawn of the first millennium, the land had been occupied by foreign powers for six centuries. Trying to live together while under the iron fist of the latest superpower, Rome, wasn't easy. Jewish attempts to achieve *co-munus*, the sharing of a world, under these politically hostile conditions took five distinct forms.

Strategy 1: Flee into the Wilderness

The first strategy was simply to leave. The group that did so was called the Essenes. The Essenes moved to the sparsely inhabited area on the west side of the Dead Sea (today's West Bank) hoping that Rome would not pay them any heed. There they built up the city of Qumran and practiced religion in diligence and peace.[33] But most of the Jews were loathe to leave Jerusalem for the desert—not because the desert meant more hardship; they had become very adept at enduring suffering. Rather, they did not want to abandon the one geographic spot where God appeared to their forefather Abraham and prevented him from sacrificing Isaac, his only son, the very site upon which Solomon built his temple.[34] But *that* place was crawling with Romans. What to do?

Strategy 2: Religious Legalism

The second strategy was to try to ignore politics in Jerusalem as best one could and stay focused on practicing religious purity until God saw fit to raise up the long-awaited military deliverer (a.k.a. the Messiah) in the style of Joshua or Gideon or any of the heroes recounted in the Hebrew Bible book of Judges. It was *Moses* and not David who represented the people's Golden Age for these religious purists. The leaders of this movement were called Pharisees and were held in high regard by the people who understood the Pharisees to be teaching them how to live under the original covenant (a.k.a. Mosaic law, which included the Ten Commandments, but also much more).

Strategy 3: Political Finesse

It might be said that the third group, the Saducees, operated more along the principle "If you can't beat 'em, join 'em." The Saducees were predominately aristocrats who, through marriage and/or crafty negotiation, had formed alliances with the local rulers (like the Idumean king named Herod) who were themselves puppets of Rome. Although the Saducees were respected for their wealth and connections, the Saducees were not the people's choice.

Strategy 4: Guerilla Warfare

The fourth group can be known as Zealots. The Zealots were the ancient Near Eastern equivalent of terrorists, perhaps often carrying a concealed weapon with which to dispatch any Roman soldier caught napping. Not that the Zealots were particularly successful or numerous. Rome had devised a particularly cruel form of public execution aimed at keeping the occupied people in shock and awe. It was called crucifixion. Anyone traveling into a Roman-governed city like Jerusalem would have had to pass by roadside crosses on which hung Zealots and other criminals.

Crucifixion might be compared to a hanging in the Old West, except infinitely more painful: it sometimes took all day to die, whereas hanging was over the instant the neck was broken. Crucifixion was the preferred *Roman* method of execution for anything that could be considered a crime against the state. For example, soldiers might be crucified for high treason, desertion to the enemy, or betraying government secrets. In addition to enforcing military discipline, crucifixion was the preferred punishment for severe crimes such as murder or piracy. But crucifixion was also used simply for "shock and awe," to preserve "stability" in society.[35]

We know that one of Jesus' disciples (Simon, not Peter) had Zealot-like sympathies. We would not have been surprised to hear of his arrest and crucifixion. But the Romans didn't execute "Simon the Zealot." They crucified Jesus. So why was the Jewish prophet named Jesus killed by means of crucifixion? After all, the local puppet of Rome, "King" Herod, was known for blocking the Jews from employing the distinctively Roman method of execution. Moreover, the Jewish religious law barred as immoral certain forms of execution, including crucifixion.[36] The Jews had their own means for killing those who violated the covenant—*stoning*.[37] So, why was Jesus *crucified* instead of stoned to death? For that matter, for what reasons was he killed at all?

Strategy 5: Love Your Enemies

Jesus was killed for political insurrection. He was considered to be a social terrorist, a corrupter of the people, a destabilizer of the government, a creator of unrest. This doesn't sound very much like baby Jesus in a manger. Of course, there were legitimate grounds for charging him with "disturbing the peace," that is, for disturbing the *Pax Romana*—the Peace of Rome. More than one of Jesus' teachings was a thinly veiled attack on the arrogance of the Caesars. For example, throughout the entire empire, the only human being who had legal claim to divine parentage was Caesar himself. The emperor alone bore the title "Son of the Gods." The populace was regularly forced to profess loyalty to the emperor by performing an act of worship, such as the public burning of incense in praise of Caesar's "divine nature." In circulation during the first century was a coin that Caesar had minted congratulating himself for being the "peacemaker" (*eirenopoieo*), which is to say, "maker and upholder of the century-long *Pax Romana*." But Jesus would have none of this. For example, in the Sermon on the Mount, Jesus turned emperor worship on its head. He proclaimed to the impoverished, downtrodden people: "Blessed are the peacemakers for they shall be called children of God."[38] Jesus used the same Greek word that appeared on the Roman coin, "peacemaker" (*eirenopoieo*), in order to deny Caesar's pretension to divinity. In other words, Jesus insisted that the *real* sons and daughters of God were those who made for a *different kind of peace* than that which was enforced at sword point.[39]

Okay, perhaps Jesus *was* something of a loose cannon and troublemaker from the vantage point of Caesar. Nevertheless, wouldn't a ruler have to be pretty insecure and petty to take notice of the ravings of an ex-carpenter in the hinterlands of the Palestinian desert? Consider the facts: Jesus had *no* army, *no* territory, *no* resources, *no* property (not even a house), *no* income, *no* weapons. He was at best a poor, fifth-place write-in candidate behind the Pharisees, Essenes, Saducees, and Zealots in competition for the imagination of a conquered people, a people that comprised the tiniest percentage of the empire's population, namely, the Jewish commoners.

Nevertheless, despite Jesus' apparent insignificance, Rome did in fact execute him as an enemy of the state, a *political* criminal deemed worthy of execution.

The word *political* comes from the Greek word *polis*, meaning "city" or "community." In fact, Jesus was a *political* activist, not simply because Rome said so, but more so because he was transforming the ways in which people lived with each other in community (*polis*). Rome knew what to do with Zealots (arrest them), with Saducees (pay them off), with Essenes (ignore them as fanatical oddballs). Rome even knew what to do with the widely respected Pharisees; Rome tolerated the Pharisees because scrupulously religious people are the easiest kind to rule. (For this reason even the Pharisees ended up serving the agenda of Caesar.) But Jesus was neither normal nor predictable. His followers began to play the game of politics by entirely different rules. And it was spreading: more and more people were living by these new and unusual *heuristics*.

HEURISTICS FROM THE NARRATIVE OF JESUS

The remainder of this chapter is an exercise in cross-domain transfer. What follows are three episodes from the story of Jesus of Nazareth and three episodes from the history of engineering. I propose that the scenes from Jesus' story display revolutionary heuristics. They were (and are) revolutionary (instead of merely reforming[40]) in the sense that the dominant culture couldn't comprehend them. We might say that these heuristics got Jesus killed. Following these heuristics also got Jesus' followers killed. In point of fact, politically and religiously motivated executions of Christians for these heuristics would stretch into the fourth century.[41] We can conclude that these heuristics are *dangerous*. To follow them once in a while may not attract much attention. But to follow them diligently may be very costly.

Of course, we might glean from Jesus other heuristics than the three offered here. But these three are enough to help us imagine how CDT between engineering and religious stories can occur. Other religious texts such as the Qur'an or the Hebrew Bible might have been used. But I will propose the following three because Jesus is the religious story with which

I am most familiar. In each case I will begin with the episode from Jesus' life, then describe the first-century context, and finally cite a contemporary event in engineering that I claim instantiates, or at least illustrates, the relevant heuristic at work.

Episode #1 from the Life of Jesus

> Now before the Feast of the Passover, Jesus knowing that His hour had come that He should depart out of this world to the Father, having loved His own who were in the world, He loved them to the end. And during supper, the devil having already put into the heart of Judas Iscariot, the son of Simon, to betray Him, Jesus, knowing that the Father had given all things into His hands, and that He had come forth from God, and was going back to God, rose from supper, and laid aside His garments; and taking a towel, He girded Himself about. Then He poured water into the basin, and began to wash the disciples' feet, and to wipe them with the towel with which He was girded. And so He came to Simon Peter. He said to Him, "Lord, do You wash my feet?" Jesus answered and said to him, "What I do you do not realize now, but you shall understand hereafter." Peter said to Him, "Never shall You wash my feet!" Jesus answered him, "If I do not wash you, you have no part with Me." Simon Peter said to Him, "Lord, not my feet only, but also my hands and my head." Jesus said to him, "He who has bathed needs only to wash his feet, but is completely clean; and you are clean, but not all of you." For He knew the one who was betraying Him; for this reason He said, "Not all of you are clean." And so when He had washed their feet, and taken His garments, and reclined at the table again, He said to them, "Do you know what I have done to you? "You call Me Teacher and Lord; and you are right, for so I am. "If I then, the Lord and the Teacher, washed your feet, you also ought to wash one another's feet. "For I gave you an example that you also should do as I did to you. "Truly, truly, I say to you, a slave is not greater than his master; neither is one who is sent greater than the one who sent him. (John 13:1–16, NASB)

A Note on the Biblical Context of John 13

A person's feet are bound to get dirty by clomping around all day on un-paved dirt roads wearing just sandals. Feet need washing. So what was the big deal? It is difficult for us to understand why Peter was so horrified by Jesus' action of footwashing. That is because Jesus' act made a decisive turning point for Western culture. In short, today we *admire* humility. Prior to Jesus, however, humility was considered *not* a good thing. Aristotle called humility a wicked habit, a vice.

In the pre-Jesus world, honor was tied up with social status. In some circles this is called an honor-shame system. In the honor-shame society, honor is not an individual's inalienable possession. While today we think of personal value (a.k.a. honor) as something inherent in each individual, in the ancient Near East (ANE), one's value was always value-in-other's-eyes.[42] Honor-shame societies were arranged hierarchically. In this context, the hierarchy reflected the way things really are. Someone's honor was not simply a matter of opinion. Rather, the honor hierarchy was also an ontological hierarchy; a monarch was more honorable because the monarch was *actually* a superior being. Each individual began the game of life by being born onto a rung of the honor hierarchy. One born into a blacksmith's family was lower on the ladder than one born into a royal family. While we think that ladders are for climbing, the ANE thought ladder climbing was itself dishonorable. One had to accept one's station (or rung) as the mandate of God, the gods, or Fate (depending on your religion). If you tried to climb the ladder, you would actually *lose* honor points for being presumptuous. The very best one could do to expand the honor capital that came with being born onto a particular rung was to (1) act in ways becoming one's rung; (2) marry well (without moving outside the rung); (3) have children; and (4) "outperform" everyone else in your class. If you were born a farmer, then act like a farmer, marry the best farmer's daughter available, have lots of children (especially boys), and be the very best farmer possible. By being better than the other farmers, one gained honor points at the expense of others (that is, by putting them to shame). There was no question of trying to be something else—farmers ought *not* to try to become aristocrats. Again, any human attempt at social climbing would result in a *loss* of honor points. If, however, a significant change in class *did* occur through no effort on the individual's part—such as when the shepherd David was anointed King of Israel—it was regarded as a miracle, as an act of God. (Case in point: David's anointing as heir to the throne was not of his own doing, but was the doing of Samuel, prophet of God.) Such an act of God brought *mega* honor points. But apart from such divine intervention, one's primary duty was to observe one's station.

In this region of the world, the honor-shame system was the basis of social stability from 2,000 BCE until the emergence of nation-states in the early modern period (ca. 1500–1800 CE). It is significant then that Jesus was widely recognized to have the mark of God's favor. Born into a carpenter's family, he was regarded as much more than a carpenter. Some referred to him as "Rabbi." Others called him a prophet. Still others whispered rumors that he might be the long-awaited military deliverer (the Messiah). When *this* Jesus washed the disciples' feet, he performed an act that threatened the very fabric of social stability. Thus Peter's confusion: "How can you be *Lord* [a.k.a. "Master" or "Your Honor"] and yet wash my feet? Don't do it!" Jesus was in fact turning social norms on their head. But he did not do this to destabilize society. Rather, Jesus was inaugurating a brand new society. In washing the feet of his inferiors, Jesus was instituting radically new rules ("follow my example") for a revolutionary way to think about honor. The one who strives after greatness, Jesus taught, must be *servant* of all.[43] By the old rules, serving others meant shame and dishonor. But Jesus changed the rules and thereby designed a whole new game.

Engineering Episode #1

FIGURE 9.6 Citicorp Tower

The Citicorp Center in Manhattan is both aesthetically stunning and architecturally marvelous. When it was completed in 1977, it was the seventh tallest building in the world.[44] The skyscraper dominates an entire city block, except for the northwest corner where St. Peter's Lutheran Church had stood since 1905. Obviously, site preparation for a fifty-nine-story skyscraper would encroach on church property. Since the Gothic-styled church was decaying, the church struck a deal: site preparation could begin so long as Citicorp agreed to raze the existing church building and rebuild a modernized version as a freestanding entity in its current location (45).[45]

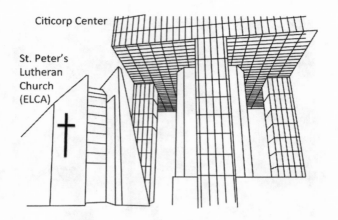

FIGURE 9.7 Nine-Story Pillars Overshadowing the Church

The catch that the church be freestanding presented a design challenge that William LeMessurier (pronounced "LeMeasure") met with vigor. He conceived of a building on nine-story pillars whose northwest corner overshadowed the church roof. Anyone looking at the building can feel the instability in the design. The structure looks to be especially susceptible to quartering winds, those that hit the building from a diagonal, because the line on which the center of gravity lies is 29 percent closer to the axis of rotation if the pillars are situated in the middle of side walls than at the corners.

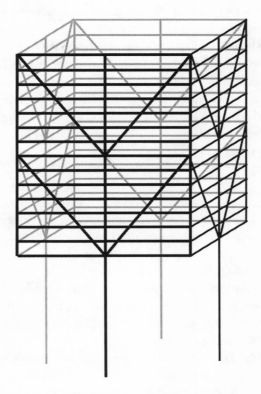

FIGURE 9.8 Chevron Bracing

LeMessurier's genius was manifest in the bracing, which he "first sketched out, in a burst of almost ecstatic invention, on a napkin in a Greek restaurant in Cambridge [Massachusetts]: forty-eight braces, in six tiers of eight, arrayed like giant chevrons behind the building's curtain of aluminum and glass" (48). LeMessurier was so proud of this design that he wished it could be on the outside of the building! According to a technical article (written by LeMessurier's partner, Stanley Goldstein), this arrangement actually made the building strong enough to deal with quartering winds that exert more strain on the building, since the winds press on two faces at once.

After receiving a phone call from a well-intentioned engineering student whose professor had accused LeMessurier of bad design, Le-Messurier introduced Citicorp as a statics problem to his own students at

Harvard Graduate School of Design. Since New York City building codes only require proof of strength in the face of perpendicular winds (a blind spot in the codes), it was simply "in the spirit of intellectual play" (46) that LeMessurier took up the task of recalculating how significant was the strain of quartering winds on the building. Although his unusual placement of pillars resulted in a 40 percent increase in strain on some members, he could also show that the welded chevrons "would have absorbed the extra load without so much as a tremor" (46). Still, just out of curiosity, he phoned his partner in charge of the day-to-day operations to see how the welding was going.

Alas! His partner earlier had approved substituting *bolted* joints for the welds in order to save $250,000 in construction costs.[46] Ordinarily this would be acceptable. But this time, the substitution was a mistake on four counts. First, the unique placement of the pillars meant that "the forty-per-cent increase in tension produced by a quartering wind became a hundred-and-sixty-per-cent increase on the building's bolts" (46). Normally, variance of conditions is accommodated by referring to standard SF (safety factor) for structural columns. But LeMessurier learned that subordinates on his team had not even applied SFs because they treated the chevron bracing as trusses, which need no SF, rather than as a kind of column. This was the second mistake.

The third mistake LeMessurier uncovered was ideal-world thinking. The deeper LeMessurier dug, which is to say, the more he tested his calculations against those of hands-on experts, the more he found his own ideal-world calculations wanting. Canadian wind tunnel experts told LeMessurier that his calculations of a 40 percent increase in strain due to quartering winds were *theoretically* correct—but *only if the wind blew at a constant speed*. In the real world, winds *gust* against a building, "setting it vibrating like a tuning fork" (47). (This would be fatal if the 410-ton tuned mass damper was on the fritz due to, say, power failure.)

Finally, bolted joints were a mistake because of the storm cycles of nature. LeMessurier's revised calculations showed increased strain on bolted joints, especially in the middle, that is, near the thirtieth floor. When these weaknesses were correlated with storm data, there was a one in sixteen chance that winds might exceed what the building could actually handle. If a sixteen-year storm should hit, the building would buckle at the thirtieth floor and collapse in a heap, killing or injuring perhaps as many as two hundred thousand people.[47] A fix was possible, but costly: a million dollars or more.[48] Moreover, the clock was ticking: "this was the end of July, and the height of the hurricane season was approaching. To avert disaster, LeMessurier would have to blow the whistle quickly on himself. That meant facing the pain of possible protracted litigation, probable bankruptcy, and professional disgrace" (48).

LeMessurier faced a problem the magnitude of which you and I will probably never encounter. According to essayist Joe Morgenstern,

> LeMessurier considered his options. Silence was one of them. . . . Suicide was another: if LeMessurier drove along the Maine Turnpike at a hundred miles an hour and steered into a bridge abutment, that would be that. But keeping silent required betting other people's lives against the odds, while suicide struck him as a coward's way out and—although he was passionate about nineteenth-century classical music—unconvincingly melodramatic. What seized him an instant later was entirely convincing, because it was so unexpected almost giddy sense of power. "I had information that nobody else in the world had," LeMessurier recalls. "I had power in my hands to effect extraordinary events that only I could initiate. I mean, sixteen years to failure—that was very simple, very clear-cut. I almost said, thank you, dear Lord, for making this problem so sharply defined that there's no choice to make. (48)

Faced with enormous personal cost, LeMessurier blew the whistle on himself and set out to make sure the problem was fixed. First, heavy steel plates (2-in. thick) were welded on each of the two hundred corner joints. Since the building already had tenants, the work was done between 5 p.m. and 8 a.m., seven days a week, for two months. Since exposure to the joints required removing drywall and carpet, rockers and carpenters worked the shift from 5 p.m. to 8 p.m., welders from 8 p.m. to 4 a.m., and cleaning crews tidied up daily from 4 a.m. until 8 a.m.

Second, an outsider with expertise in both disaster management and structural engineering was brought on site. Although Leslie Robertson and LeMessurier were peers, they were not friends per se. Yet LeMessurier *invited* Robertson's jurisdiction—an act of humility. Third, strain gauges were placed on individual members and closely monitored. Fourth, backup generators were purchased and technicians were brought on site to keep the tuned mass damper running flawlessly at all times. Fifth, multiple weather experts provided wind predictions four times each day. Finally, emergency evacuation plans were drawn up—just in case.

Throughout it all, LeMessurier seemed almost unconcerned with his reputation. As one city official described LeMessurier, "It started with a guy who stood up and said, 'I got a problem, I made the problem, let's fix the problem.'" (51). Perhaps the greatest test of LeMessurier's character was precipitated by *The New York Times* catching whiff of a scandal. On August 9, LeMessurier's wife told him that a reporter had been trying to reach him all day. As Morgenstern aptly put it, "That worried him greatly; being candid with city officials was one thing, but being interrogated by *The New York Times* was another" (51). LeMessurier decided simply to tell the truth. But then something wonderful happened: "Two minutes after six o'clock, LeMessurier called *The New York Times* switchboard. As he braced himself for an unpleasant conversation, he heard a recording. *The New York Times*, along with all the other major papers in the city, had just been shut down by a strike." The newspaper strike may have saved LeMessurier's career. The strike lasted until November 5, a month after Citicorp Center had been fully repaired. But LeMessurier had already proven what sort of person he was—self-effacing, self-sacrificing, others-serving.

LeMessurier died in 2007 at the age of eighty-one. Toward the end of his life, LeMessurier repeatedly recounted the summer of 1978 with his Harvard students. "You have a social obligation," he would tell them. "In return for getting a license and being regarded with respect, you're supposed to be self-sacrificing and look beyond the interests of yourself and your client to society as a whole. And the most wonderful part of my story is that when I did it nothing bad happened" (53).

Episode #2 from the Life of Jesus

> Now there was a woman who had been suffering from hemorrhages for twelve years; and though she had spent all she had on physicians, no one could cure her. She came up behind him and touched the fringe of his clothes, and immediately her hemorrhage stopped. Then Jesus asked, "Who touched me?" When all denied it, Peter said, "Master, the crowds surround you and press in on you." But Jesus said, "Someone touched me; for I noticed that power had gone out from me." When the woman saw that she could not remain hidden, she came trembling; and falling down before him, she declared in the presence of all the people why she had touched him, and how she had been immediately healed. He said to her, "Daughter, your faith has made you well; go in peace." (Luke 8:43–48, NRSV)

A Note on the Biblical Context of Luke 8

The cultural context of this passage is extremely difficult for us to imagine. Disease has always been a bad thing. But in the ancient Near Eastern world, disease was sometimes also considered symptomatic of deeper problems. If someone was seriously ill, others assumed that the cause of the disease could be traced back to poor character or some nefarious sin. In the case of this story, both Jesus and the woman were Jewish. And in Jewish eyes, disease was defined as the absence of health. As an absence or lack of the good, disease was classified as a kind of *evil*. Often this evil had *nothing* to do with the character of the sufferer. The Hebrew Bible story of Job makes it clear that Job's suffering was not related to some moral failure on his part. But this same story also makes it clear that it was very, very natural for Job's friends to jump to the conclusion that something *must* be wrong with Job. "Is not your wickedness very great?" asks Job's neighbor Eliphaz.

Jews were conditioned to treat disease as a kind of impurity. If one's illness wasn't symptomatic of a deeper moral failing (e.g., high cholesterol resulting from gluttony), the sickness itself nevertheless rendered one unworthy to appear before God. This is an extension of Jewish purity laws. Jews had been offering animal sacrifice to God for two thousand years before this story took place. According to the Jewish law (Torah), only the very best animal—one free from sickness and deformity—was acceptable to God. A similar logic was applied to people. If you were sick, you stayed home from temple. (This had the social advantage of preventing the spread of sickness.) The technical term was *unclean*. The law was binding on this point; so long as you were sick, you were unclean and had to stay away from religious gatherings and festivals.[49]

Perhaps more disturbing than the length of time this woman suffered ostracization (twelve years!) was the gender-specific account of her suffering. Women were already restricted to an outer court in the temple.[50] But her "bleeding" was likely a menstrual bleeding, which meant she couldn't even get into the Court of Women. Although menstruation is a natural event created by God, purity laws were explicit: a woman was banned from temple worship so long as she was menstruating. But since this woman had been bleeding for twelve years, she had been excluded from the most important social gatherings of the community for her entire adult life. We must keep in mind that for Jews, virtually every celebration and holiday was a *religious* one, a holy day on which the community gathered, often at or near the temple.[51] As a result, this woman was essentially an outcast.

She was invisible, virtually unknown to everyone who otherwise most certainly would have been her peers.

But that isn't even the end of the bad news. As a reproductive disease, her bleeding meant that she was unable to bear children. Therefore she was also unmarriageable. And remember that in this honor-shame society, two of the ways to increase social standing were to marry well and to bear children. If her parents had already died, she would be left virtually all alone, with neither son nor husband to be her champion and provider.[52] She is utterly alone.[53]

Engineering Episode #2

FIGURE 9.9 Treadle Pump in Malawi[54]

As the planet continues to heat up due to climate change, the people who live closest to the equator will suffer the most. The key to their survival is getting water for irrigating arid lands. The treadle pump is an ingenious device that is so mechanically efficient that even a child can operate it.[55] The frame can be constructed out of local materials such as bamboo, and, if PVC is unavailable, the tube-well also can be made of bamboo. When properly constructed the treadle pump is able to generate just over a liter per second with a maximum lift of about five meters. When more than a third of the world lives on $2 a day or less, a pump that costs less than $20 may be a real lifesaver. At last count, over 1.4 million treadle pumps have been installed worldwide for impoverished farmers.[56]

Episode #3 from the Life of Jesus

> And two others also, who were criminals, were being led away to be put to death with Him . . . And those passing by were hurling abuse at Him, wagging their heads and saying, "You who are going to destroy the temple and rebuild it in three days, save Yourself! If You are the Son of God, come down from the cross." In the same way the chief priests also, along with the scribes and elders, were mocking Him and saying, "He saved others; He cannot save Himself. He is the King of Israel; let Him now come down from the cross, and we shall believe in Him. "He trusts in God; let Him deliver Him now, if He takes pleasure in Him; for He said, 'I am the Son of God.'" And the robbers also who had been crucified with Him were casting the same insult at Him. . . . And when they came to the place called The Skull, there they crucified Him and the criminals, one on the right and the other on the left. But Jesus was saying, "Father, forgive them; for they do not know what they are doing." And they cast lots, dividing up His garments among themselves. . . . And one of the criminals who were hanged there was hurling abuse at Him, saying, "Are You not the Christ? Save Yourself and us!" But the other answered, and rebuking him said, "Do you not even fear God, since you are under the same sentence of condemnation? "And we indeed justly, for we are receiving what we deserve for our deeds; but this man has done nothing wrong." And he was saying, "Jesus, remember me when You come in Your kingdom!" And He said to him, "Truly I say to you, today you shall be with Me in Paradise. (Luke 23:32; Matthew 27:39–44; Luke 23:33–34, 39–43, NASB)

A Note on the Context of the Passion of Jesus

The above use of the word *Passion* comes from the Latin *passio*, which simply means "suffering." The New Testament gives four different accounts of the one event known as the suffering death of Jesus. The four accounts have different emphases. Here the accounts as told by Luke and Matthew mention two additional criminals condemned to die. As noted above, crucifixion was a Roman method of execution reserved for those criminals significant enough to pose a threat to the state. The way Matthew and Luke tell the story, these two felons did not deny their guilt. That they lived hard lives shows itself in the abuse that they were quick to heap upon Jesus, as if they wanted to distance themselves from him. But one had a change of heart *after* he saw Jesus freely offer forgiveness to his executioners.

Engineering Episode # 3

What we today call the nation-state is a recent invention. In the medieval period, governance was a reflection of the class system; one's claim on social power (including the scope of one's oversight, whether one ruled a country, a castellany, an estate, or a small farm) was the result of the class into which one was born, because one's class was an ontological fact. The king ruled because he was ontologically the greatest being in the land; the baron ruled the estate because he was ontologically superior to anyone else on the estate. And so on. (Thus, in the Middle Ages, a pauper like Abraham Lincoln could *never* have risen to the level of ruler.) Title and wealth (especially land) not only marked one as authorized to rule others; it was *incumbent* upon such a one to rule. The higher one's rank, the greater one's *duty* to rule. Those who didn't have rank were beholden to those who did. Those in the middle, between the extremes of emperor and pauper, were always looking to increase their holdings by strategic alliances (e.g., a felicitous marriage) or by nefarious schemes (e.g., by plunder). This picture was complicated by the reality of the double realm: as far as medieval Europe was concerned, every city was both the realm of a governmental ruler *and* the realm of the pope as the supreme religious ruler. Both state and church were arranged hierarchically. Ecclesiastical titles arranged by rank included pope, cardinal, archbishop, bishop, priest, monk, and friars. Secular titles arranged by rank are (roughly) as follows: emperor, king, viceroy, grand duke, archduke, prince, duke, marquess (marquis), earl (or count), viscount, baron, baronet, knight, and gentleman. Not all titles included "sovereignty," the authority to rule some sector of the population, but many did. Similarly, title did not always imply wealth and land holdings (e.g., a castle), but often did. Thus the Holy Roman Empire did not set stable political boundaries as in today's Europe. Rather, it was subdivided into regions ruled by persons of varying rank, power, and wealth, and also of varying loyalties. This ever-changing situation describes the location of engineering episode #3: the Mediterranean shoreline of southern France during the twelfth century.

Our idea of "nation" cannot be easily read backwards into an era when borders were constantly shifting and one's most important enemy may be one's peer in rank and title. The baron whose land abuts yours may speak the same language as you but may be out to undermine your power by making alliances with other barons, viscounts, or counts. You did not want to come up on the short end of that stick. For that reason, rivers were a most natural and politically crucial property marker. You can relocate a fence, but you can't move the river.

But rivers are also troublesome things. The Rhone River in southern France is cold, swift, and wide. In December 2003, the high waters of the Rhone during the region's rainy season claimed the lives of seven persons. How much less equipped to tackle the Rhone was the technologically primitive medieval peasant? A river like the Rhone—a half-mile wide at its mouth—was a hazard that one dared to cross with the greatest reluctance. As often as not, there was nothing for the peasants to do but ply their wares on one bank but not the other.

In addition to the physical danger the river posed, the Rhone River served as a secure political border between the County of Toulouse, on the one hand, and the County of Maurienne (of the old kingdom of Arles, the lower part of Burgundy), on the other. Toulouse and Maurienne were on poor terms for several reasons. First, Toulouse was suspicious of foreigners, especially the power-hungry dukes to the north. The region of Aquitaine, to the north, was in perpetual turmoil: anyone with a castle seemed to think himself free to rule as he saw fit.[57] These Aquitaine dukes were not shy of trying to plunder their southern neighbors. Case in point: when Pope Innocent III called all noblemen to a crusade (1204), these Aquitaine dukes used the call as a pretext for invading Toulouse en route to Jerusalem!

Second, Toulouse was tetchy because of empire-wide religious intolerance. Toulouse had originally been settled by a Germanic tribe (the Visigoths) who had converted to Christianity except in one point: they denied the full divinity of the Second Person of the Trinity[58] (a doctrinal position called Arianism). Although the Visigoths were conquered in the sixth century, their beliefs lingered on for centuries in this region such that orthodox Christians considered the region of Toulouse as religiously dangerous. The religion of the Toulousians was declared to be "a cancer in the body of European civilization that had to be rooted out at all costs."[59] This was thought to be a problem of such significance that in 1208, a crusade was declared directly against Toulouse.[60] But as early as 1163, the Council of Tours had called upon the secular powers to dispossess the "heretics" of their land.[61] In other words, for forty-five years, "good" Christians were religiously *obligated* to enforce "a social and economic boycott so that [the heretics] may be forced through the loss of human comfort to repent of the error of their way of life."[62]

This story of religious intolerance makes us feel uncomfortable because the "good" guys don't look to be very good. I don't mean only that this story chafes against our contemporary sense of religious toleration. I mean particularly that the actions of "good" Christians made life worse for the Toulousians—especially for the impoverished. As far as the region's poor were concerned, there was no difference between starvation by boycott and starvation by famine.

How does one change such a messy situation? The local politics are so unpredictable and messy that nothing you and I might design would likely work. In fact, anything we might concoct would be roundly ignored, for we would have been mere commoners. Nevertheless, in the year 1177, a teenage sheepherder named Bénezet undertook the construction of a bridge at Avignon. That this was an engineering marvel is uncontested. (The lad single-handedly positioned as the first stone one weighing more than thirty men could lift.) But more than a marvel, the bridge was an act of mercy: peasants on each bank could now profit from cross-river trading, and enemies could now become friends. For this act, Bénezet, who died before the completion of the bridge, was canonized as Saint Bénezet the Bridge Builder.

FIGURE 9.10 *Le pont d'Avignon depuis l'île de la Barthelasse*[63]

CONCLUSION

I have purposely left unspoken the connections between each story and engineering. The simple fact that I see connections doesn't do you any more good than if I point to the duck-rabbit and insist that it is also a duck, although all you can see is the rabbit. The important claim for this chapter is that practical reasoning—whether solving a design problem or constructing an ethical argument—*may* be assisted by cross-domain transfer. In particular, I have claimed that religious narratives can serve as one kind of source for CDT that lies outside engineering proper. The question that remains is whether you see it.

DISCUSSION QUESTIONS

1. (a) Describe what features of the first episode from Jesus' life "fit" with the story of William LeMessurier's Citicorp Tower. Do you notice anything that makes you hesitate to put these two together? (What aspects of the one don't seem to go with the other?) (b) Summarize in

a short sentence the heuristic that you think covers the two stories—
what "rule of thumb" seems to be at work in both?

2.   (a) Poke around on the Internet to describe the features of the treadle
     pump. Describe what features of the second episode from Jesus' life
     "fit" with the story of the treadle pump. Do you notice anything that
     makes you hesitate to put these two together? (What aspects of the
     one don't seem to go with the other?) (b) Summarize in a short sen-
     tence the heuristic that you think covers the two stories—what "rule
     of thumb" seems to be at work in both?

3.   (a) Describe what features of the story of Jesus' Passion "fit" with the
     story of Bénezet's bridge at Avignon. Do you notice anything that
     makes you hesitate to put these two together? (What aspects of the
     one don't seem to go with the other?) (b) Summarize in a short sen-
     tence the heuristic that you think covers the two stories—what "rule
     of thumb" seems to be at work in both?

4.   No one is canonized for building a bridge today. Nevertheless, tech-
     nology can play a role in building bridges between people. Describe
     a recent event in which social media (like Facebook[64]) established
     friendly lines of communication between former strangers who were
     potential enemies.

5.   Suggest some piece of culturally appropriate technology and explain
     the way it resonates with an episode from the story of Jesus (you may
     cite a passage other than the three listed above).

NOTES

1.   This is not to say that scientific knowledge and theoretical reason-
     ing are unimportant to the engineering design process. Rather, it is to
     note with Walter Vincenti that what engineers call "science" is already
     a *subset* of scientific knowledge, preselected for its *usefulness* by the
     community of engineering practitioners. Vincenti argues that the *kind*
     of science used by engineers is neither "new" knowledge produced by
     research nor "basic" science. Thus, while a science such as physics is
     after knowledge per se, engineering seeks *usefulness-in-context*, where
     the "context" in question is the current state of engineering excellence.
     Vincenti, "Control-Volume Analysis."

2. Vincenti, "The Davis Wing and the Problem of Airfoil Design." NACA stands for National Advisory Committee for Aeronautics. For illustration of how NACA number works, see Ferguson, *Engineering and the Mind's Eye*, 52.

3. "The first digit of the designation gives the maximum height of the camber line in percent chord, the second the location of this maximum height in tenths of chord aft of the leading edge, and the final two the maximum thickness in percent chord." Ibid., 742.

4. Cited in Ferguson, *Engineering and the Mind's Eye*, 54. Emphasis added.

5. "To argue, as I have . . . that engineering skills are rarely theoretical and often not even technical is different from arguing that engineering is unskilled work. To the contrary, engineering often involves highly complex skills, many of which are learned only through industrial practice and over the course of a long career. But these skills require experience and a *'feel'* for things—for a particular machine or process, for an organization and its personnel—as much, if not more, than scientific training." Zussman, *Mechanics of the Middle Class*, 75. Emphasis added.

6. Importantly, it was the shape of the fuselage that turned out to be the key to reducing high-speed drag.

7. Hands-on observation coupled with drawing has the effect of training one's imagination to follow certain tracks. A biology student named Samuel Scudder has immortalized this in his turn-of-the-century essay, "The Student, the Fish, and Agassiz," widely available on the web.

8. The story is told by Gardner, "Mathematical Games."

9. A creative commons image; http://en.wikipedia.org/wiki/File:Smith_diagram.png.

10. Koen, *Discussion of the Method*, 35.

11. If you are baking a cake from scratch, eggs are a *necessary* condition: you can't bake it without them. But if eggs were a *sufficient* condition, then eggs would be all you need.

12. Vincenti, "The Scope for Social Impact in Engineering Outcomes."

13. Ibid., 764.

14. The term is Mark Schwehn's; see Schwehn, "Local Genius."

15. For a helpful introduction to sustainable design for buildings, see the 2006 PBS series *Design e2: The Economies of Being Environmentally Conscious.*

16. McDonough and Braungart, *Cradle to Cradle*, 135–36.

17. Root-Bernstein, "Visual Thinking," 51. The example is given from the 1870s of one brilliant chemist who wrote poetry of such high quality that it was praised by Coleridge.

18. Gelernter, *Machine Beauty*, 130–31.

19. Public Domain source: http://en.wikipedia.org/wiki/File:Cristo_de_San_Pl%C3%A1cido,_by_Diego_Vel%C3%A1zquez.jpg.

20. Graham, "Palchinsky's Travels."

21. Soudek, "Humanist Engineer of Aleksandr Solzhenitsyn," 58.

22. Ibid.

23. Ibid.

24. Graham, "Palchinsky's Travels," 30.

25. The term is Koen's. The transom view holds that no overlap exists between the skills of society and of the engineer, and therefore "the duty of the society is to pose the problems it wants solved, and the duty of the engineer is to solve them using the best techniques available." Koen fears that engineering in America is rapidly becoming, or has already become, a transom window affair. By contrast, he advocates for what we have called an IDEO approach, where design teams comprised of both non-engineers and engineers produce the very best design solutions. Koen, *Discussion of the Method*, 56.

26. Cited in Soudek, "Humanist Engineer of Aleksandr Solzhenitsyn," 58.

27. Famously, political philosopher Alasdair MacIntyre argued, "Deprive children of stories and you leave them unscripted, anxious stutterers in their actions as in their words." In his epoch-making work, *After Virtue*, MacIntyre goes on to show that dependence on stories for getting our moral bearings is something we *never* outgrow. MacIntyre, *After Virtue*, 216.

28. http://whatwouldjesusdrive.info/intro.php.

29. Thus we expect Jesus to rule out the Hummer (H1) in favor of, perhaps, the European SmartCar. (The original European version, built in France, was made of 98 percent recycled materials and got 60 mph.)

30. The library at Alexandria was the largest in the world: one hundred thousand scrolls, or about ten thousand books.

31. The destruction of Solomon's Temple is painfully ironic since Solomon expected that this building would in some sense tether God to a geographic location. Consider the almost magical flavor of Solomon's lengthy prayer of dedication for the grand temple recorded in 2 Chron 6:12–42.

32. See 2 Chron 34:8–13 and the book of Ezra; the repairing of the walls is reported in Neh 2:11—6:19.

33. This community is famous for preserving the Jewish Scriptures from waves of anti-Semitic persecution that resulted in the burning of Hebrew Scriptures. The scriptures preserved in the caves of Qumran are called the Dead Sea Scrolls.

34. Cp. Genesis 22, and 2 Chron 3:1 and 1 Chron 21:18–22. See Terrien, "The Metaphor of the Rock in Biblical Theology."

35. Crucifixion was sometimes used randomly by a tyrant to instill fear and foster submission by a conquered people. For example, when rumors of slave uprising were quashed, suspect rabble-rousers were forced to walk around the forum with a signboard listing their impending cause of death and then were crucified publicly, for all to see. Thus the line of crosses outside the city was a constant reminder of the power of Rome. See Hengel, *Crucifixion in the Ancient World and the Folly of the Message of the Cross.*

36. The Jewish law says anyone hanging on a tree is cursed, Deut 21:23.

37. Famously, in the early days of the church, Stephen was stoned to death while young Saul (as the Apostle Paul was known before his conversion) stood by and watched approvingly. Acts 7:54–61.

38. Matt 5:9.

39. Bainton, *Christian Attitudes toward War and Peace*, 64.

40. On the crucial difference between reform and revolution, see McCabe, *Law, Love and Language*, 133–38, but also 10, 26, 61, 13, 44, 54, 60.

41. By the time Constantine became emperor, the number of Christ-followers had swelled to roughly 5 percent of the population. Constantine legalized Christianity by 317 and a later emperor, Theodosius, made Christianity mandatory in 387.

42. Malina, *The New Testament World.*

43. Mark 9:35.

44. http://upload.wikimedia.org/wikipedia/commons/1/1d/Citicorp. JPG.

45. All page numbers come from Morgenstern, "The Fifty-Nine-Story Crisis." See also Pritchard, "Responsible Engineering."

46. Karagianis, "The Right Stuff."

47. The estimated death toll was calculated by the Red Cross. Kremer, "(Re)Examining the Citicorp Case," 323. Note: a functioning tuned mass damper reduces the probability to 1 in 55. But if the electricity was compromised by a severe storm, so might the tuned mass damper. Morgenstern noted that the backup generators for the twin towers lasted only fifteen minutes!

48. LeMessurier's first guess was $1 million for the retrofix. Other estimates ranged from $4.3 million to $8 million. Morgenstern, "Fifty-Nine-Story Crisis," 52.

49. Leviticus chapters 12 and 15 cover some of these purity laws.

50. The temple was constructed roughly as a series of concentric rooms. Men could go one ring closer than women; male priests closer yet; the High Priest alone once a year could enter the innermost room, called the Holy of Holies.

51. The one important exception was the Sabbath meal celebrated with one's family every Friday evening.

52. Bruce Malina underscores the absolute importance of the eldest son in this culture: by far the strongest relationship a woman can ever have is not with her husband but with her first male child. We see this in the way Mary, especially since the death of her husband, relied heavily on Jesus. Even in his dying moments, Jesus makes sure to delegate to his disciple John the ongoing care for his mother (John 19:26–28). See Malina for other cultural examples.

53. It is even possible that "bleeding" is a euphemism for some more unspeakable disease. Surgeon-turned-author Verghese recounts a condition called *vesicularvaginal fistula,* which, if uncorrected surgically, will produce not only a continual discharge of pus, blood, and urine, but a horrific stench that would have kept any sympathizers far, far away. Verghese, *Cutting for Stone,* 349f., 467–68.

54. Image is public domain: http://en.wikipedia.org/wiki/File:Treadle_pump_malawi.jpg.

55. Picture of the treadle pump is public domain: http://commons.wiki-media.org/wiki/File:Treadle_pump_malawi.jpg.

56. http://www.ideorg.org/OurTechnologies/TreadlePump.aspx

57. "Capable of magnificent feats in order to achieve expansion, the dukes [of Aquitaine, just to the north of Toulouse] had poor control over a vaguely defined area, subject to anarchic forces. The collapse of the Carolingian structures had given way to a whole system of relations, more or less binding, based on a temporary *convenientiae*. Ducal suzerainty was inconsistent, many-layered and unstable, castellanies virtually independent. All this was further aggravated by ecclesiastical privileges and a rapid decline in the public peace." Bur, "Kingdom of the Franks from Louis VI to Philip II," 543.

58. Cantor, *Civilization of the Middle Ages*, 113. Their belief, called Arian-ism, was determined to be heterodox at the Council of Nicaea in 325 CE.

59. Ibid., 389.

60. In 1208, a papal legate had been murdered in Toulouse. The Count of Toulouse was himself implicated in the crime. Ibid., 424.

61. Robinson, "The Papacy, 1122–1198," 337.

62. Ibid., 336.

63. Two world wars have been unkind to this bridge. Nevertheless, four of the original twenty-two arches that span the nine-hundred-foot-wide Rhone River at Avignon are still standing. Photo by Chimigi: http://commons.wikimedia.org/wiki/File:Le_pont_d%27Avignon_depuis_l%27%C3%AEle_de_la_Barthelasse.jpg.

64. See, for example, Bronner, "Virtual Bridge Allows Strangers in Mid-east to Seem Less Strange."

10

ENGINEERING AS CHRISTIAN VOCATION[1]

RECENT TRENDS IN JOB data seem to indicate that twentysomethings are likely to hold as many as ten different long-term jobs and to have, on average, three different careers. This is quite different from the experience of our great-grandparents, who tended to have one career while living in one town their entire adult lives. So what accounts for the new career mobility? Is it simply the global economy that forces us to choose and rechoose? Or does it have more to do with the way contemporary culture has burdened us with a nearly limitless range of choices, and it is hard to make up our minds? Or maybe some people choose and rechoose jobs and careers because they are looking for something special. Truth be told, what we really seem to long for is *a job that picks me* rather than a job I pick. At the very least, the notion of "job picks me" suggests the intriguing possibility of a deep resonance between the requirements of a job and who I really am in the deepest sense—all my skills and knowledge and personality. At its best, the phrase sounds like destiny: "I was fated and slated for just this job."

But it is still just a metaphor, right? After all, a job is not a living agent that can knowingly "pick" anything. But is it merely a metaphor? I propose that the language of "job picks me" is a loose translation, a shadowy imitation of the deeper and richer historical idea of *vocation*.[2]

We hardly know what to do with the term *vocation* today. We figure that those who go in for "vocational counseling" are those who are having trouble getting a job. And those who go to vo-tech (vocational-technical) schools are sometimes looked down upon because supposedly they are not going to "real" colleges. But such colloquial uses of *vocation* are not very helpful. What *is* helpful is the realization that better than the luck of "job picks me" is the possibility of having a *calling*. That's what *vocation* means, after all: *vocare,* to call, and *vocatio,* that to which one is called. So vocation is the more extreme and concrete form of "job picks me." A vocation refers to God's inviting you into a career that both *matters* and *fits who you are.*

Reading this chapter will probably not settle for you what your vocation is, much less whether there really is a God who calls. But this chapter sets its sights on a more doable task of answering a straightforward question: Is engineering the sort of occupation to which God might call someone, and if so, why? The way we will proceed in answering this question is by thinking about *practical wisdom.* As you recall, practical wisdom is the disposition (or "habit" or "virtue") of doing practical reasoning well.

There are two ways practical reasoning can go wrong. German engineers under the Nazi regime built gas chambers and cremation ovens using top-quality materials and the "finest" workmanship to produce ovens that were highly efficient.[3] This is an instance of good *means* but of a horribly bad *end* (or aim). Conversely, Nazi physicians perfected the refrigeration of meat—a good end—by studying the effects of freezing and thawing (and then refreezing and re-thawing) the limbs of *living* victims (the process was repeated until, in some cases, the limbs simply fell off)—a case of good ends (medical research) but evil means.[4] But as we learned in the chapter on practical reasoning, both means *and* ends must be good in order to say that an act of practical reasoning is good.

In this chapter we will apply these two metrics to the enterprise of engineering as a whole. It seems logical to suppose that if the enterprise fails to meet one or both metrics, it cannot be a viable candidate for vocation. I shall argue that engineering, viewed theologically, *fulfills both metrics.* This won't *prove* engineering to be a vocation (much less prove engineering to be *your* vocation), because there may be metrics that we have not yet considered. The furthest our investigation will be able to go is to conclude that by fulfilling these two metrics, engineering becomes a plausible candidate for vocation. To say the same thing differently, by the end of this chapter, you will be able to explain two ways in which engineering resembles medicine, ministry, social work, teaching, and other bona fide vocations.

Metric #1: Does engineering have a (Christianly) good end?

Claim #1: Jesus is the end (or aim) of engineering as a Christian vocation.

True or false, "Honor is always bestowed on those who deserve it." Hmm—the trouble with this sentence is the ambiguity around the meaning of *deserve*. What counts as "deserving" changes from time to time. Social esteem is a shape-shifter. As late as the 1960s, surgeons in Russia were classified with manual laborers, because they worked with their hands. In contrast, in America doctors have long since occupied the top of the social pecking order, and the highest paid doctors are the ones who work with their hands, namely, *surgeons* (orthopedic surgeons). It may be a matter of cultural luck that today's engineers are held in such regard. But the esteem engineers enjoy today was not inevitable. In other times and places, engineers were honored much less than today. Recall that being an engineer in Stalin's era was likely to get you imprisoned, exiled, and possibly killed.[5] Nor does the honor that a society pays the professional always reflect the inherent worth of the profession. If it did, millions of dollars would be paid to schoolteachers rather than to straight-out-of-high-school athletic phenoms. I raise the point about the fickleness of social esteem to remind us that the worth of engineering is not a no-brainer. We cannot count on society's opinion (currently high) to assure ourselves that engineering matters. To reach this conclusion we must think a little harder.

At first glance, history is not entirely reassuring. Looking at the broad sweep of history, we can observe a greater tendency to bestow honor more quickly and in greater measure on those who *owned* technology than on those who designed and built technology.[6] Medieval farmers who *owned* heavy plows increased in prosperity, and thus social status, but no one remembers who invented the heavy plow to begin with.[7] Medieval knights were grateful to the blacksmiths who made and improved their armor. Despite the fact that knights owed their success in battle to the smithy, it was the knights and not the smithy who received honor.

Between the demise of the Jewish kingdom once ruled by Solomon (587 BCE) and the birth of Christianity (first century CE), the dominant technological culture that arose in the West was Greece, followed by Rome. Both cultures produced engineering marvels such as the Parthenon and the aqueducts. But when we ask who got the honor, it was decidedly *not* the mechanical reasoner. The glory of the Colosseum belonged to the emperor. This wasn't mere neglect—mechanical reasoners (a.k.a. proto-engineers) were stuck near the bottom of the social pecking order of the day. The smartest people in the ancient world thought mechanical reasoning was *undignified*!

[N]ot only are the arts which we call mechanical [*banausikai*] generally held in bad repute, but States also have a very low opinion of them,—and with justice. For they are injurious to the bodily health of workmen and overseers, in that they compel them to be seated and indoors, and in some cases also all day before a fire, and when the body grows effeminate, the mind also becomes weaker and weaker. *And the mechanical arts, as they are called, will not let men unite with them care for friends and State, so that men engaged in them must ever appear to be both bad friends and poor defenders of their country.* And there are States . . . in which not a single citizen is allowed to engage in mechanical arts [*banausikas technas*].[8]

—Socrates, fifth century BCE

. . . any occupation, art, or science, which makes the body or soul or mind of the freeman less fit for the practice or exercise of excellence, is mechanical; wherefore *we call those arts mechanical which tend to deform the body . . . for they absorb and degrade the mind.*[9]

—Aristotle, fourth century BCE

In other words, mechanical reasoning was fit only for *slaves*. The early Roman historian Plutarch, looking back on Greek history, concluded that even if Archimedes had saved Athens by his mechanical contraptions (we now know he didn't), he would have done so *shamefully* because it involved machines![10]

Although Plutarch had been born a Greek, he became a naturalized citizen of Rome. So advanced was Rome in its heyday that some tiny nations reportedly declared "war" on Rome with the intent of immediate surrender, because to be "conquered" by Rome meant better roads, better policing, better mail, and, in some cases, the hope of better water and even indoor plumbing (via the Roman aqueduct system[11]). As far as these outlying peoples were concerned, Rome was much more like their savior than their conqueror. Perhaps this is why Plutarch transferred allegiance from Greece to Rome. But for Plutarch's contemporaries who were Jewish—like Rabbi Gamaliel and Jesus of Nazareth—the culture of the occupying force was *not* kindly viewed. The ubiquitous military presence of Rome was something to be *regretted*.

In the hinterlands of the empire at the turn of the new millennium, a tiny but devout Jewish sect called "The Way" slowly gained Rome's attention.[12] We learned in chapter 9 that by the end of the first century, members of the Way, eventually called "Christians," were persecuted—some even to the point of death.[13] Sporadic waves of persecution against Jews, Jewish-Christians, and eventually non-Jewish Christians, especially in large cities, would last for several centuries. So, it is not surprising that writers of the Christian New Testament didn't care two figs for the technological marvels produced by the very empire that was feeding Christians to the lions for sport. As far as the New Testament is concerned, salvation was decidedly *not* found in Roman (or Greek) technology. This is not the same thing as saying mechanical reasoning is evil. But the New Testament is noticeably silent on topics of technological skill (*technē*) and mechanical arts (*banausikas technas*).

While Christianity grew in strength and intellectual acumen, Rome as a culture appeared simultaneously to rot from within (at least that is how historians today diagnose the rule of monsters like Nero and Caligula and Domitian). In the fourth century, then-Roman-emperor Constantine opted to establish his throne in the *eastern* side of the world, making Constantinople the new imperial city instead of Rome. It was Constantine who finally ended the ban on Christianity circa 315 CE and who emblazoned the militia's shields with the Christian symbol of the cross. A later emperor, Theodosius, went further in 387, declaring that Christianity was not only legal, it was the *mandatory* religion. The division of power between the old imperial city of Rome and the new one, Constantinople, contributed to vulnerability in the defenses of Rome. By the end of the fourth century, Rome was being repeatedly sacked and torched by "marauding hordes of barbarians" from the north. (Were they *really* barbarians, or is "barbarian" simply the name any nation gives to its enemy?) Many began to grumble that the gods whose job it was to protect Rome had turned their backs on the city, the gods having been snubbed by the rise of the rival religion of Christianity. Thus was the demise of Rome blamed on Christians.

A former philosopher named Augustine converted to Christianity and defended Christianity against its accusers in terms that the educated elite could understand.[14] The books he wrote span many feet of shelving. But on the issue of technology, Augustine is virtually silent. In one of the last books he wrote (the one in which he defended Christianity against the charge of ruining Rome), Augustine expressed guarded admiration for Roman technology. But his treatment consisted of only two paragraphs.[15] Later Christian theologians followed suit and simply stepped over the topic of technology in their writings.

The one exception is St. Isidore—today Isidore has been deemed the patron saint of the Internet—whose seventh-century encyclopedia gives a detailed account of the state of human learning. As far as Isidore was concerned, human learning was expanding. Some disciplines, such as the study of clays, sands, and minerals (and their related properties), were relatively new. But how to classify this new kind of learning? He decided he could not subsume mineralogy under "geometry" or under "music." Neither could he dismiss this new branch of knowledge as fit only for slaves, as Socrates had done. Isidore decided to place "mechanical" arts *alongside* other noble disciplines. At the hand of Isidore materials science becomes noble in its own right.[16] Unfortunately, Isidore also set engineering back a few paces. His blundering fascination with etymology led him to mistakenly think that the Latin *mechanicus* was derived from the Greek *moichos*, meaning "adulterer," rather than from *mechane* (i.e., machine) or *mechos* (i.e., a means, something expedient, a remedy). Christian thinkers after Isidore—and in this age virtually every "thinker" was explicitly a theologian—understood "mechanical" to be synonymous with "adulterate"![17] The lingering implication is that the practice of *ars mechanicus* by any Christian may taint one's soul and thus require confession and penance.

These one thousand years of scattered historical anecdotes yield a puzzling picture. We know that in the West today engineering is held in very high regard. Many suppose that the nineteenth-century industrial revolution had something to do with this.[18] But the industrial revolution spawned both technological marvels *and* horrific human suffering.[19] Shouldn't the social esteem of engineering suffer losses as well as gains? Just as puzzling is the way the high esteem of engineering was correlated with a nearly instantaneous upturn in opinion by Christian theologians. So complete was their praise that in some circles engineers imagined themselves to be "saints."[20]

If we graph the limited anecdotal data we have, we get this sort of result:

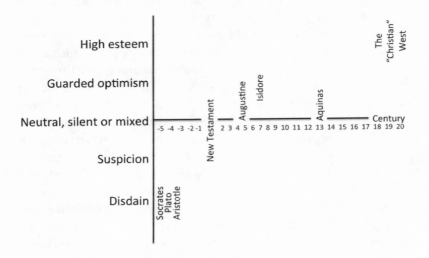

FIGURE 10.1 Cultural Esteem of Engineers in the West

In short, ancient Greeks disdained technology, and twelve centuries of theologians were middling at best. Yet by the nineteenth and twentieth centuries, the opinion of Christian thinkers is very high.

The gap between the middling outlook toward engineers by most medieval Christian thinkers to the extremely high opinion of engineers by the end of the twentieth century is a puzzle requiring a solution. The gap-filler is a twelfth-century monk living in Paris name Hugh of St. Victor.[21] To him we turn for an explanation that engineering matters because it is inherently good, and it is inherently good because it can, and often does, aim at God-approved ends.

1.1 Hugh of St. Victor

Hugh's work on technology is found in the book called *The Didascalicon: A Medieval Guide to the Arts.* In fact, it is not a book on mechanical arts per se; mechanical arts show up as a side issue. But his handling of mechanical arts sets an entirely new theological trajectory, one that will help us appreciate engineering as a *Christian* vocation. The most concise way to spell out Hugh's line of reasoning is by the following three points.

1.1.1 (Moral) Entropy Happens

Hugh's positive account of engineering begins with the admission of something very negative. If you or I set out to defend engineering, we would probably begin by pointing to engineering *successes*. But Hugh begins at the very bottom, as it were, with the reality of moral entropy.

Moral entropy—for example, that it is easier to fall into bad habits than into good ones—poses something of an enigma for Abrahamic faiths since the most fundamental aspect of the universe is a good God. "In the beginning God . . . " In the very beginning, there were not two things in conflict, but One,[22] namely, God whose name is Love, Peace, Nearness, Mercy, Justice, Compassion, Light, Forgiveness, and so on.[23] God is, by definition, goodness itself. God's goodness is so excessive and his delight in goodness so abundant that God is delighted for his goodness to "bubble over." This "bubbling over" of the Goodness that is God is called "creation."[24] "God saw everything that he had made, and indeed, it was *very* good."[25]

If everything was so peachy, where does moral entropy come from?

Hugh follows the historical Christian answer that the entirely good God created all and only good things, but created them *in a particular order* of value.[26] Each item in creation has its own inherent degree of worth or honor. We rightly love horses more than slugs because, on this view, horses are higher on the order of things. (Today we might say "more complex" instead of higher, but the idea is similar.) The answer to the mystery of where moral entropy comes from is that because human beings were created as free moral agents, we can pour out love in greater or lesser quantities as we choose. *Sometimes we choose incorrectly.* Most of the time we don't notice our choices. Yet the pattern of our choosing is manifest in our form of life. A positive example is the way we instinctively spend time with a dog, giving it treats, affection, care, and a name, while we do these things to a far lesser degree for a potted plant. We *could* lavish affection on a potted plant and neglect Fido, but to do so would be inordinate, out of whack, messed up. The origin of "out of whackness" is referred to as the Fall. Poetically it is told as the episode of the snake and the apple in the Garden of Eden.[27] The choice made by the human couple was not to love a potted plant too much, but to place God *lower* than rational mammals on the honor scale.[28] From the vantage point of theology, the fallen state is extensive, though perhaps not intensive. We may not be as bad as we can be (i.e., intensive depravity), but every arena (i.e., extensive) of human experience feels the pull of a distorting influence.

The origin of evil is a complex philosophical matter.[29] But two things concern us in Hugh's account. First, the free choice that rearranged the value system, putting God on the discount rack, as it were, resulted in the disordering of the *human ranking faculty*. Once humans got God's pricing wrong, we couldn't get any other values correct. Humans lost their bearings, as it were. In other words, the human faculty of love became disordered and confused. On the one hand, we love ourselves too much. Love that is inordinate is no longer genuine love, but something vicious and possessive, something idolatrous and obsessive.[30] Thus, disordered human love manifests itself sometimes as greed, other times as jealousy, covetousness, pride, and so on. Human love is not *entirely* messed up; but we cannot ever completely escape the distorting pull of moral gravity. (Thus a parent may fly into a rage and strike the very child he or she would otherwise die for.) At its worst, this is pseudo-love. Such narcissistic affection results in warping our outlook: we can't help misperceiving the object of our obsession; namely, we misperceive *ourselves*. In short, we no longer remember who we really are. Nor does the bad news stop there, according to Hugh. By loving ourselves wrongly we fail to love God rightly. By failing to "love" God enough, we are also failing to love God genuinely. In our sinful state we mistakenly think we "love" God just the right amount. In reality the "love" we aim at God is not love at all but something defective, tame, commodified; we don't actually love God, we hold God in mere sentimental regard. Moreover, just as in the former case of misperceiving ourselves, in sentimentalizing God we *misperceive* God. As sociologist Christian Smith points out, young Americans think of God as nice, helpful, safe.[31] As a result of our dually disordered love, fallen human beings have forgotten who they are and Whose they are.

In addition to self-perpetuating moral myopia, the second result of the Fall is that creation is under a "curse." I am speaking neither about magic nor science. I am speaking as a theologian.[32] According to Hugh, once human beings, viceroys of creation, became incapable of rescuing themselves (*nonposse nonpeccare*, not able not to sin), creation itself, which they were supposed to tend, fell into randomness. Christian Scripture aptly expresses it this way: "For the anxious longing of the creation waits eagerly for the revealing of the sons of God. For the creation was subjected to futility . . . in hope that the creation itself also will be set free from its slavery to corruption into the freedom of the glory of the children of God. For we know that the whole creation groans and suffers the pains of childbirth together until now."[33]

Whether we call this futile, corrupt state "sin" or "entropy" makes little difference for Hugh's argument. The fact of the matter is that iron rusts, people sicken and die, tsunamis occur, meanness happens, and things fall apart.

You'll forgive me for speaking in the broadest terms. Scientifically minded theologians do not today glibly equate physical entropy with moral evil. Some of the things people call "evil" are not the result of primordial fallenness from perfection but simply the by-product of finitude. Physical bodies, being finite in space and time, will sometimes collide in painful, though not necessarily evil, ways.[34] Nevertheless, if we think like a *medieval* and grant these starting points to Hugh—namely, that something is out of whack about people and creation—we'll be able to understand his defense of engineering as good. To summarize the first point, none of us can escape the down drag of entropy in all its forms.

1.1.2 Moral Entropy Motivates a Quest

There is a map of the word that was discovered at a convent in Ebstorf in northern Germany. It dates from the thirteenth century. It shows the known world—centered on Jerusalem—as the body of Christ. (See Figure 10.2 on the following page.)

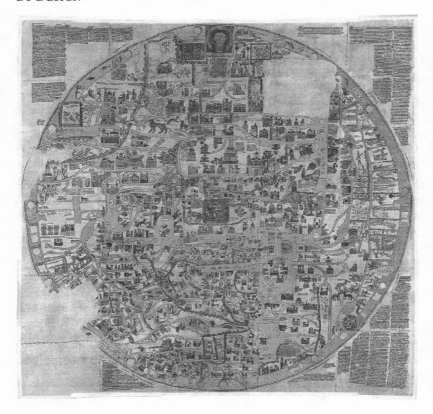

FIGURE 10.2 Ebstorf Map Reproduction[35]

Christ's head is at the top (= east[36]), feet at the bottom, and his hands open to the northern and southern poles. *Theological* legitimacy for this (very odd to us!) picture is the notion that the Second Person of the Trinity, who according to Christians became incarnate as Jesus Christ, was the *exemplar* or *formal cause* of creation. (A formal cause is like a blueprint, with the caveat that the kind of modeling involved in formal causes is not strictly "one-to-one onto" like it is for blueprints.) In other words, theologians claim that the world was *modeled* after Christ. In terms more familiar to us, our world and Christ are *dynamically similar* rather than scalar or proportional (see ch. 6).[37] As you recall, engineers need top-flight training to be able to work the dynamical similarity between the childhood toy (Pénaud flyer) and the full-scale working helicopter. So, if we are charitable, we may grant that it is logically possible that theological philosophers *may* have undergone training adequate for really seeing the similarity between Christ and the world. At least Hugh claimed to see it. The opening line of his book is, "Of all things to be sought, the first is that Wisdom in which the Form of the Perfect Good stands fixed." This phrase, "the Form of the Perfect Good," is technical terminology as far as theologians are concerned: it was a special name for Jesus the Christ.[38]

Thinking of Jesus as the end (*telos*) or aim of creation may not be as odd as we might think. St. Paul's first-century letter to the church in Colossae refers to Christ as "the image [*eikon*] of the invisible God . . . for in [*en*] him were all things created, in the heavens and upon the earth, things visible and things invisible, whether thrones or dominions or principalities or powers; all things have been created through [*dia*] him, and unto [*eis*] him; and he is before all things, and in him all things consist."[39]

The three prepositions *in, through,* and *unto* express the Christian belief in the extensiveness of Christ's involvement in creation. I used an older translation because newer ones mistranslate the third preposition as *for* ("all things have been created for him"). But the Greek term connotes direction rather than instrumentality: all things are created *unto* or *toward* Christ. This is the language of modeling. Just as Jesus is the visible image (*eikon*) of the invisible Deity, so too all created things are, or ought to be, the visible expression of Christ.

Hugh sees Jesus as the model (or prototype) for putting things to right that are currently out of whack. As is the case at the beginning of a quest (or dynamical modeling), we are not likely to have a crystal clear idea where we are going. Clarity is achieved slowly as the quest (design process) moves forward. But Hugh suggests that Jesus presents us with at least a foggy notion of where to begin. Admittedly, these first two principles make for thick theological weeds. However, we need only to be able to imagine how these concepts worked for thirteenth-century thinkers to see that they lead, finally, to Hugh's following conclusion.

1.1.3 A Complete Quest Team Necessarily Includes Engineers

The quest for Wisdom is necessarily a *team* sport. The Ebstorf map pictures the world community as a giant body. Each inhabitant of the world is like an organ of the body whose overall health is intertwined with the health of all the organs. Given the interdependence of "organs" within the "body" of Christ,[40] we should not expect any one individual to possess expertise in all three of the modes of reasoning needed to set the world to right (theoretical reasoning, practical reasoning, and mechanical reasoning).

The important point for us is that Hugh is perhaps the very first person in Western history to say that *mechanical reasoning plays a crucial role in the quest.* As we have seen, thinkers prior to the Christian era often misunderstood *ars mechanicus*, if they mentioned it at all. In striking contrast, Hugh's treatment was an immediate and lasting catalyst for regarding mechanical arts in positive ways. Within the very next generation, one of the towering figures in theology, St. Bonaventure (1221–1274), credits Hugh with near genius understanding of *ars mechanicus.*[41]

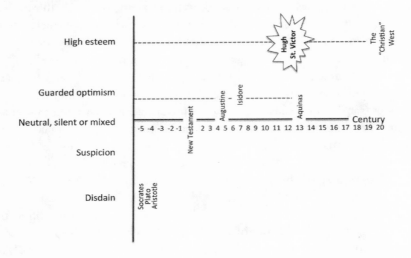

FIGURE 10.3 Hugh's Influence on Western Esteem for Engineering

This is not to say that all confusion about mechanical reasoning was erased. (It doesn't occur to Hugh that *mechanicus* does *not* mean "adulterate"![42]) But it does mean that Hugh understood mechanical reasoning as something wonderful rather than dirty, as something good in itself, because it could cooperate with God's designs for human rescue and therefore serve a unique, positive role in human redemption. Hugh's conclusion was based on the pragmatic truism that no one can pursue God once he or she is dead. Therefore, anything that forestalls death and decay must be good, because it gives people more time to pursue God. Hugh says simply, "the intention of all human action is resolved in a common objective: either to restore in us the likeness of the divine image *or to take thought for the necessity of this life* which, the more easily it can suffer harm from those things which work to its disadvantage, the more does it require to be cherished and conserved."[43]

As far as Hugh can see, human beings have two jobs to occupy their attention: (1) to restore our pre-fall likeness to Christ, and, since this takes time, (2) to win more time by ministering to the necessities of the body—in particular, by feeding the body, fortifying it against harms, and contriving mechanical remedies for harms already assailing us.[44]

This way of putting things might tempt us to think that mechanical reasoning serves a menial, or perhaps preparatory, role for doing the real important work of restoring the divine likeness (which for Hugh involves the dual activity of contemplation on truth and the practice of virtue by which we "resemble" God[45]). But that can't be true, because engineering design is simultaneously practical reasoning *and* mechanical reasoning.[46] The two forms of reasoning simply cannot be pulled apart—something we now understand but that in the thirteenth century Hugh couldn't quite comprehend. Any nonliving, material artifact can *embody* social-moral goodness.[47] This can be shown by an example from Greek-speaking Christianity that was unknown to Hugh.

1.2 Basil's Famine Relief and Cities of Refuge— Fourth-Century Engineering Projects

Concrete examples help us learn how to apply concepts. In the late fourth century, a number of charitable soup kitchen–hospital complexes were built around Asia Minor, in the region of Cappadocia (present-day central Turkey)—roughly the "left hip" on the Ebstorf map—about 450 miles north-northwest of Jerusalem. As engineering projects, these complexes will help us understand Hugh's mysterious claim that Christ is the "end" (or aim, or *telos*) of mechanical reasoning. They show engineering to be simultaneously practical reasoning and mechanical reasoning.

In its heyday, the Roman Empire was very large. But this was not the first "world" empire. Two centuries earlier, the "known" world had been conquered by a Greek named Alexander the Great. By the time the Roman Caesars came into power, all the world was fluent in the Greek language. (Even as late as the first century, "street Greek" was spoken in the Palestinian markets through which Jesus walked.) The western side of the empire slowly lost its fluency in Greek. (It wasn't until the thirteenth century that Greek was reintroduced to Western scholarship. This was a very big deal; it helped trigger the Renaissance and the rise of humanism.) In the regions closest to Rome, Latin became the common tongue. As one heads eastward, the line extending south from Turkey through Syria to

Egypt marks the division of the empire along language lines. Important thinkers like Aristotle (incidentally, Alexander the Great's teacher) were virtually lost to the West for hundreds of years. So, it is not surprising that the Latin-speaking Hugh would have been unaware of the following example, since all the records of it were from Greek language sources.

1.2.1 Famine in Cappadocia

In the year 369 CE, the region surrounding the town of Caesarea—one hundred miles from anywhere—was devastated by famine. An extremely dry winter was followed by a spring without rain.[48] The local pastor of the church in Caesarea, a man named Basil (one of the three famous "Cappadocian Fathers," whose fingerprints are all over the Nicene-Constantinopolitan Creed and the doctrine of the Trinity), said that the sky—"shut up, naked and cloudless"—had left the fields "little more than withered clods, unpleasant, sterile, and unfruitful, cracked and pierced to the depths by the hot sun. The rich and flowing streams have fled away and the torrential paths of the great rivers are exhausted. Little children walk in them, and women cross them [in a single step], laden with bundles. Many of our wells have dried up and we lack the basic necessities of life . . ."[49]

The hot spring and summer were followed by another tough winter that made travel from the landlocked town physically impossible. Those who could afford to do so had begun hoarding grain, while the commoners became "walking cadavers" as they slowly starved. Basil laments:

> [F]amine is a slow evil, always approaching, always holding off like a beast in its den. The heat of the body cools. The form shrivels. Little by little strength diminishes. Flesh stretches across the bones like a spider web. The skin loses its bloom, as the rosy appearance fades . . . and blood melts away. Nor is the skin white, but rather it withers into black while the livid body, suffering pitifully, manifests a dark and pale mottling. The knees no longer support the body but drag themselves by force, the voice is powerless, the eyes are sunken as if in a casket, like dried-up nuts in their shells; the empty belly collapses, conforming itself to the shape of the backbone without any natural elasticity of the bowels.[50]

Today people are hardened to the horrors of death by starvation because the images are shown so frequently on television. But imagine being a *pastor* whose job it is to care for these walking cadavers and their children with swollen bellies. There is evidence that the poor were desperate enough even to sell their own children as slaves to the rich. For their part, the rich had the gall to haggle over the purchase price, even though their hoarding of grain made the scarcity problem worse.[51] It was under these cruel conditions that Basil, the local priest, went to work.

1.2.2 Basil's Cities

The son of a nobleman and therefore independently wealthy, Basil sold his own inheritance, bought grain from the hoarders, and set up a famine relief center on what used to be the family's summer estate. He organized soup kitchens, built dormitories, constructed a hospital—one of the first mercy hospitals on record, if not the very first—and hired bona fide physicians and nurses to attend the sick. This "Patron House for the Poor" (*ptochotropheion,* from *ptchoi* [poor] and *trepho* [to be a patron to]), became a model for all the monasteries Basil would found: a group of monks would locate *outside* the walls of a large city and provide food, shelter, and medical treatment for the urban poor. Not only did Basil oversee the logistics of food acquisition and distribution, he himself could often be found ministering directly to those in need. (Basil had studied medicine before becoming a pastor.[52]) Basil's *ptochotropheion* was large enough to create a mid-sized economy of its own, enabling the poor to first be trained and then actually to serve in various trades.[53] The sheer scale of these complexes earned them the nickname Basil's Cities.

Basil's activities during this period encompassed all three kinds of reasoning detailed in Hugh's taxonomy. As a theologian, Basil did *theoretical* reasoning. As a pastor/ethicist, Basil engaged in practical reasoning—especially in his homilies, letters, conversations, and other strategies intended to persuade the rich to donate foodstuffs. But also at every turn, Basil was engaged in *design.* The placement of buildings, layout of each building (whether dormitory or hospital or kitchen), logistics of food acquisition and distribution, procurement of doctors and medicines, day-to-day care for the sick, and jobs training program were all instances of design. And we understand that design is a form of practical reasoning. But more particularly, these activities were also instances of *mechanical* reasoning. To borrow Hugh's terminology, the layout and arrangement and construction of buildings belongs to "Armament." Food preparation and distribution falls under "Hunting." Medicine was its own class of mechanical reasoning. And logistics—the flow of goods and the coordinated efforts of many people—was classified by Hugh as "Theatrics." These odd terms make it pretty obvious that Hugh himself was an outsider to mechanical reasoning. Perhaps if Hugh himself had actually done some mechanical reasoning, as Basil did, he would have come up with more fitting names than "Hunting" and "Theatrics." While Hugh *thought* about mechanical reasoning, Basil actually engaged in design.

In addition to engaging in important activities that exemplify Hugh's categories, Basil's Cities have Christ as their aim. What does this mean? Old maps like *Ebstorf mappa mundi* (Figure 10.2) show the belief in dynamical similarity between Christ and geography. Of course, these theological mapmakers didn't actually think Jesus' physical head lay to the east. But they did see some kind of (dynamical) similarity between the character of Jesus and the layout of the world. Basil's Cities help us glimpse how.

When Jesus announced to the skeptics, "The kingdom of God is in your midst,"[54] he was referring to *himself* as the first-order instantiation of the new kind of human friendship that he was inaugurating. At that moment, Jesus was the kingdom; later there were a dozen, then five hundred, then three thousand, and so on.[55] This new "kingdom" would be marked by a distinct manner of relating, which we will examine below. It is not an accident that Basil's *ptochotropheion* were nicknamed *basileia* (Basil's Cities) because the Christian New Testament word for "kingdom of God" was *basileia theou*. When Christians pray the Lord's Prayer, they ask for God's kingdom (*basileia*) to come in the same breath that they ask God to provide bread. In Basil's mind, Jesus' kingdom shows up when bread is provided to the poor of God. Thus, Basil's cities were *christomorphic*, that is, shaped (*morphe*) like Christ's kingdom. Basil's cities look (dynamically) like Christ Jesus.

More similarities can be drawn. Ancient Jewish law required lepers to live "outside the city."[56] That's why Jesus met and healed the ten lepers outside the city wall.[57] Because Jesus befriended the sick and unclean "outside the city," that is where the author of Hebrews tells us we should go.[58] "Outside the city" is where Christ can always be found. Christ went outside the city to suffer and die for the people. And that is the logic behind Basil's intention to build his monasteries *outside* the walled enclaves of the rich city-dwellers. Christ welcomed society's "least"; so, too, Basil's complexes welcomed the poor, destitute, crippled, sick, and starving. As Christ said, whatever is done for the poor person is actually done for Christ himself.[59] And just as Christ rose from the dead on the third day that we might have life, so the formerly hopeless walking cadavers found hope of a brand new life through the sacrifices of another. Like Christ, Basil's complexes made all the difference for the survival of the poorest of the poor. Today many people commonly suppose the poor to be the necessary casualties of the market economy, and thus they deserve, at best, our pity. In Basil's world, rather than being objects of pity, the poor were *blessed*. As Luke records Christ's Sermon on the Mount, "*Blessed* are you poor [*ptochoi*], for yours is the kingdom [*basiliea*] of God."[60]

To summarize: requirement #1 is fulfilled. Hugh has shown, and Basil has illustrated, that engineering qualifies as vocation, because mechanical reasoning plays a crucial role in the human quest that aims at the Wisdom personified in Christ. The second requirement for engineering to qualify as vocation is that it not only have a good *end*, but that it be practiced in a good *manner*.

Metric #2: Can engineering be practiced in a (Christianly) good manner?

Claim #2: Grace is the manner of engineering as a Christian vocation.

Engineering is a *practice*.[61] Whether or not non-engineers honor engineering as a practice, the fact remains that engineering is an evolving practice that runs on time-tested heuristics and is teeming with its own built-in rewards (recall ch. 8).[62] This is a great gift. As Wittgenstein would advise us, "Remember how great the grace of work is."[63] But what is "grace"?

One of the ways we use the word *grace* today is in describing the elegant beauty of a dancer or gymnast. We readily understand "graceful" to be a measure of the athlete's skill. And there certainly was a skillfulness in Bail's execution of these large-scale engineering projects. All the dimensions of designing, constructing, staffing, and supplying these complexes were accomplished with so much skill that even nonmechanical types were impressed: Basil was promoted to ecclesiastical overseer, a.k.a. bishop. In addition to the sheer skillfulness of his work, I want to focus on three other ways Basil's engineering displayed grace. These will not exhaust all that can be said of grace, but will give our imaginations a framework for getting a grip in engineering as vocation because of the manner of its execution.

2.1 GRACE AS RECEPTIVITY

Hugh of St. Victor contrasts *worldly* reasoning with *graced* reasoning.[64] By "worldly" Hugh means something that begins with the less complex and tries to comprehend the more complex. In Hugh's mind this plan is flawed; it would be a little like the inhabitants of a two-dimensional world trying to fathom what three-dimensionality is like. No matter how hard the Flatlander tries, her 2D mind simply cannot translate 3D into terms that 2D can understand. What is the 2D thinker supposed to imagine—that a hemisphere is the infinite piling up of ever-smaller circles on top of one another? The key phrase, "on top of," *has no meaning* in Flatland. Yet comprehension moving in the other direction is not so thwarted; a 3D thinker like you or I *can imagine* what description of 2D objects means in a place like Flatland, even if we wouldn't want to live there.[65]

Worldly thinking is like tugging on one's bootstraps in order to jump higher. Because it starts with the empirical world, it is stuck with the empirical world, stuck in Flatland, as it were. But *graced* thinking, as Hugh sees it, is not self-generated bootstrap pulling. Rather, grace comes from outside the self, from above, from a third dimension, as it were. If moral entropy is the current that constantly pulls us downstream, grace is the wind that enables us to sail upstream (see ch. 7).

This illustration is quite abstract. The point is that mechanical reasoning, when it is *graced*, involves a receptivity to, and cooperation with, an additional dimension, namely, God. This additional dimension doesn't change how design works or artifacts function. (We are not speaking about interventionist miracles.) But it *may* change the manner in which one *sees*, and thus tip the balance in favor of some satisfactory designs over other satisfactory proposals. Remember that the teenage Mary, trembling before the angel who brought the terrifying news that would change her life forever, replied simply, "May it be done to me as you have said." Thinking in 2D, Mary would have immediately understood that as an unmarried, pregnant, teenage Jewish girl, she would be ostracized forever. She was certain to lose her fiancé, Joseph, who was not the child's father. Life as she knew it was over. Nevertheless, Mary was not stuck in 2D thinking. Her reply indicates receptivity to the divine dimension: "May it be done to me as you have said."[66] Similarly, St. Paul urges us to "keep in step with the Spirit."[67] A graced reasoning process begins by trying to detect where God is involved in order to cooperate. If God is on the side of the poor, as Basil thought and Scripture claims,[68] then mechanical reasoning that is graced seeks to fit with God's program by designing products for the other

90 percent of the world rather than products that benefit only the richest 10 percent of the world.[69]

2.2 GRACE AS GIFT

In our society, gift giving is often a matter of keeping score. If you give me a gift on my birthday, I feel a sense of obligation to reciprocate in kind and give you a gift (with a similar price tag) on your birthday. This transaction settles the score and we both can relax; debts have been discharged.

But true gift giving is not a kind of scorekeeping. In 2010–2011, Liberty Mutual Life Insurance broadcast touching commercials that followed a string of random acts of kindness.[70] The lady observing a kind deed is motivated herself to do a kind deed. But wait, someone else is watching her do the kind deed and is himself motivated to do another kind deed. The chain continues until the last person to benefit from the string of kindnesses is the very woman who initiated the sequence. This commercial is a little like the "gift economies" made well known by Marcel Mauss and Lewis Hyde.[71] But gift economies have two important improvements over Liberty Mutual: (1) the string of giving never ends, and (2) the chain is not a single strand, but a network of strands. As Mauss and Hyde describe, entire societies are known to have thrived on a "pay it forward" logic rather than the simple one-to-one reciprocity that typifies Western consumer culture.[72]

Such were Basil's Cities. One astute observer likened Basil to Joseph—the guy with the multicolored robe who, after being sold by his brothers into slavery in Egypt, miraculously rose to a position of leadership in Egyptian agriculture and thus was in the right place at the right time to save from starvation an entire country (not to mention his own brothers). But unlike Joseph, who grew wealthy and powerful from his oversight of the Egyptian grain industry, *Basil did it all for free.* As one fourth-century onlooker summarizes:

> There was a famine, the most severe one ever recorded. The city was in distress and there was no source of assistance. . . . The hardest part of all such distress is the insensibility and insatiability of those who possess supplies. . . . Such are the buyers and sellers of corn. . . . But . . . by his word and advice [Basil] opened the stores of those who possessed them, and so, according to the Scripture, dealt food to the hungry and satisfied the poor with bread. . . . And in what way? . . . He gathered together the

victims of the famine with some who were but slightly recover-
ing from it, men and women, infants, old men . . . and obtaining
contributions of all sorts of food which can relieve famine, set
before them basins of soup and such meat as was found preserved among us, on which the poor live. Then, imitating the
ministry of Christ . . . he attended to the bodies and souls of
those who needed it, combining personal respect with the supply of their necessity, and so giving them a double relief. Such
was our young furnisher of corn, and second Joseph. . . . [But
unlike Joseph, Basil's] *services were gratuitous* [i.e., grace-filled,
or free] *and his succour of the famine gained no profit*, having
only one object, to win kindly feelings by kindly treatment, and
to gain by his rations of corn the heavenly blessings.[73]

Engineering projects undertaken in the spirit of grace necessarily
have a not-for-profit motivation. Perhaps an individual (like Fred Cuny[74])
or a firm (such as Engineering Ministries International[75]) offers services
for free to the needy. Or perhaps firms adopt an "open source" approach
to patents (like Eco-Patent Commons[76]) or work exclusively on devices for
those who need them most but can afford them the least.

2.3 Grace as Reconciliation

A third feature of grace as the manner in which mechanical reasoning
ought to be performed is the reconciliatory nature of grace. Grace entails
forgiveness. Forgiveness that comes with a price tag is not really forgiveness. If forgiveness comes with a catch—"I'll forgive you, if you do X for
me"—it creates a kind of bondage or servitude. So forgiveness, to be au-
thentic, must be freely offered.[77] When forgiveness is offered for free, with
no strings attached, it may generate *friends*.

Oftentimes friendships begin spontaneously. And we tend to think
that our very best friends virtually never stand in need of forgiveness. (If
they often do those things that require forgiveness, they would not likely
become our friends in the first place.) But grace is so powerful that occasionally it turns enemies into friends. Stories like the Amish community
actually *forgiving* the murderer of five schoolchildren in Nickel Mines,
Pennsylvania, leave us breathless.[78] Stories like that of Mary Johnson's forgiveness and virtual adoption of Oshea Israel—her son's murderer, who
by Mary's invitation lives next door!—leaves us wondering whether we
could be this brave.[79] It makes sense to label these incidents as moments
of "grace." But it also makes sense to label *artifacts* that bring healing as

moments of grace. Recall the story from chapter 9: when a seventeen-year-old French shepherd boy named Bénezet undertook to build the only bridge he ever attempted (he died before the bridge was finally completed), his undertaking earned him a new name: St. Bénezet the Bridge Builder. The site he proposed was the mouth of the Rhone River, which for some years divided two nations at war. The bridge embodied grace in two ways. On the one hand, it was a work of mercy that enabled the poor of Toulouse to ply their wares on the other side of the river in the rich city of Avignon, in the kingdom of Arles. On the other hand, the bridge removed a natural political and military barrier. Both sides wanted the advantages that a bridge would bring (economic and otherwise). But these advantages came at a cost: the kingdoms on opposing banks would need to learn to get along. In this way, Bénezet's bridge was a catalyst for reconciliation. It was this reconciling function of technology that Hugh had in mind when he said that mechanical reasoning "reconciles nations, calms wars, strengthens peace, and commutes the private good of individuals into the common benefit of all."[80]

Conclusion

I've argued that in order for us to be justified in claiming that engineering is a legitimate candidate for Christian vocation, we must be able to articulate how engineering meets the two requirements of practical reasoning: that the engineering enterprise has, or may have, *good ends and good means*. To this end, I have drawn heavily on the theology of Hugh of St. Victor. Hugh is perhaps the very first to say clearly that mechanical reasoning plays a crucial role in God's redemptive plan. So crucial is mechanical reasoning, in fact, that the community that lacks mechanical reasoners will have an incomplete grasp on the Good. In other words, engineers are not simply the slaves who do the bidding of other, smarter people who comprehend what needs to be done.[81] Rather, *there is a mechanical component of the Good that will only be rightly understood by those skilled at mechanical reasoning*. Thus has Hugh opened the door for us to see mechanical reasoning as actually *participating* in and contributing to Christian discipleship (a.k.a. our painstakingly slow progress toward resembling the divine). To be most specific, what Hugh has said explicitly, and Basil and Bénezet have materially exemplified, is that engineering meets both requirements for being considered a Christian vocation: The end of Christian engineering is Christ; the manner of Christian engineering is grace.

Notes

1. A draft of this material was presented at the Christian Engineering Education Conference, 30 June 2001, in Vancouver, BC.

2. Because Jewish, Christian, and Muslim ethics have an overlapping concept of "divine command ethics," they also share similar notions of vocation.

3. Recovered correspondence between various German firms and concentration camps include sentences like this: "We are submitting plans for our perfected cremation ovens which operate with coal and have hitherto given full satisfaction. . . . We guarantee their effectiveness, as well as their durability, the use of the best material and our faultless workmanship." Cited in Merton, *Conjectures of a Guilty Bystander*, 241.

4. McNeill, *The Ethics and Politics of Human Experimentation*.

5. Graham, *The Ghost of the Executed Engineer*; Graham, "Palchinsky's Travels"; Soudek, "The Humanist Engineer of Aleksandr Solzhenitsyn."

6. Postman, *Technopoly*.

7. The heavy plow, so efficient that it could be pulled by a lone horse rather than a team of oxen, was especially helpful in the clay-ridden soils of northern Europe, which were too dense for the scratch plow to work well. White, *Medieval Technology and the Social Change*; White, "The Expansion of Technology, 500–1500."

8. Xenophon, *Economist of Xenophon*, IV.2 pp. 22–23.

9. Aristotle, *Politics*, 8.2, 1337b. Emphasis added.

10. Plutarch reports that had Archimedes saved Athens with his contraptions (we now know he did not), he did so *shamefully*, in light of Plato's "indignation at [mechanical arts], and his invectives against it as the mere corruption and annihilation of the one good geometry." Plutarch, *Marcellus*, 376.

11. Hodge, *Roman Aqueducts and Water Supply*; Chanson, "The Hydraulics of Roman Aqueducts."

12. Acts 24:14, 22. In the town of Antioch, members of the Way were called "Christians," and this name stuck. Acts 11:26.

13. The New Testament records the martyrdom of Stephen and foreshadows the deaths of many more. Tradition has it that ten of the original

twelve disciples died martyrs' deaths; Judas, of course, committed suicide. John reputedly survived both exile and boiling in oil. For a moving account of two women martyrs, see "The Martyrdom of Saints Perpetua and Felicitas."

14. Augustine's neoplatonic vision of Christianity would go largely unrevised for the next eight hundred years. Eventually, an equally compelling synthesis of theology and philosophy would be penned by St. Thomas.

15. St. Augustine, *City of God*, bk. xxii, ch. 24, pp. 526–27 in this edition.

16. Thus does Isidore break with the myth of the perfect seven. Since seven was regarded as the perfect number, medieval scholars assumed that complete human learning reduced to seven domains: the classical quadrivium was comprised of arithmetic, music, geometry, and astronomy, while the trivium was comprised of grammar, rhetoric, and logic.

17. Thus Martin of Laon (d. 680 CE): "from 'moechus' we call 'mechanical art' any object which is clever and most delicate and which, in its making or operation, is beyond detection, so that beholders find their power stolen from them when they cannot penetrate the ingenuity of the thing." Cited by Taylor, in Hugh of St. Victor, *Didascalicon*, 191n64.

18. The historical picture is more complicated; engineers had to claw their way to respectability. See Layton, *Revolt of the Engineers*, ch. 2.

19. One only need read the novels of Dickens to see how bad things were in London during this era.

20. In 1933, a pageant was written for the fiftieth anniversary celebration of the American Society of Mechanical Engineers (ASME). One of the characters declares: "Major Premise: the highest authority states 'the earth is the Lord's and is the inheritance of the saints' . . . Minor Premise: WE are the saints!" Baker, *Control*, 44. A messianic spirit in Western engineering can be traced to the influence of Joachim of Fiore. See Noble, *The Religion of Technology*.

21. Perhaps Hugh derived some ideas from John Scotus Erigena. But he developed these ideas much further than his predecessor.

22. Deut 6:4.

23. 1 John 4:8, Eph 2:14; Ps 75:1 and Jer 23:23; Ps 145:8–9; Ps 37:28; 1 John 1:5; Num 14:7.

24. St. Thomas Aquinas, *Summa theologica*, I.1 QQ44–45.

25. Gen 1:31.

26. It has been extremely common to think of *order* as just as real as the things themselves. So the sequence □△○ contains *four* things rather than three: the three shapes *plus* the order they are in. After all, □△○ is different from ○△□.

27. Apple in Latin is spelled *malum*. "Evil" in Latin is spelled *malus*. However, when *malus* takes the action of a verb (e.g., "choose"), it is spelled *malum*. Thus Eve, choosing evil (accusative case, *malum*), is mistakenly thought to have chosen an apple (*malum*).

28. Eventually this leads to a state in which God is treated as lesser in value than critters (Rom 1:25) and even lower than material possessions.

29. A standard place to begin is Hick, *Evil and the God of Love*.

30. Aristotle's description of virtue as the mean that lies between extremes of excess and deficiency. We can love too much or love too little. Both would be vice rather than virtue.

31. When C. S. Lewis's character Lucy asks Mr. Beaver whether Aslan is *safe*, Mr. Beaver replies: "'Course he isn't safe. But he's good. He's the King, I tell you." Christian Smith's term for the uninformed, un-Christian outlook that construes God as predominately safe is "moral therapeutic deism." See Smith and Denton, *Soul Searching*.

32. Science and theology do not have rival and competing descriptions of a single reality. Rather, the descriptions given by science constitute one world, and the descriptions given by theologians constitute another world. Whether or not these worlds are the "same" or even "similar" is a complicated matter. See Goodman, *Ways of Worldmaking*.

33. Rom 8:19–22.

34. This observation dates to Leibniz's distinction between metaphysical evil (= finitude) and physical evil (finite bodies bumping into each other) and moral evil. From §21 of his *Philosophical Writings*, bk. vi.

35. WikiCommons: http://en.wikipedia.org/wiki/File:Ebstorfer-stich2.jpg.

36. East at the top is reasonable considering the biblical account of Jesus as the "bright and morning star" (Rev 22:16). The morning star is Venus when it appears on the eastern horizon at dawn.

37. Kallenberg, "Dynamical Similarity and the Problem of Evil."

38. Taylor explains: "The commentary tradition on the *De consolatione* identifies the Boethian 'Form of the Good' with the Second Person of the Trinity, to whom is assigned the role of formal cause or exemplar of creation." In Hugh of St. Victor, *Didascalicon*, 175n1.

39. Col 1:15–17 (ASV).

40. Eph 4:25; 1 Cor 12:4–12; etc.

41. *Opusculum de reductione artium ad theologiam*. English translation of "Retracing the Arts to Theology" can be found at http://people. uvawise.edu/philosophy/phil205/Bonaventure.html.

42. Hugh of St. Victor, *Didascalicon*, 55, 56.

43. Ibid., 54.

44. Ibid., 55.

45. Once again, this "resemble" cannot be scalar proportionality. God is *not* just like us only bigger, stronger, and faster. The similarity achievable by human beings and God is *dynamical* rather than *dimensionless*. See ch. 6.

46. This gets the most explicit treatment in the works of Caroline Whitbeck. See Whitbeck, "Ethics as Design." Even Aristotle, who disdained mechanical reasoning, observed an overlap between technological knowing (*technē*) and ordinary knowing (*episteme*). See Joseph Dunne, *Back to the Rough Ground*, 237–357. See also Angier, *Technē in Aristotle's Ethics*. With his culturally inspired disdain, Aristotle could not help seeing mechanical reasoning as mere "production." Today we split the concept of *technē* into (1) technique that is universalizable, and (2) the non-universalizable *tacit* dimension of mechanical reasoning.

47. See the work of Langdon Winner, esp. "Do Artifacts Have Politics?".

48. "The winter was dry with no moisture; everything froze and dried out, since there were neither snowflakes nor showers. The spring gave us the other extreme,—the heat, I mean—but again without rain. Feverish heat and icy cold, unforeseen, exceeded the boundaries of creation

and conspired with evil to do us damage, to drive people from life and livelihood." St. Basil, "In Time of Famine and Drought," 185.

49. Ibid., 184.

50. Ibid., 190.

51. Holman, *Hungry Are Dying*, 69.

52. Miller, *Birth of the Hospital in the Byzantine Empire*, 57.

53. Holman, *Hungry Are Dying*, 74.

54. Luke 17:21.

55. 1 Cor 15:6; Acts 2:41.

56. Num 5:1–4.

57. Luke 17:12.

58. Heb 13:13.

59. Matt 25:34–40.

60. Luke 6:20.

61. *Practice* is a technical term. See MacIntyre, *After Virtue*, esp. 187ff. For a less technical, educational approach, see Wenger, *Communities of Practice*.

62. Even the menial and boring and disgusting aspects of a practice may, in time, become sources of great delight. As Basil's brother reminds us, the cure for our natural aversion to the grotesque or loathsome sick is actually caring for the sick! "For hard exercise has a surprising effect even on the most difficult people, in that it creates a long-term sense of enjoyment. Let no one say this is laborious duty, for it is useful to those who perform it. In time we will change and laborious effort will become sweet. If I must make it even more clear, sympathy toward the unfortunate is, in this life, profitable for the healthy. For it is beautiful for the soul to provide mercy to others who have fallen on misfortune. For all humanity is governed by a single nature, and no one possesses any guarantee of continual happiness." St. Gregory of Nyssa, "On the Love of the Poor."

63. Cited in Klagge, *Wittgenstein in Exile*, 125.

64. "Invisible things can only be made known by visible things, and therefore the whole of theology must use visible demonstrations. But worldly theology adopted the works of creation and the elements of

this world that it might make its demonstration in these. . . . And for this reason, namely, because it used a demonstration which revealed little, it lacked ability to bring forth the incomprehensible truth without stain of error. . . . In this were the wise men of this world fools, namely, that proceeding by natural evidences alone and following the elements and appearances of the world, they lacked the lessons of grace." Hugh of St. Victor, from "Exposition of the Heavenly Hierarchy," cited in Taylor, "Introduction," 35.

65. Abbot, "Flatland."

66. Luke 1:26–38.

67. Gal 5:24.

68. E.g., Ps 146:7–8; Prov 22:22–23.

69. "Design for the Other 90%" was the title of an exhibit by Cooper-Hewitt, National Design Museum. For information, see http://other90.cooperhewitt.org/.

70. See http://www.youtube.com/watch?v=wMwoexR1evo.

71. Mauss, *The Gift*; Hyde, *The Gift*.

72. See Kallenberg, *God and Gadgets*, 98–105.

73. Gregory of Nazianzus, cited in Holman, *Hungry Are Dying*, 65. Emphasis added.

74. For more details on Fred Cuny's disaster relief, see the National Academy of Engineering's Web site: http://www.onlineethics.org/Topics/ProfPractice/Exemplars/BehavingWell/cunyintro.aspx.

75. http://www.emiusa.org/. See also Engineers without Borders (http://www.ewb-international.org) and Engineers with a Mission (www.engineerswithamission.org).

76. Eco-Patent Commons is part of the World Business Council for Sustainable Development (WBCSD). For a list of one hundred open patent products, see http://www.wbcsd.org/work-program/capacity-building/eco-patent-commons.aspx.

77. The people who nailed Christ to the cross apparently will not be held responsible for that barbaric act, because Christ explicitly forgave them (Luke 23:34). They may be held responsible for other dastardly deeds. But they will not be held guilty for aiding and abetting the murder this Innocent Man.

78. Kraybill, Nolt, and Weaver-Zercher, *Amish Grace.*

79. Hartman, "Love Thy Nieghbor." For another example, see Ramsey, "Ohio Man Seeks Forgiveness of Mourning Mother."

80. Hugh of St. Victor, *Didascalicon*, 77.

81. Koen calls this instrumental view of engineering the "transom window" view. Koen, *Discussion of the Method*, 56.

Appendix

FOLLOWING THE RULES IN DESIGN

ONCE UPON A TIME there was a very zealous engineer who contacted me with an agenda. This gentleman was a safety engineer at a nuclear facility, and so fell under the watchful eye of one or more state or federal agencies.[1] Engineers, especially civil and nuclear engineers, who work closely with governmental agencies are typically required to have earned their Professional Engineering license.[2] This nuclear engineer—let's call him Tom—was a deeply religious man who seemed to feel that the quality of engineering in America was in moral peril. During a series of e-mail exchanges, Tom wrote that "Engineering Ethics, as presently implemented, is fundamentally unethical because the profession that supposedly promotes and implements the ethical code has no intention of doing anything but say 'good luck' to any engineer who places him/herself at any degree of professional risk to adhere to them in their employment when the employer wishes otherwise." According to Tom, "The large majority of engineers are employees in 'at-will' employment situations, and the major engineering professional societies are co-opted by employers of engineers, who pay a significant portion of their operating expenses." In Tom's eyes, this constitutes a conflict of interest, since the only knowledgable people capable of bringing to light any unjust practices of the corporation are themselves on the payroll of the corporation under scrutiny! Tom claims that this present arrangement means that engineering ethics is seriously "in the ditch" and that the engineers themselves are "in denial" about the problem.

As a nineteen-time whistleblower himself, Tom raises important concerns about the challenges and risks of whistleblowing. Whether the moral character of engineering as a whole is in jeopardy or decline is outside the scope of this present chapter. But what is of interest to us is the remedy Tom zealously offers to overcome the conflict of interest problem: *compel more engineers to earn P.E. licensure.* (Currently only about one in six engineers is a P.E., and the bulk of them are concentrated in firms associated with municipal, state, and federal contracts.[3]) P.E. licensure requires four years of practical engineering experience after the university degree as well as at least two exams: the Fundamentals of Engineering (the "F.E.," two four-hour portions covering 180 discipline-specific questions) and the Principles and Practice of Engineering (the "P.E."). Achievement of licensure subsequently qualifies one to belong to the National Society of Professional Engineers and be governed by the NSPE Code of Ethics.

Hmm . . . Will a college degree make one more moral? Will four years of practical experience improve one's ethics? Will two daylong exams raise the level of one's character? Will upping the ante to include a second professional code of ethics (e.g., ASCE *plus* NSPE code) drastically improve morality among engineers? Will all these together do the trick? A qualified "maybe" is the best answer we can give to these questions.[4] We saw in chapter 7 that under certain conditions, experience in engineering *may* in fact improve one's character. And we saw in the chapters on modeling and practical reasoning that the kinds of activities that ready one for the P.E. exams can themselves be morally formative with or without a written exam. To really appreciate how this might be, however, we need to be clearer on what is meant by "moral improvement" and the relatively limited role that rules—such as those found in professional codes of ethics— play in measuring moral improvement or, alternatively, moral decline.

In this Appendix I will compare two rival models for assessing morality. Roughly speaking, both have to do with something called "following the rule." The first model is the Stipulation Model. It compares morality to a three-step process of *commanding-interpreting-applying.* As we shall see, this model comes up short even though it seems very intuitive. The second approach is called the Heuristic Model. I will argue that this approach is truer to moral assessment, and it has the added benefit for us of resonating well with engineering design.

THE STIPULATION MODEL

We generally assume that rule-following implies the presence of some authority who issues an actual command. More than one moral philosopher has argued that morality becomes unintelligible apart from the notion of an authority.[5] If the English language is a map of how we think, it is significant that we have such a large number of words to convey what happens when the sergeant tells the private to "drop and gimme twenty [pushups]." We say that the sergeant issued a *command, order, directive, imperative, instruction, prescription, injunction, requirement*, and so on. Similarly, a "standing" order can just as easily be called a *rule, regulation, law, protocol, ordinance*, or *stipulation*. The model we are considering first is called the Stipulation Model because the word *stipulation* carries with it the idea of a command that leaves little to chance because it spells out in sufficient detail that which is binding: "Do twenty pushups, chest to floor, back straight, full extension, head up, *now!*"

As a positive command, "Do twenty pushups, now!" is actually the less usual form of rule-following that we run into. The more common form of stipulation seems to be *negative* rather than positive. Thus we think of things like "Thou shalt *not* steal" as typifying the stipulation form. Perhaps this has something to do with why ethics often carries such a negative connotation today. Ethics boards seek to sniff out "violations" and "violators" rather than to reward truly good persons.

Most folk think of morality as the space fenced in by prohibitions. Crossing the line is called *trespassing, transgressing, violating*, or *breaking*. Cross the line and you're punished (or *shamed, shunned, penalized, fined, imprisoned, exiled, executed*, etc.). Live within the fence and, well, nobody pays much notice, because that is where you're *supposed* to live. The moral "fence" has other names. If something is prohibited, it is also sometimes called *off-limits, forbidden, verboten, proscribed*, or *taboo*.[6]

The last term, *taboo*, has a curious history. It entered the English language in 1777 when explorer Captain James Cook heard it used by natives of Polynesia and Micronesia. Today we live in a global society in which exposure to different systems of morality and different styles of ethical reasoning is increasingly common. But for Captain Cook, and for Victorian English society generally, morality was naturally understood to be of only one kind—the British kind and, incidentally, the *right* kind. Thus ethicists in nineteenth-century Britain classified Polynesian morality rules as "primitive." For example, Cook observed that the typical state of Polynesian dress (or rather, undress) lacked decorum, and the frequency and familiarity of sexual contact between men and women struck the prudish Victorians as horrifyingly lax. At the same time, Polynesian men were strictly forbidden to sit at the same table as women to eat a meal! When asked why the sexes were separated during meals, the Polynesians simply said, "taboo." Rather than ask what the story was behind "taboo," ethicists in Victorian England tended to assume "taboo" was the Polynesian equivalent to the British "moral rule." Notice that the concept "rule" was assumed to be universal in form even if the content varied form culture to culture. If Polynesians had a rule prohibiting mixed-gender dining, then the rule must function in exactly the same manner as British morality rules. The Brits had decided in advance that any difference in morality between two cultures could never be a difference in how rules *function* but simply a difference of *content*. The Victorians concluded that the Polynesian taboos held *primitive* versions of the fully evolved content of the moral rules of the British Empire. (It doesn't take much to spot the arrogant colonialism of this line of reasoning.) And for the Victorian thinkers, ethics is, above all, a following of rules-as-stipulations.

We have a difficult time imagining what things were like in the nineteenth century. The device of the century was the steam engine, whose application in railroads meant that news could travel from New York to San Francisco in just over a week! (Until the telegraph, the Pony Express was still faster than trains, setting the land record for this nearly three-thousand-mile journey in seven days, seventeen hours at an average speed of almost eleven mph.) But while technology has changed a great deal in the decades since, the way we think about morality has not changed much, if at all. Despite the exponential growth of technology since the days of the steam engine, our present culture retains a strong memory of Victorian culture's morality. Although we think of ourselves as less prudish than the Victorians, four other marks of Victorian ethics are stunningly similar to the way we think today. Consider MacIntyre's summary:

1. Compartmentalization—Like Victorian-era English, we tend to assume that actions begin as neutral but become moral when a moral ingredient is added. This myth results in our classifying human behaviors into two sorts: moral acts and neutral acts.

2. Ethics for the Victorians meant rule-following, plain and simple. When the British ruled India, they were frustrated by the answer that Indians gave to British requests for enumeration and explication of indigenous moral principles. Unlike the Polynesians, who, in an equally frustrating way, explained their moral norms with an undefined word (*taboo*), the Indians inevitably and simply pointed to actual persons who were judges of such matters in local context. To the Brits, this was clunky, subjective, and inefficient. The British insisted that morality

must be *codified* into rules or laws. So, too, for us. We assume today that moral norms can always be written down.

3. Prohibitions are instinctively held to be much more morally important than positive injunctions. For example, the Bible commands us positively to give money to charity, and it commands us negatively not to steal. Our tendency, like our British forebears, is to assume that "Thou shalt not" is a bigger deal than "Thou shalt." Thus Western Christians would never dream of taking money from a neighbor's wallet but consistently fail to bring the "whole tithe into the storehouse" (Mal 3:10); the average giving among conservative, *biblicist* Christians hovers around 3 percent, only slightly higher than the national average of 2.5 percent.

4. Also like the Victorians, we tend to unquestioningly assume that *our* moral rules are timelessly true, culturally transcendent, universal principles toward which all *homo sapiens* are evolving as a species.[7]

These four marks characterize contemporary Western assumptions about morality and point to why the Stipulation Model of ethics has such a strong grip. The Stipulation Model works a little like geometry. We know that there can be no absolutely perfect triangle in architecture and that true knowledge of the properties of triangles is not a matter for laboratory measurement. Rather, our mind perceives the timeless principles of triangularity (e.g., that the sum of interior angles is always 180°). We envision these principles as existing in some sense "behind" the ever-imperfect actual triangles in architecture. So it goes with moral stipulations: our job, we think, is to ferret out the timeless principle that lies "behind" ordinary commands. Why think that we need to discover an underlying principle? Because ordinary commands sometimes can be confusing.

For example, at first blush, the prohibition "Thou shalt not kill" seems clear enough. But does the command work the same way in every instance? Consider these scenarios.

- I am in a heated argument with my neighbor about the superiority of the Dayton Flyers basketball team.

- A hunter has his crosshairs set on a deer; venison is on the dinner menu.

- The family dog is sixteen years old, can no longer walk or control its bladder, and appears to be in constant pain.

- A soldier on a combat mission "acquires a target."

- You surprise a burglar who pulls a knife; you happen to be toting your child's baseball bat.

The proscription "Thou shalt not kill" would seem to prohibit death in each of the above cases. It appears, on its own, to be a stand-alone, one-size-fits-all rule. And, clearly, I ought *not* to kill my neighbor just because he champions another college basketball team. But the other four cases don't seem to fit. In response to the deer and the dog, one might object that the non-killing rule doesn't apply to animals. The rule, so the objection goes, is better stated, "Thou shalt not kill *human beings.*" Okay, but what of the burglar? Well, the burglar's death isn't at all certain. If it does happen, it may be accidental, since you are not likely trained in baseball bat combat. So perhaps the rule ought to be modified again, "Thou shalt not *intentionally* kill human beings." If this is the clarified rule, what of the soldier? The soldier intends to kill (i.e., killing *is* the aim), and a human being is understood as the target. Despite having clarified the language of the rule, many will say that the stipulation doesn't apply in the soldier's case, because war is the *exception* to the rule.[8]

So far, in this section, we've been looking at one model of ethical rule-following. We call it the Stipulation Model. We have seen that according to this model, there are several parts working together:

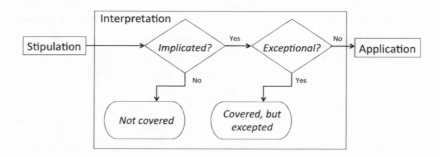

FIGURE A The Stipulation Model of Rule-Following

But wait a minute—something seems fishy. The flowchart looks like a works-every-time mechanism. (Why is it that we so naturally and eagerly reach for *mechanism* as the guiding metaphor?) There are, as it were, only two positions for the "internal gears"—either in the "yes" position, or in the "no" position. But mechanisms work best in an ideal world of frictionless bearings, point masses, completely elastic collisions, and instant accelerations. But that is not our world. We live in the messy world where things bend, break, bind, melt, and generally fall apart.[9] So perhaps we ought to suspect the tidiness of the flowchart as something that leads us astray.

If we view ethics through the lens of a *design* paradigm, we may get clearer about the *variety of ways* in which rules actually work.[10] For example, what is the relationship of rules to good design? Imagine a designer trying to make the strongest case to a group of venture capitalists for the superiority of his firm's widget: "Ours is the superior design, *because we broke no rules*"!? Can any engineer convincingly claim, "I contrived an excellent design—see, I broke no rules!" I suppose some engineers do make such a claim. But if made, it is only of minimal value. This is not to say that rules are irrelevant. There are many relevant rules, such as federal specs, state licensure laws, legal precedents, laws pertaining to contracts, city building codes, and so on. But *rules by themselves do not compel excellence in design*. Rather, rules are the ground floor beneath which design best not sink. To say the same thing differently, there is much more to excellence in *any* skilled practice—not just engineering, but also music, medicine, farming, carpentry, and so on—than strict conformity to stipulations.

What can be said of practices such as medicine or engineering can be said of human living in general: rules-as-stipulations only have minimal connection to excellent living. After all, who on their deathbed would say, "I have lived well; see, I have broken no rules." That would be a sad testimony to hear on the lips of the dying person. What of friendships? What of accomplishments? What of fulfillment? Nearly everything worth living for falls outside the pale of "I broke no rules."

If all we have is a stipulation model of ethics, then ethics has something to say only when things go *wrong* (i.e., because a rule has been broken). But ethics has far more to say than simply pointing out those instances when we stand in violation. More than adherence to rules, ethics is concerned with living *well*. For the remainder of this essay, I want to propose a better model for thinking about rule-following. The better account attends to the contrast between stipulations and monastic orders, between "Thou shalt *not*" and "Thou *shalt*," between individual efforts to not trespass negative prohibitions and the complex practice of friendship among religious faithful. There is, on the one hand, the "order" that a commanding officer might issue and, on the other, what is called a religious "order." There are rules, and then there is the Rule of St. Benedict. But first the hard case: mathematical rules. Surely if rules were always and only stipulations, then the Stipulation Model could help students learn mathematical rules. Or not.

FOLLOWING MATHEMATICAL RULES

If we are concerned (as we should be) with designing well rather than simply avoiding designing poorly, if we are concerned (as we should be) with living well rather than merely avoiding living badly, we'd do well to focus on positive kinds of rules rather than negative prohibitions. When we focus on prescription ("Thou shalt") rather than proscription ("Thou shalt not"), we see that the Stipulation Model comes up short. Surprisingly, mathematics can show us why.

When my nephew Robert was about three, his eight-year-old sister tried to teach him to play cards. For a three-year-old, card playing is daunting—one needs to recognize fourteen different cards, separated into four suits, and to rank order the cards. Like any three-year-old, Robert was learning to parrot—"*Onetwothreefourfivesixseveneightnineten*"—but was a little unclear on the *concept* of counting. At one point, I overheard Julia quizzing the befuddled Robert. Showing him a ten of spades, she asked, "What is this?" He was stumped. So she hinted, "What comes after nine?" Still stumped. So she adds, "Can you *count* them?" More silence. The trouble was, of course, that the concept of counting that Julia used as a hint was *more difficult* than learning to "read" the numeral 10. After all, even three-year-olds can "read" the word *Coke* as a logo long before they can sound it out as a word. But to Julia, the notions of *numeral recognition* and *rank ordering* were equally simple, *because she'd mastered both*. At eight years of age, Julia had already forgotten what it was like to be three years old.

The sort of forgetfulness that afflicted Julia also afflicts us. Because we have mastered so many skills, we think that rule-following is a straightforward, stepwise process of stipulation → interpretation → application. But let's take a closer look with another example.

Imagine instructing a child, one who knows the ordinals from one to ten, to continue a particular series. (Perhaps, like me, you remember painstakingly constructing the series of all integers from one to one thousand in first grade.) Suppose you give this child the series {2, 4, 6, . . .} and tell the child to "continue the next four in the series." According to the Stipulation Model, the child supposedly performs a mental act of interpretation, first ferreting out the precise rule governing the series, and subsequently applying it to his case. (*We* might say that the "rule" is "add two," although young children must be *taught* that the activity called "addition" is uniform across all real numbers.) Along the way, the child may blurt out: "Oh, I get it!" Can we take her word for it? Has she "gotten it"? How do we know for sure? We can only know for sure by seeing what she writes out.

So we ask her to write it down. Suppose she then writes the following: {12, 10, 8, 14}. Would we be suspicious of her ability to continue the series {2, 4, 6, . . .}? After all, the numerals are all there—but the order is strange. Then again, suppose she writes {10, 12, 14, 16}, missing the 8. We might reasonably suppose that this is merely a slipup. So we ask her to do it again and she complies: {10, 12, 14, 16}. How do we understand her mistake? It turns out that there is a *large variety* of ways she might have gone wrong.

- Perhaps she doesn't know the numeral 8, the way Robert didn't know the numeral 10.

- Perhaps she thinks that the ellipsis, symbolized by ". . ." in our original order, is itself another way to write 8, and so she needn't repeat it but begins with 10.

- Perhaps she thinks the symbol ". . ." is a taboo command, indicating she is to skip any integer containing the numeral 8. (In other words, she also intends to skip 18, 28, 38, etc.)

For adults who long ago mastered counting by twos, these creative ways to "get it wrong" seem far-fetched. But notice that our imaginary student does not *think* she is getting anything wrong. She thinks she is doing it right, where "it" means following the rule. In other words, while *we* think the rule is "add two," *she* might think the rule is "add two except 8's, which are taboo." Still sound far-fetched? Maybe. But the point is that *the Stipulation Model allows for such goofy scenarios to be plausible, because teachers have virtually no control over what goes on "inside" a student's head.* In other words, the inherent weakness of the Stipulation Model lies in involving a step (interpretation) about which nothing can be known.

But hold it right there. Perhaps the haze surrounding interpretation burns off under the sunshine of step 3, application. Philosophers observe that there is no clear boundary between a random mistake and a systematic mistake.[11] Perhaps teachers really do not need to straighten out what is "going on in the student's head" so long as they produce the correct answer. Well, what goes on in *your* head when *you* count by twos? Do you really do addition? Do *you* pause slightly after 12,346 in order to calculate the sum "12,346 + 2 = 12,348"? Or do you write *automatically* 12,348? Does it really matter *how* you go about generating the correct answer, so long as it is the correct answer?

Might we not dispense with interpretation altogether? (But what becomes of the Stipulation Model without this step?) Suppose the teacher works with the student until she automatically writes {8, 10, 12, 14} and so on until she nears 200, at which point the student writes {196, 198, 200, 204, 208, 212, . . .}. Here we go again? The teacher interrupts her work, "Excuse me, but you aren't continuing the series." The student answers, "Of course I am! You said, 'Count by twos.' (And *this* is how *I* interpret the rule 'count by twos.')" How can the teacher criticize the student's error? If this a case of the student's *interpretation* versus the teacher's *interpretation*, who is to say that only the teacher's interpretation is correct? I suppose there is a way to proceed: only if there is a higher court of appeal can we be sure that the teacher's interpretation is the right one. But what kind of "higher court" do we need? Well, maybe there is a loftier principle or higher rule that is the metric for correct interpretations of the command "count by twos." We might call this a *super-rule*. But now the wheels come off.

If we say that the writing of a series is governed by one's *interpretation* of a rule or command, and we are assured that our *interpretation* is correct by appeal to a super-rule that tells us how the rule *ought* to be interpreted, are we not faced with another problem? Namely, how do we know that we are interpreting the super-rule correctly? Doesn't this line of reasoning imply the need for a *super-duper-rule* to tell us how to interpret the super-rule?

This chain of interpretation—rule, super-rule, super-duper-rule, super-duper-duper-rule—never ends. It is called an infinite regress. As you might suspect, if an application of a rule requires an *infinite* sequence of interpretations, we'll never get around to writing an answer. In philosophy, this conundrum produces a state called skepticism: we can never know with certainty that we are following a rule correctly.[12] But of course we *do* know how to follow a rule.[13] So what is wrong with the picture?

The philosophically minded engineer Ludwig Wittgenstein observes that the stalemate between the imaginary student and teacher shows that *we* are looking at "rules" in the wrong way. "This [becomes] our paradox: no course of action could be determined by a rule, because every course of action can be made out to accord with the rule. . . . if everything can be made to accord with the rule, then it can also be made out to conflict with it. And so there would be neither accord nor conflict here." In other words, who is to say who is right? Both student and teacher can say, "You're not following the rule!" as well as shoot back, "Yes I am!" Whose interpretation *wins*? Is our only conclusion that the one with the most power wins? The problem is that we mistakenly assume that rule-following depends on "interpretation." Again, Wittgenstein: "It can also be seen that there is a misunderstanding here from the mere fact that in the course of our argument we give one *interpretation* after another; as if each one contented us at least for a moment, until we thought of yet another [rule, super-rule, super-duper-rule] standing behind [each interpretation]. What this shows is that *there is a way of grasping a rule which is not an interpretation*, but which is exhibited in what we call 'obeying the rule' and 'going against it' in actual cases."[14] In short, the key to the puzzle is in paying attention to the fact that *we count by twos automatically, reflexively, almost without thinking, and* not *by stepwise application of a rule that needs interpretation at each step along the way.*[15]

When you see an arrow pointing to the right (→), why do you turn right? It sounds like a silly question. But what *makes* you turn right? Is there some mysterious force at play? No, of course not. Yet everyone always *does* turn right. They turn right, some say, "by force of habit." This means that somewhere along the way, wittingly or unwittingly, we were all *trained* to respond to → by looking or going to the right. Are we neurologically wired to respond to arrows this way? Yes, perhaps—but only as the result of recent learning. We certainly were not *born* that way. Rather, we got neurologically "rewired" by training.[16]

We must tread carefully here. Wittgenstein is not saying that interpretation *never* occurs. Rather, he wants us to see that 1) interpretation doesn't always occur, and 2) interpretative activity is logically subsequent to *non-interpretive*, regular, automatic behaviors. We can only do interpretation because we *already do by habit* things that do not depend on interpretation.

The missionary linguist Don Richardson tells the amusing story of trying to translate the language of a tribe indigenous to Iran Jaya (Indonesia). But every item he pointed to he got the same word back, which he later learned was the word for "finger"! What he had assumed was universal—the gesture of pointing with one's finger—was simply not how Iran Jayans pointed. *The natives point with their lips!* So every time he extended his American finger to point at a new object (☞) and asked, "What's this?" his lips lined up with his extended finger. Since his lips lined up with his extended finger, they told him, "It's a finger." (They must have thought Americans to be extremely stupid.) Even seemingly universal gestures, such as pointing, are based upon culturally specific habits learned from childhood. Similarly, at the bottom of our ability to learn rules is the notion of custom or habit. Such *customs and habits are non-interpretive regularized behaviors.* "It is not possible that there should have been only one occasion on which someone obeyed a rule. It is not possible that there should have only been one occasion on which a report was made, an order given, and so on.—To obey a rule, to make a report, to give an order, to play a game of chess, are *customs* (uses, institutions). . . . *Following a rule is analogous to obeying an order. We are trained to do so; we react to an order in a particular way.*[17]

Two lessons follow. First, in order for us to follow a rule—whether an arrow, a finger, a mathematical series, a moral command—there must already be in place the regular use of these things by the people who surround us.[18] Second, we must learn or be trained to follow the sign, series, or rule in (roughly) the same way everyone else does, and to do so without stopping to interpret. What happens if we don't? That depends on which rule we are talking about. We can at least say this much: those who turn left, or miscount, or disobey a moral rule, *stop being able to get along;* they get into difficulties with others around them, like trying to walk against the flow of a parade.[19]

THE HEURISTIC MODEL AND THE RULE OF ST. BENEDICT

Imagine living in a nation ruled by an iron-fisted but not very bright tyrant. Having heard that all things snazzy—from the iPhone to Hoover Dam, from drywall to the SmartCar—were built by people called "enjineerz," this dictator decrees that everyone in the land must become engineers on pain of imprisonment and execution.

As hare-brained as this ruler's scheme is, for your own part, you are not worried because you happen to like math and sciences and show aptitude for several branches of engineering. Admittedly, you feel a bit sorry for those poor people who barely passed geometry and have little or no mechanical aptitude. After all, while award-winning design firms like IDEO fruitfully employ *non*-engineers in the design process, these same folk are pretty worthless when engineering *science* needs to be done. But you are hopeful that, eventually, real engineers—like yourself—will rise to power and become this nation's decision-makers who will put things to right. But in the meantime, a fair number of decisions will be made by techno-dunderheads. Alas. To make matters worse, you have to put up with working alongside various fakers, triflers, and pretenders. You have a growing fear that you may be the only person in your corporation who actually understands, say, $F = m \times a$.

What relief and joy it is one day to finally bump into another *bona fide* engineer. The two of you hit it off instantly and try as much as possible to work together. Together you hatch a plan to draw other genuine engineers into a small cohort. Because you all love engineering, you voluntarily work long hours; this fact alone is enough to keep most of the triflers and knuckleheads away. In fact, this becomes a recipe for success; because of your joint love for engineering, the seriousness with which you apply yourselves to technical tasks, and the sheer energy and focus that comes when like-minded friends cooperate, the group begins to grow in number *and* make real strides in engineering.

This account of the evolution of a practice like engineering (and it might be retold similarly for medicine, farming, shipbuilding, violin playing, violin making, etc.) seems very plausible. In point of fact, this fanciful tale has more than one historical analogue. Consider the virtue-inculcating social practice called monasticism. In its early years, Christianity was illegal in the Roman Empire. Despite growing waves of persecution and execution, the number of Christ followers grew steadily from a dozen or so, until they comprised something like 10 to 15 percent of the empire.[20] At the turn of the fourth century CE, then-Emperor Constantine is credited with overturning the illegal status of Christianity. Oddly, the pendulum kept moving until a later emperor named Theodosius eventually made Christianity the *mandatory* religion of the empire (late 300s CE). You can imagine the confusion this caused. People who didn't want to be "Christian" now at the very least had to pretend to be Christian just to keep their jobs and avoid prison. Almost overnight, the population density of "registered" Christians in each parish increased by a factor of seven. Forget about the three-year-long catechesis advised by Hippolytus! Pastors were kept very busy just trying to baptize the enormous influx of pretenders.

You can get a sense of how this state of affairs was similar to our imaginary engineering firm. True believing practitioners were vastly outnumbered by triflers, pretenders, and cheats. It should not surprise us that some religious believers banded together for the sheer love of the game[21] and volunteered to put in long hours practicing the religion they loved. Thus were born monastic orders.

In our contemporary age, we sometimes assume that we know what monastic life was like. After all, haven't we seen it depicted vividly in film?

But Hollywood's portrayal of monastic life almost always is drawn from the High Middle Ages, some time after 1000 CE. But what was monastic life like five hundred years earlier? Whatever excess or oddities typified later centuries, at the outset monastic life aimed simply to be a banding together of friends for the voluntary intense practice of the religion they were devoted to.[22] One of their number, St. Benedict, wrote a handbook on friendship that we know as the Rule of St. Benedict. It wasn't the earliest rule.[23] But it was certainly the one with the widest influence, because it was imitated by so many other monastic orders and put into practice by many laity as well. Understanding the four differences between "following the Rule" and "following the rule" will help us learn something important about engineering and engineering ethics.

First, the Benedictine Rule is very brief—only seventy-three "rules" in all. The longest of these is an essay on humility, a chapter of less than five pages. The shortest is barely forty words.

Second, the Rule has to do with an entire way of life rather than discrete commands regarding stand-alone actions. Rather, individual imperatives make the most sense in light of the whole. While many moral stipulations ("Thou shalt not tell lies") make sense as stand-alone injunctions, the Benedictine Rule is all of a piece: one can best understand a part by comprehending the shared form of life. The author fruitfully compares the manner of their life together to that of (1) a combat unit, (2) a workers' guild, (3) a large family of siblings, and (4) a classroom of students. In each case, the day-to-day activity of living together sheds light on the meaning of the more obscure passages.

Third, stipulations per se are surprisingly rare. There are specifics, for example, about how many times to pray together and which psalms ought to be used when. But where we might expect black-and-white stipulations, we instead find fuzzy rules of thumb known more technically as "heuristics." A standard definition of heuristic is "anything that provides a plausible aid or direction in the solution of a problem but is in the final analysis unjustified, incapable of justification, and potentially fallible."[24] In short, heuristics are tips for proceeding that require skilled judgment to utilize well. For example, the parent figure (a.k.a. the abbot who functions like a "teacher," "leader," "commanding officer," "trainer," etc., depending on the metaphor in play) is warned that when exercising discipline on novices, "he must act sensibly and not be excessive, in case he should damage the pot while trying to scrub the dirt away" (par. 64). Clearly the heuristic in play for the abbot is something like, "Balance mercy with justice."

For another example, consider paragraph 37, here quoted in its entirety: "Although people naturally show compassion towards old people and children, the authority of the Rule should also provide for them. One should always bear in mind their weakness and, with regard to good, the Rule should not be applied very strictly to them. Rather, they should be treated with loving consideration and allowed to eat before the regular hours."[25] Children and old persons may not have great physical stamina. But like the case of tailoring discipline to a person, no one-size-fits-all principle regarding fasting can be spelled out in advance. Once again, skilled judgment is required because human needs vary according to situation and context.

Finally, the aim of the Rule is not conformity but individual growth and development. Just as parents raising children sometimes have household rules ("Always say 'Please' and 'Thank you'!"), the goal in parenting is not to raise rule-followers but rather well-mannered children for whom politeness and pleasantness have become second nature. In this spirit, Benedict concludes the Rule by saying, in effect, this Rule is for its followers *only the beginning*. Some monks will go on to make progress more quickly than others, but *progress* is the expectation, not perfection. Thus St. Benedict circles back to the point he made in the prologue: "As we make progress in our way of life and in faith, as our heart expands with the inexpressible sweetness of love, we shall run along the path [initially felt to be narrow] of God's commandments."[26]

Taken together, the ideas of "progress," "heart expansion," and learning to "run" with endurance suggest a good illustration of the contrast between the Stipulation Model and the Heuristic Model. Recall from chapter 4 the difference between the following two commands:

Stipulation: "Every day thou shalt not eat a quarter-pound stick of butter."

Heuristic: "Every day run ten minutes longer than is comfortable."

Notice that both commands appear to aim at health. If I *break* the stipulation by eating a stick of butter every day, my health will eventually be jeopardized. Of course, refusing to eat butter daily doesn't force health upon me. After all, I might forego the butter but eat a daily pail of ice cream or package of raw bacon. Yet we must admit proscription does make for an easy check-off: "Hmm—have I eaten a quarter-pound stick of butter today? No! *Check*. Hurrah for me!"

In contrast, it is tougher to know if I can "check off" the completion of a heuristic statement because I'm never sure I did it correctly, or enough. "When did genuine discomfort set in, and have I been running a full ten minutes since then?" The worse one's physical endurance, the easier it is to specify when discomfort begins. But the curious thing about running is that as the weeks pass, the onset of those first pangs of discomfort are slowly delayed. We might say the heuristic makes for a training regimen that is *self-transforming*. The meaning of "when discomfort begins" changes as discomfort sets in later and later in the daily run. But not only does the meaning of the command change as one gains endurance. The heuristic is self-transforming in a second way as well: *it can be discarded!* A marathoner has a built-in indicator that tells him or her what makes for a good training run on this particular day (automatically factoring in recent food intake, water intake, sleep, etc.). This built-in indicator has nothing to do with time increments as short as ten minutes. The habitual marathoner rarely runs less than an hour. (For some runners, the tendency is to *over*train—100-plus miles per week—rather than undertrain.) Moreover, sensing "discomfort" is confused by both the brain's release of endorphins at about the six-mile mark and by the runner's previous practice at "breaking through the wall" (i.e., when the aerobic fuels are used up and the muscles begin to digest themselves for energy). While the beginning runner needs a concrete prescriptive command to keep him or her on track, the marathoner has long since internalized it.

CONCLUSION

In this Appendix we have examined two kinds of rule-following. One the one hand is the Stipulation Model, according to which one succeeds or fails in light of his or her strict conformity to black-and-white, easily checked off imperatives. On the other hand, there is a kind of rule-following that happens when one is attempting to "fit" with the Rule of St. Benedict. Following the Rule of St. Benedict is a team sport; it only makes sense (and seems doable) in light of an entire way of life. The point of the Rule for monks was not to live identically, as if they were clones of each other (boring!), but to live in a manner that resonates with the spirit of the whole. This kind of Rule-following produces something like the "clicking" that some athletic teams experience on good days. Since strict conformity is not the goal, the Rule can be followed in surprising, unexpected, innovative bursts of creativity that can still be seen as "in keeping with" the Rule.

But since these creative bursts are dependent upon the team "clicking," the Rule aims at creating conditions under which genuine progress happens, where "genuine progress" means that one finds the Rule easier and easier to follow.

What, then, of stipulations? Stipulations are not entirely done away with in the Heuristic Model. On the contrary, stipulations simply become the simplest case. Recall that Einstein didn't replace Newton. Rather, Newtonian kinematics is the simplified case, when velocity is very, very small with respect to the speed of light (as Lorentz transformations show[27]). A similar analogy holds for stipulations: complicated moral and engineering heuristics reduce to simple stipulations when the age of the practitioner is relatively young. It is, of course, possible for one slavishly and strictly to follow the prescription "run ten minutes longer than is comfortable," keeping a careful record in a training log. But eventually the stipulation is internalized and becomes second nature. At this point the runner can understand that the stipulation was not a stipulation after all but a heuristic.

What the Heuristic Model has that the Stipulation Model lacks is the possibility of *growth in skill over time*. For the group that begins to internalize what it means to follow the Rule, their skilled judgment likewise improves. As internalized and skillful judgment improves, there occasionally evolve new and better ways to live in the manner and spirit of the Rule. These new ways cannot be described in terms of narrow stipulations. Yet from the vantage of the Heuristic Model, the new ways that evolve still fit the spirit and manner of following the Rule.[28] It may not be accidental that the earliest example of a working waterwheel in western Europe happens to be at a monastery (St. Ursus at Loches, sixth-century France[29]). Read under the lens of the Stipulation Model, the Rule of St. Benedict makes no explicit provision for technology, and thus newfangled gizmos ought not to be allowed. But read under the lens of the Heuristic Model, the Rule allowed that a community of like-minded friends might creatively employ technology (like waterwheels that mill grain for people too poor to afford oxen) in the service of other and the honor of God. This is not to say that "newfangled" technology was never opposed. Undoubtedly the debates were long and intense. But on the Stipulation Model, such debate is simply shut down. The extent to which the medieval monks were able to keep the argument going is evidence that the Heuristic Model, rather than the Stipulation Model, was in play.

NOTES

1. Such strict oversight is as it should be. Langdon Winner has observed that the inherent danger of nuclear energy requires citizens to swap some freedoms for needed safety. See Winner, "Do Artifacts Have Politics?"

2. Approximately one in four practicing engineers have this license. The number has been in decline.

3. Tom does not think this increase in P.E. can be legislated—too many loopholes are currently (and likely will continue to be) built into the laws governing who may and who may not become a P.E. As a result, Tom crusades to convince clients to always opt for P.E.-certified contracts even when not required by law.

4. For his part, Tom is more optimistic that I am. In a private phone conversation, he seemed to argue that once an engineer was within the ambit of licensure, U.S. laws can be devised to *compel* the P.E. to perform more morally.

5. See Anscombe, "Authority in Morals." See also the first chapter of Pinckaers, *The Sources of Christian Ethics.*

6. Violations have other names, too, such as trespasses, sins, infractions, and so on.

7. The story of "taboo" and our memory of Victorian culture is explored by MacIntyre in his *After Virtue,* 27–28.

8. Those who take this view may say, for instance, that under certain conditions—though not all conditions—war may constitute an exception to the stipulation against killing human beings. This view is called the just war theory and has a long and noble history. See Bainton, *Christian Attitudes toward War and Peace.*

9. "The machine as symbolizing its action: the action of a machine—I might say at first—seems to be in it from the start, What does that mean?—If we know the machine, everything else, that is its movement, seems already completely determined. We talk as if these parts could only move in this way, as if they could not do anything else. How is this—do we forget the possibility of their bending, breaking off, melting, and so on? Yes; in many cases we don't think of that at all." Wittgenstein, *Philosophical Investigations,* §193.

10. See Kallenberg, "Teaching Engineering Ethics by Conceptual Design."

11. Wittgenstein, *Philosophical Investigations*, §143.

12. This is the one of the conclusions drawn by Saul Kripke in his *Wittgenstein on Rules and Private Language*.

13. McDowell, "Non-Cognitivism and Rule-Following,"; McDowell, "Wittgenstein on Following a Rule."

14. Wittgenstein, *Philosophical Investigations*, §201. Emphasis added.

15. Wittgenstein is suggesting a model of rule-following that is much broader than the Stipulation Model. The model he alludes to comes from engineering itself and makes sense of all kinds of rules, of proscriptions but also prescriptions too. It even helps our understanding of ordinary things like signposts.

16. For an account of how training affects our brains, see ch. 7.

17. Wittgenstein, *Philosophical Investigations*, §§199, 206. Emphasis added.

18. "Is what we call 'obeying a rule' something that it would be possible for only one man to do, and to do only once in his life?" Ibid., §199.

19. Wittgenstein observes that even the rules of logic are no more compelling than other laws of society; strictly speaking, neither is *unbreakable*. ". . . thinking and inferring (like counting) is of course bounded for us, not by an arbitrary definition, but by natural limits corresponding to the body of what can be called the role of thinking and inferring [and counting] in our life. For we are at one over this, that the laws of inference [a.k.a laws of logic] do not compel him to say or write such and such like rails compelling a locomotive. . . . Nevertheless the laws of inference can be said to compel us; in the same sense, that is to say, as other laws in human society. The clerk who infers [see example in an earlier paragraph, §17] *must* do it like that; he would be punished if he inferred differently." Wittgenstein concludes: "If you draw different [i.e., illogical] conclusions you do indeed get into conflict, e.g., with society; and also with other practical consequences." Wittgenstein, *Remarks on the Foundations of Mathematics*, I§116, p. 81. Here Wittgenstein appears to be contrary to Aquinas. But appearances can be deceiving. Aquinas observes in the *Summa* that noncontradiction is the precondition to *lex naturalis*. If Bourke is trustworthy, "*lex*" in Aquinas tends to connote what humans can say or write about what is natural. Wittgenstein here is only saying that noncontradiction doesn't compel us to follow it, rather that in our society, an individual

who ignores noncontradiction in communication will fail to achieve communication, which is to say, fail to achieve *co-munus*, a sharing in a world-of-meanings. See ch. 8 for discussion of McCabe, *Law, Love and Language.*

On the question of whether an entire language might be constructed without explicit use of noncontradiction, consider the account of the Pirahã tribe: "One morning last July, in the rainforest of northwestern Brazil, Dan Everett, an American linguistics professor, and I stepped from the pontoon of a Cessna floatplane onto the beach bordering the Maici River, a narrow, sharply meandering tributary of the Amazon. On the bank above us were some thirty people—short, dark-skinned men, women, and children—some clutching bows and arrows, others with infants on their hips. The people, members of a hunter-gatherer tribe called the Pirahã, responded to the sight of Everett—a solidly built man of fifty-five with a red beard and the booming voice of a former evangelical minister—with a greeting that sounded like a profusion of exotic songbirds, a melodic chattering scarcely discernible, to the uninitiated, as human speech. Unrelated to any other extant tongue, and based on just eight consonants and three vowels, Pirahã has one of the simplest sound systems known. Yet it possesses such a complex array of tones, stresses, and syllable lengths that its speakers can dispense with their vowels and consonants altogether and sing, hum, or whistle conversations." Colapinto, "The Interpreter."

Additionally, on noncontradiction, consider advances made in computer programming by means of "fuzzy" logic where bivalency of "A or not-A" is discarded in favor of a trivalent system.

20. No one knows for sure what the population distribution was. Rodney Stark has created a numerical model that estimates the growth of Christian converts to be around nine million, or about 14.8 percent of the empire, by the year 312 CE. Stark, *Cities of God*, 67.

21. See Leclercq, *The Love of Learning and the Desire for God.*

22. Friendship was crucial in the development of Christianity. See White, *Christian Friendship in the Fourth Century.*

23. Benedict's was preceded by Rules written, for example, by Saints Pachomius, Augustine, and Basil.

24. Koen, *Discussion of the Method*, 28.

25. Benedict, *Rule of St. Benedict*, 60. I have added the capitalization of the word "Rule" for clarity.

26. Ibid., 9.

27. For example, displacement along the x axis is given by $x' = \gamma(x\text{-}vt)$ where γ, the Lorentz factor, is given by $\gamma = 1/\sqrt{[1\text{-}(v^2/c^2)]}$.

28. It was the possibility of evolution in community that made the Rule of St. Benedict such good news. Although the percentage of the population that was monks has always been quite small, it is widely acknowledged by historians that the Rule made a positive impact on Western culture. The medieval era may have been "dark," but it wasn't dark inside the early monasteries. See Numbers, *Galileo Goes to Jail*.

29. White, "Technology, Western."

BIBILIOGRAPHY

Abbot, Edwin A. *Flatland: A Romance of Many Dimensions*. Public domain. Online: http://www.math.brown.edu/~banchoff/gc/Flatland/.

Ackermann, Inge, Robert Ackermann, and Betty Hendricks. "Wittgenstein's Fairy Tale." *Analysis* 38:3 (1978) 159–60.

Allen, Barry. *Artifice and Design: Art and Technology in Human Experience*. Ithaca: Cornell University Press, 2008.

Amato, Joe. "Unwritten Laws: Engineering Ethics in a Narrative Context." PhD diss., State University of New York at Albany, 1989.

Angier, Tom. *Technē in Aristotle's Ethics: Crafting the Moral Life*. New York: Continuum, 2010.

Anscombe, G. E. M. "Authority in Morals." In *Ethics, Religion and Politics*, 43–50. Minneapolis: University of Minnesota Press, 1981.

———. "Modern Moral Philosophy." *Philosophy* 33 (1958) 1–19.

———. "Under a Description." *Noûs* 13:2 (1979) 219–33.

Appelbaum, Binyamin. "As U.S. Agencies Put More Value on a Life, Businesses Fret." *New York Times*, 16 February 2011. Online: http://www.nytimes.com/2011/02/17/business/economy/17regulation.html?pagewanted=all.

Aquinas, Thomas, Saint. *Summa theologica*. Translated by Fathers of the English Dominican Province. New York: Christian Classics, 1981.

Aristotle. *Nicomachean Ethics*. In *The Complete Works of Aristotle: The Revised Oxford Translation*, edited by Jonathon Barnes, 1729–867. Bollingen Series 71:2. Princeton: Princeton University Press, 1984.

———. *Politics*. In *The Complete Works of Aristotle: The Revised Oxford Translation*, edited by Jonathon Barnes, 1986–2129. Bollingen Series 71:2. Princeton: Princeton University Press, 1984.

Associated Press. "Engineer Becomes First Sentenced under Economic Espionage Act." *FoxNews.com*, 18 June 2008. Online: http://www.foxnews.com/story/0, 2933,368681,00.html.

Augustine, Saint. *The City of God*. An abridged version from the translation by Gerald G. Walsh et al. Edited by Vernon J. Bourke. Garden City, NY: Doubleday, 1960.

Bainton, Roland. *Christian Attitudes toward War and Peace: A Historical Survey and Critical Re-Evaluation*. Nashville: Abingdon, 1960.

Baker, George Pierce. *Control: A Pageant of Engineering Progress*. New York: American Society of Mechanical Engineers, 1930.

Basil, Saint. "In Time of Famine and Drought (*Homila Dicta Tempore Famis Et Siccitatis; Hom 8*)." In *The Hungry Are Dying: Beggars and Bishops in Roman Cappadocia*, translated from *Patrologiae Cursus Completus, Series Graeca* 31.303–28 by Susan R. Holman, 179–92. New York: Oxford University Press, 2001.

Bibiliography

Benedict, Saint. *The Rule of St Benedict*. Translated by Carolinne White. London: Penguin, 2008.

Binswanger, Hans Christoph. "The Challenge of Faust." *Science* 281 (1998) 640–41.

Bloom, Paul. "The Moral Life of Babies." *New York Times Magazine*, 10 May 2010. Online: http://www.nytimes.com/2010/05/09/magazine/09babies-t.html?pagewanted=all.

Boltzmann, Ludwig. "Model." In *Theoretical Physics and Philosophical Problems: Selected Writings*, edited by Brian McGuiness, 213–20. Dordrecht, Holland: Reidel, 1974.

Bronner, Ethan. "Virtual Bridge Allows Strangers in Mideast to Seem Less Strange." *New York Times*, 9 July 2011. Online: http://www.nytimes.com/2011/07/10/world/middleeast/10mideast.html?_r=1&nl=todaysheadlines&emc=tha26.

Bucciarelli, Louis L. "Between Thought and Object in Engineering Design." *Design Studies* 23 (2002) 219–31.

———. "Designing, Like Language, Is a Social Process." In *Engineering Philosophy*, 9–22. Delft, Netherlands: DUP Satellite (Delft University Press), 2003.

———. *Designing Engineers*. Edited by Wiebe E. Bijker, Bernard Carlson, and Trevor Pinch. Inside Technology. Cambridge: MIT Press, 1994.

———. *Engineering Philosophy*. Delft, Netherlands: DUP Satellite (Delft University Press), 2003.

———. "Knowing That, and Knowing How." In *Engineering Philosophy*, 43–75. Delft, Netherlands: DUP Satellite (Delft University Press), 2003.

Bur, Michel. "The Kingdom of the Franks from Louis VI to Philip II: The Signeuries." In *The New Cambridge Medieval History*, edited by David Luscombe and Jonathan Riley-Smith, IV/2:530–48. Cambridge: Cambridge University Press, 1995.

Cantor, Norman F. *The Civilization of the Middle Ages: A Completely Revised and Expanded Edition of Medieval History, the Life and Death of a Civilization*. San Francisco: HarperCollins, 1993.

Caro, Robert A. *The Power Broker: Robert Moses and the Fall of New York*. New York: Knopf, 1974.

Chanson, H. "The Hydraulics of Roman Aqueducts: What Do We Know? Why Should We Learn?" Paper presented at the Proceedings of World Environmental and Water Resources Congress 2008, Ahupua'a, Hawaii, 13–16 May 2008. Online: http://espace.library.uq.edu.au/view/UQ:138266.

Colapinto, John. "The Interpreter: Has a Remote Amazonian Tribe Upended Our Understanding of Language?" *New Yorker*, 16 April 2007, 120–39.

Crawford, Matthew B. *Shop Class as Soulcraft*. New York: Penguin, 2009.

Dalrymple, Dana. "The American Tractor Comes to Soviet Agriculture: The Transfer of Technology." *Technology and Culture* 5 (1964) 191–214.

Damasio, Antonio. *Descartes' Error: Emotion, Reason, and the Human Brain*. New York: Penguin, 2005.

Damasio, Hanna, et al. "The Return of Phineas Gage: Clues about the Brain from the Skull of a Famous Patient." *Science* 264:20 (1994) 1102–4.

Datz, Todd. "Eating Processed Meats, but Not Unprocessed Red Meats, May Raise Risk of Heart Disease and Diabetes." *Harvard School of Public Health Press Release*, 17 May 2010. Online: http://www.hsph.harvard.edu/news/press-releases/2010-releases/processed-meats-unprocessed-heart-disease-diabetes.html.

Davis, Michael. *Thinking Like an Engineer*. Oxford: Oxford University Press, 1998.

Diamond, Cora. "Martha Nussbaum and the Need for Novels." *Philosophical Investigations* 16:2 (1993) 128–53.

Drury, Maurice O'C. "Madness and Religion." In *The Danger of Words and Writings on Wittgenstein*, 115–37. Bristol, UK: Thoemmes, 1996.

Dunne, Joseph. *Back to the Rough Ground: Practical Judgment and the Lure of Technique.* Notre Dame: University of Notre Dame Press, 1993.

Eisenberg, Anne. "New Puzzles that Tell Humans from Machines." *New York Times*, 23 May 2009. Online: http://www.nytimes.com/2009/05/24/business/24novelties. html?_r=1&scp=1&sq=new puzzles that tell humans from machines&st=cse.

Fahrenthold, David A. "Cosmic Markdown: EPA Says Life Is Worth Less." *Washington Post*, 19 July 2008. Online: http://www.washingtonpost.com/wp-dyn/content/article/2008/07/18/AR2008071803235.html.

Federal Aviation Administration. "Airworthiness Directives: Boeing Model 757-200 Series Airplanes." Online: http://rgl.faa.gov/Regulatory_and_Guidance_Library/rgAD.nsf/0/e22075f4705e6c2086256e8d0055fe44!OpenDocument&ExpandSection=-5.

Ferguson, Eugene S. *Engineering and the Mind's Eye*. Cambridge: MIT Press, 1993.

———. "How Engineers Lose Touch." *American Heritage of Invention and Technology* 8 (1993) 16–24.

Firmage, D. Allan. *Modern Engineering Practice*. New York: Garland STPM, 1980.

Gardner, Martin. "Mathematical Games." *Scientific American* 199 (1958) 136–42.

Gelernter, David Hillel. *Machine Beauty: Elegance and the Heart of Technology*. New York: Basic Books, 1998.

Gispen, Kees. *New Profession, Old Order: Engineers and German Society, 1815–1914.* Cambridge: Cambridge University Press, 1989.

Glick, Daniel. "Building Bridges of Hope " *Parade Magazine*, 7 March 2010. Online: http://www.parade.com/news/2010/03/07-building-bridges-of-hope.html.

Goodman, Nelson. *Ways of Worldmaking*. Indianapolis: Hackett, 1978.

Gotterbarn, Don. "Not All Codes Are Created Equal: The Software Engineering Code of Ethics, a Success Story." *Journal of Business Ethics* 22 (1999) 81–89.

Graham, Loren R. *The Ghost of the Executed Engineer: Technology and the Fall of the Soviet Union*. Cambridge: Harvard University Press, 1993.

———. "Palchinsky's Travels: A Russian Engineer's Adventures among Gigantic Projects and Small Minds." *Technology Review* 96:8 (1993) 22–31.

The Greek New Testament. Edited by Kurt Aland et al. 3rd ed. Stuttgart: United Bible Societies, 1983.

Gregory of Nyssa, Saint. "On the Love of the Poor, 2: On the Saying, 'Whoever Has Done It to One of the Least of These Has Done It to Me' (*De Pauperibus Amandis: Quaetenus Uni Ex His Fecistis Mihi Fecistis*)." In *The Hungry Are Dying: Beggars and Bishops in Roman Cappadocia*, translated from PG 46.471–90 by Susan R. Holman, 201–6. New York: Oxford University Press, 2001.

Grose, Thomas K. "Opening a New Book." *Prism (American Society for Engineering Education)* 13:6 (2004). Online: http://www.prism-magazine.org/feb04/new_book.cfm.

Große, Christian, and Markus Krüger. "Inspection and Monitoring of Structures in Civil Engineering." *The E-Journal of Non-destructive Testing* 11:1 (2003) no pages.

Grossman, Dave. *On Killing: The Psychological Cost of Learning to Kill in War and Society*. Boston: Little Brown, 1995.

Bibiliography

Hartman, Steve. "Love Thy Nieghbor: Son's Killer Moves Next Door." *CBSNews.com* (2011). Online: http://www.cbsnews.com/stories/2011/06/07/eveningnews/main20069849.shtml#ixzz1PSOvnjiQ.

Hauerwas, Stanley. *With the Grain of the Universe: The Church's Witness and Natural Theology.* Grand Rapids: Brazos, 2001.

Hengel, Martin. *Crucifixion in the Ancient World and the Folly of the Message of the Cross.* Minneapolis: Fortress, 1977.

Herdt, Jennifer A. *Putting on Virtue: The Legacy of the Splendid Vices.* Chicago: University of Chicago Press, 2008.

Hertzberg, Lars. "On the Attitude of Trust." *Inquiry* 31:3 (1988) 307–22.

Hick, John. *Evil and the God of Love.* London: Collins, 1968.

Hill, Percy H. *The Science of Engineering Design.* New York: Holt, Rinehart & Winston, 1970.

Hippocrates. "Ancient Medicine." In *Hippocrates*, translated by W. H. S. Jones, 1:13–63. Cambridge: Harvard University Press, 1984.

————. "Decorum." In *Hippocrates*, translated by W. H. S. Jones, 2:267–302. Cambridge: Harvard University Press, 1981.

————. "The Oath." In *Hippocrates*, translated by W. H. S. Jones, 1:299–301. Cambridge: Harvard University Press, 1984.

Hodge, A. T. *Roman Aqueducts and Water Supply.* 2nd ed. London: Duckworth, 2001.

Hoffman, W. Michael. "The Ford Pinto." In *Case Studies in Business Ethics*, edited by Thomas Donaldson and Al Gini, 207–15. 4th ed. Upper Saddle River, NJ: Prentice Hall, 1996.

Holman, Susan R. *The Hungry Are Dying: Beggars and Bishops in Roman Cappadocia.* New York: Oxford University Press, 2001.

Hugh of St. Victor. *The Didascalicon of Hugh of St. Victor: A Medieval Guide to the Arts.* Translated by Jerome Taylor. New York: Columbia University Press, 1961.

Hughson, Roy V., and Philip M. Kohn. "Ethics." *Chemical Engineering* 87 (1980) 132–47.

Hyde, Lewis. *The Gift: Creativity and the Artist in the Modern World.* 2nd ed. New York: Vintage, 2007.

Inskeep, Steve. "Atul Gawande's 'Checklist' for Surgery Success." *Morning Edition*, 5 Jan 2010. Online: http://www.npr.org/templates/transcript/transcript.php?storyId=122226184.

Juarerro, Alicia. *Dynamics in Action: Intentional Behavior as a Complex System.* Cambridge: MIT Press, 2002.

Kallenberg, Brad J. "The Descriptive Problem of Evil." In *Physics and Cosmology: Scientific Perspectives on the Problem of Natural Evil*, edited by Nancey Murphy, Robert John Russell, and William R. Stoeger, 297–321. Vatican City: Vatican Observatory Press, 2007.

————. "Dynamical Similarity and the Problem of Evil." In *God, Grace and Creation*, edited by Philip J. Rossi, 163–83. Annual Publication of the College Theology Society 55. Maryknoll, NY: Orbis, 2010.

————. *Ethics as Grammar: Changing the Postmodern Subject.* Notre Dame: University of Notre Dame Press, 2001.

————. *God and Gadgets: Following Jesus in a Technological World.* Eugene, OR: Cascade Books, 2010.

————. "Phronesis and Divine Command Ethics." Paper presented at the annual meeting of the Society of Christian Ethics, January 4–7, 2007, Dallas, Texas.

————. "Praying for Understanding: Reading Anselm through Wittgenstein." *Modern Theology* 20:4 (2004) 527–46.

————. "Professional or Practitioner? What's Missing from the Codes?" *Teaching Ethics: The Journal of the Society for Ethics across the Curriculum* 3 (2002) 49–66.

————. "Rethinking Fideism through the Lens of Wittgenstein's Engineering Outlook." *International Journal for the Philosophy of Religion* 71 (2012) 55–73.

————. "Teaching Engineering Ethics by Conceptual Design: The Somatic Marker Hypothesis." *Science and Engineering Ethics* 15:4 (2009) 563–76. Online: http://www.springerlink.com/openurl.asp?genre=article&id=doi:10.1007/s11948-009-9129-2.

Kaplan, Sheila. "Boeing Whistleblowers Say Planes Must Be Grounded." *Mother Jones*, November 2005. Online: http://www.motherjones.com/politics/2005/11/flight-risk.

Karagianis, Liz. "The Right Stuff: A Question of Ethics." *Spectrum* (Winter 1999). Online: http://spectrum.mit.edu/articles/intro/the-right-stuff/.

Kennedy, Pagan. "Necessity Is the Mother of Invention." *New York Times*, 30 November 2003. Online: http://www.nytimes.com/2003/11/30/magazine/30MIT.html?ei=5070&en=2b0652694b32018f&ex=1189742400.

Kenny, Anthony. *A Brief History of Western Philosophy*. Oxford: Blackwell, 1998.

————. "Practical Reasoning and Rational Appetite." In *Will, Freedom and Power*, 70–96. New York: Barnes & Noble, 1976.

Kim, Jim Yong, et al., editors. *Dying for Growth: Global Inequality and the Health of the Poor*. Monroe, ME: Common Courage, 2000.

King, W. J. "Unwritten Laws of Engineering: Part 1—What the Beginner Needs to Learn at Once." *Mechanical Engineering* 66 (1944) 323–26.

————. "Unwritten Laws of Engineering: Part 2—Relating Chiefly to Engineering Executives." *Mechanical Engineering* 66 (1944) 398–402.

————. "Unwritten Laws of Engineering: Part 3—Purely Personal Considerations for Engineers." *Mechanical Engineering* 66 (1944) 459–62.

Klagge, James C. *Wittgenstein in Exile*. Cambridge: MIT Press, 2011.

Koen, Billy Vaughn. *Discussion of the Method: Conducting the Engineer's Approach to Problem Solving*. Oxford: Oxford University Press, 2003.

Krabbe, Alexander. "Senseless Deaths in Bad Reichenhall." *Ohmynews International*, 18 Jan 2006. Online: http://english.ohmynews.com/articleview/article_view.asp?menu=c10400&no=267651&rel_no=1.

Kraybill, Donald B. *The Riddle of Amish Culture*. Rev. ed. Center Books in Anabaptist Studies. Baltimore: Johns Hopkins University Press, 2001.

Kraybill, Donald B., Steven M. Nolt, and David L. Weaver-Zercher. *Amish Grace: How Forgiveness Transcended Tragedy*. San Francisco: Jossey-Bass, 2010.

Kremer, Eugene. "(Re)Examining the Citicorp Case: Ethical Paragon or Chimera." *Cross Currents* 52:3 (2002) 315–29. Online: http://www.crosscurrents.org/kremer2002.htm.

Kripke, Saul. *Wittgenstein on Rules and Private Language: An Elementary Exposition*. Cambridge: Harvard University Press, 1982.

Kuhn, Thomas S. *The Structure of Scientific Revolutions*. 2nd ed. Chicago: University of Chicago Press, 1970.

Ladd, John. "The Quest for a Code of Professional Ethics: An Intellectual and Moral Confusion." In *Ethical Issues in Engineering*, edited by Deborah G. Johnson, 130–36. Upper Saddle River, NJ: Prentice Hall, 1991.

Layton, Edwin T. *The Revolt of the Engineers: Social Responsibility and the American Engineering Profession*. Baltimore: John Hopkins University Press, 1986.

Leclercq, Jean. *The Love of Learning and the Desire for God: A Study of Monastic Culture*. Translated by Catharine Mishari. New York: Fordham University Press, 1961.

Liptak, Adam. "Religious Groups Given 'Exception' to Work Bias Law." *New York Times*, 11 January 2012. Online: http://www.nytimes.com/2012/01/12/us/supreme-court-recognizes-religious-exception-to-job-discrimination-laws.html?_r=1.

Løgstrup, Knud E. *The Ethical Demand*. Translated by Theodor I. Jensen. Philadelphia: Fortress, 1971.

Ludden, Jennifer. "Unlimited Vacation Time Not a Dream for Some." *All Things Considered*, 12 August 2010. Online: http://www.npr.org/templates/transcript/transcript.php?storyId=129137542.

MacIntyre, Alasdair. *After Virtue: A Study in Moral Theory*. 2nd ed. Notre Dame: University of Notre Dame Press, 1984.

———. *A Short History of Ethics*. New York: Collier, 1966.

———. *Whose Justice? Which Rationality?* Notre Dame: University of Notre Dame Press, 1988.

Macmillan, Malcolm. *An Odd Kind of Fame: Stories of Phineas Gage*. Cambridge: MIT Press, 2000.

Malina, Bruce J. *The New Testament World: Insights from Cultural Anthropology*. Atlanta: John Knox, 1981.

"Margie Pinnell, an Ethos of Service." n.d. Online: http://www-ig.udayton.edu/Stories/Story/?contentId=10856.

"The Martyrdom of Saints Perpetua and Felicitas." In *The Acts of the Christian Martyrs*, edited by Herbert Musurillo, 107–31. Oxford: Clarendon, 1972.

Mauss, Marcel. *The Gift: Forms and Functions of Exchange in Archaic Societies*. Translated by Ian Cunnison. New York: Norton, 1967.

May, William F. "Code, Covenant, Contract, or Philanthropy." *Hastings Center Report* 5 (1975) 29–38.

———. *The Physician's Covenant*. Philadelphia: Westminster, 1983.

McCabe, Herbert. "Aquinas on Good Sense." *New Blackfriars* 67 (1986) 419–31.

———. *Law, Love and Language*. New York: Continuum, 2004.

McCarthy, David Matzko, editor. *The Heart of Catholic Social Teaching: Its Origins and Contemporary Significance*. Grand Rapids: Brazos, 2009.

McDonough, William, and Michael Braungart. *Cradle to Cradle: Remaking the Way We Make Things*. New York: North Point, 2002.

McDowell, John. "Non-Cognitivism and Rule-Following." In *Wittgenstein: To Follow a Rule*, edited by Steven H. Holtzman and Christopher M. Leich, 141–62. London: Routledge & Kegan Paul, 1981.

———. "The Role of *Eudaimonia* in Aristotle's Ethics." In *Essays on Aristotle's Ethics*, edited by Amélie Oksenberg Rorty, 359–76. Berkeley: University of California Press, 1980.

———. "Wittgenstein on Following a Rule." In *Meaning and Reference*, edited by A. W. Moore, 257–93. Oxford: Oxford University Press, 1993.

McGuinness, Brian, editor. *Wittgenstein: A Life: Young Ludwig, 1889–1921.* Berkeley: University of California Press, 1988.

McNeill, Paul M. *The Ethics and Politics of Human Experimentation.* Cambridge: Cambridge University Press, 1993.

Meiskins, Peter. "The 'Revolt of the Engineers' Reconsidered." *Technology and Culture* 29:2 (1988) 219–46.

Merle, Renae, and Jerry Markon. "Ex-Pentagon Official Admits Job Deal; Civilian Got Boeing Offer while Overseeing Air-Tanker Contract." *The Washington Post*, 21 April 2004.

Merton, Thomas. *Conjectures of a Guilty Bystander.* Garden City, NY: Image, 1966.

Miller, Timothy S. *The Birth of the Hospital in the Byzantine Empire.* Baltimore: John Hopkins University Press, 1997.

Mitchell, Sandra D. *Unsimple Truths: Science, Complexity, and Policy.* Chicago: University of Chicago Press, 2009.

Monk, Ray. *Ludwig Wittgenstein: The Duty of Genius.* New York: Viking Penguin, 1990.

Morgenstern, Joe. "The Fifty-Nine-Story Crisis." *The New Yorker*, 29 May 1995, 45–53.

Morison, Elting. "The Works of John B. Jervis." In *From Know-How to Nowhere: The Development of American Technology*, 40–71. New York: Basic Books, 1974.

Mulhall, Stephen. "The Mortality of the Soul: Bernard Williams's Character(s)." In *Wittgenstein and the Moral Life: Essays in Honor of Cora Diamond*, edited by Alice Crary, 355–79. Cambridge: MIT Press, 2007.

Murphy, Nancey C. *Reasoning and Rhetoric in Religion.* Valley Forge, PA: Trinity, 1994.

Noble, David W. *The Religion of Technology: The Divinity of Man and the Spirit of Invention.* New York: Penguin, 1999.

Numbers, Ronald, editor. *Galileo Goes to Jail: And Other Myths about Science and Religion.* Cambridge: Harvard University Press, 2010.

Pearson, Lee M. "The 'Princeton' and the 'Peacemaker': A Study in Ninteenth-Century Naval Research and Development Procedures." *Technology and Culture* 7 (1966) 166–83.

Peil, Udo. "Life-Cycle Prolongation of Civil-Engineering Structures Via Monitoring." *The E-Journal of Non-destructive Testing* 11:1 (2003): no pages.

Petroski, Henry. *Design Paradigms: Case Histories of Error and Judgment in Engineering.* Cambridge: Cambridge University Press, 1994.

———. "Past and Future Failures." *American Scientist* 92:6 (2004) 500–504.

———. *To Engineer Is Human: The Role of Failure in Successful Design.* New York: Vintage, 1992.

Phillips, D. Z. *Religion and the Hermeneutics of Contemplation.* Cambridge: Cambridge University Press, 2001.

Pilloton, Emily, and Allan Chochinov. *Design Revolution: 100 Products that Empower People.* New York: Metropolis, 2009.

Pinches, Charles. *Theology and Action: After Theory in Christian Ethics.* Grand Rapids: Eerdmans, 2002.

Pinckaers, Servais. *The Sources of Christian Ethics.* Maryknoll, NY: Orbis, 1995.

Plutarch. *Marcellus.* In *The Lives of the Noble Grecians and Romans.* Translated by John Dryden. New York: Modern Library, 1932.

Pojman, Louis P. *Ethical Theory.* Belmont, CA: Wadsworth, 1989.

Polanyi, Michael. *The Tacit Dimension.* Garden City, NY: Doubleday, 1966.

Bibiliography

Polkinghorne, John. *Science and Providence: God's Interaction with the World.* Boston: Shambhala, 1989.

Postman, Neil. *Technopoly: The Surrender of Culture to Technology.* Rev. ed. New York: Vintage, 1993.

Pritchard, Michael S. "Responsible Engineering: The Importance of Character and Imagination." *Science and Engineering Ethics* 7:3 (2001) 391–402.

Pugh, Stuart. *Creating Innovative Products Using Total Design: The Living Legacy of Stuart Pugh.* Edited by Don Clausing and Ron Andrade. Reading, MA: Addison-Wesley, 1996.

Ramsey, Krista. "Ohio Man Seeks Forgiveness of Mourning Mother." *The Cincinnati Enquirer,* 5 Nov 2011. Online: http://content.usatoday.net/dist/custom/gci/InsidePage.aspx?cId=cincinnati&sParam=37867095.story.

"A Reaffirmation of the Synod's Position on Close(d) Communion: A Statement of the Praesidium of the Lutheran Church—Missouri Synod." 21 August 1996. Online: http://www.iclnet.org/pub/resources/text/wittenberg/mosynod/web/clcommunion.html.

Richards, Frederick. *Sue the Bastards: Handbook for the Field Engineer.* Pittsford, NY: Richards, 1976.

Ricks, Thomas E. "Separation Anxiety: Life in the 'New' Marine Corps." *The Wall Street Journal* 226:18 (1995) A1, A4.

Rittel, Horst W. J., and Melvin M. Webber. "Planning Problems Are Wicked Problems." In *Developments in Design Methodology,* edited by Nigel Cross, 135–44. New York: Wiley, 1984.

Robinson, I. S. "The Papacy, 1122–1198." In *The New Cambridge Medieval History,* edited by David Luscombe and Jonathan Riley-Smith, IV/2:317–83. Cambridge: Cambridge University Press, 1995.

Root-Bernstein, Robert Scott. "Visual Thinking: The Art of Imagining Reality." *Transactions of the American Philosophical Society* 75:6 (1985) 50–67.

Rorty, Amélie Oksenberg. "How to Harden Your Heart: Six Easy Ways to Become Corrupt." *Yale Review* 86:2 (1998) 104–12.

Russell, Robert John, Nancey Murphy, and Arthur R. Peacocke. *Chaos and Complexity: Scientific Perspectives on Divine Action.* Vatican City: Vatican Observatory, 1995.

Schwehn, Mark. "Local Genius." Paper presented at the University of Dayton, OH, December 2004.

Searle, John R. "The Myth of the Computer." *The New York Review of Books,* April 29, 1982. Online: http://www.nybooks.com/articles/6628.

Seely, Bruce. "Scientific Mystique: Highway Research at the Bureau of Public Roads, 1918–1940." *Technology and Culture* 19 (1978) 675–702.

Seife, Charles. *Proofiness: The Dark Arts of Mathematical Deception.* New York: Viking Penguin, 2010.

Severance, Kristi, Lisa Spiro, and Patricia H. Werhane. "W. R. Grace & Co. and the Neemix Patent (a)." In *Ethical Issues in Business : A Philosophical Approach,* edited by Thomas Donaldson, Patricia H. Werhane, and Margaret Cording, 399–409. Upper Saddle River, NJ: Prentice Hall, 2002.

Shah, Taimoor, and Graham Bowley. "U.S. Sergeant Is Said to Kill 16 Civilians in Afghanistan." *New York Times,* 12 March 2012. Online: http://www.nytimes.com/2012/03/13/world/asia/us-army-sergeant-suspected-in-afghanistan-shooting.html?_r=1&hp=&pagewanted=all.

Smith, Christian, with Melinda Lundquist Denton. *Soul Searching : The Religious and Spiritual Lives of American Teenagers.* New York: Oxford Univesity Press, 2005.

Smith, Cynthia E. *Design for the Other 90 Percent*. Paris: Editions Assouline, 2007.

Soudek, Ingrid H. "The Humanist Engineer of Aleksandr Solzhenitsyn." In *Social, Ethical, and Policy Implication of Engineering: Selected Readings*, edited by Joseph R. Herkert, 57–60. New York: IEEE, 2000.

Spelt, P. D. M., and Brian McGuinness. "Marginalia in Wittgenstein's Copy of Lamb's *Hydrodynamics*." In *From the Tractatus to the Tractatus and Other Essays*, edited by Gianluigi Oliveri, 131–48. Frankfurt am Main: Lang, 2001.

Spiegel, Alix. "When the 'Trust Hormone' Is Out of Balance." *All Things Considered*, 22 April 2010. Online: http://www.npr.org/templates/story/story.php?storyId=126141922.

Stark, Rodney. *Cities of God: The Real Story of How Christianity Became an Urban Movement and Conquered Rome*. San Francisco: HarperSanFrancisco, 2006.

Staudenmaier, John M. "Perils of Progress Talk: Some Historical Considerations." In *Science, Technology, and Social Progress: Research in Technology Studies*, edited by Steven L. Goldman, 2:268–93. Bethlehem, PA: Lehigh University Press, 1989.

Steffens, J. H., et al. "Panel Discussion: Ideas for Better Code." Paper presented at the Conference on Engineering Ethics, Baltimore, MD, 18–19 May 1975.

Sterrett, Susan G. "Physical Pictures: Engineering Models circa 1914 and in Wittgenstein's *Tractatus*." In *History of Philosophy of Science: New Trends and Perspectives*, edited by Michael Heidelberger and Friedrich Stadler, 121–35. Dordrecht: Kluwer Academic, 2002.

———. *Wittgenstein Flies a Kite: A Story of Models of Wings and Models of the World*. New York: Pi, 2006.

Stohr, Kate, and Cameron Sinclair. *Design Like You Give a Damn: Architectural Responses to Humanitarian Crises*. New York: Metropolis, 2006.

Sturt, George. *The Wheelwright's Shop*. Canto ed. Cambridge: Cambridge University Press, 1993.

Taylor, Jerome. "Introduction." In *The Didascalicon of Hugh of St. Victor: A Medieval Guide to the Arts*, translated by Jerome Taylor, 3–42. New York: Columbia University Press, 1961.

Terrien, Samuel. "The Metaphor of the Rock in Biblical Theology." In *God in the Fray: A Tribute to Walter Brueggemann*, 157–71. Minneapolis: Fortress, 1998.

Tilley, Maureen A. "The Ascetic Body and the (Un)Making of the World of the Martyr." *Journal of the American Academy of Religion* 59:3 (1991) 467–79.

Verghese, Abraham. *Cutting for Stone*. New York: Knopf, 2009.

Vincenti, Walter G. "Control-Volume Analysis: A Difference in Thinking between Engineering and Physics." *Technology and Culture* 23:2 (1982) 145–74.

———. "The Davis Wing and the Problem of Airfoil Design: Uncertainty and Growth in Engineering Knowledge." *Technology and Culture* 27:4 Special Issue: Engineering in the Twentieth Century (1986) 717–58.

———. "The Scope for Social Impact in Engineering Outcomes: A Diagrammatic Aid to Analysis." *Social Studies of Science* 21 (1991) 761–67.

———. *What Engineers Know and How They Know It: Analytical Studies from Aeronautical History*. Baltimore: John Hopkins University Press, 1990.

Wade, Nicholas. "We May Be Born with an Urge to Help." *New York Times*, 2 December 2009.

Wakin, Daniel J. "Seeing Heresy in a Service for Sept. 11: Pastor Is under Fire for Interfaith Prayers." *New York Times*, 8 February 2002, C16.

Bibiliography

Wald, Matthew L. "Late Design Change Is Cited in Collapse of Tunnel Ceiling in Boston." *New York Times*, 2 November 2006. Online: http://www.nytimes.com/2006/11/02/us/02dig.html?ex=1163221200&en=f6b033108cd97aca&ei=5070&emc=eta1.

Weil, Simone. "The Love of God and Affliction." In *Waiting for God*, 117–36. New York: Harper & Row, 1951.

Wenger, Etienne. *Communities of Practice: Learning, Meaning, and Identity*. Learning in Doing. Cambridge: Cambridge University Press, 1999.

Weston, Anthony. *A Rulebook for Arguments*. Indianapolis: Hackett, 1992.

Whitbeck, Caroline. "Ethics as Design: Doing Justice to Moral Problems." *Hastings Center Report* 26:3 (1996) 9–16.

———. *Ethics in Engineering Practice and Research*. Cambridge: University of Cambridge Press, 1998.

———. "Teaching Ethics to Scientists and Engineers: Moral Agents and Moral Problems." *Science and Engineering Ethics* 1:3 (1995) 299–308.

White, Carolinne. *Christian Friendship in the Fourth Century*. Cambridge: Cambridge University Press, 1992.

White, Lynn. "Eilmer of Malmesbury: An Eleventh-Century Aviator: A Case Study of Technological Innovation, Its Context and Tradition." *Technology and Culture* 2:2 (1961) 97–111.

———. "The Expansion of Technology, 500–1500." In *The Fontana Economic History of Europe*, edited by Carlo M. Cipolla, 1:143–71. New York: Barnes & Noble, 1976.

———. *Medieval Technology and Social Change*. London: Oxford University Press, 1962.

———. "Technology, Western." In *Dictionary of the Middle Ages*, edited by Joseph R. Strayer, 11:650–64. New York: Scribner, 1982.

Wiggins, David. "Deliberation and Practical Reason." In *Essays on Aristotle's Ethics*, edited by Amélie Oksenberg Rorty, 221–40. Berkeley: University of California Press, 1980.

Wilson, Andrew D. "Hertz, Boltzmann and Wittgenstein Reconsidered." *Studies in History and Philisophy of Science* 20:2 (1989) 245–63.

Winner, Langdon. "Do Artifacts Have Politics?" In *The Whale and the Reactor: A Search for Limits in an Age of High Technology*, 19–39. Chicago: University of Chicago Press, 1986.

Wittgenstein, Ludwig. *Culture and Value*. Translated by Peter Winch. Edited by G. H. von Wright and Heikki Nyman. 2nd. ed. Oxford: Blackwell, 1980.

———. *Notebooks, 1914–1916*. Edited by G. H. von Wright and G. E. M. Anscombe. Chicago: University of Chicago Press, 1961.

———. *On Certainty*. Translated by Denis Paul and G. E. M. Anscombe. Edited by G. E. M. Anscombe and G. H. von Wright. New York: Harper Torchbooks, 1972.

———. *Philosophical Grammar*. Translated by Anthony Kenny. Edited by Rush Rhees. Berkeley: University of California Press, 1974.

———. *Philosophical Investigations*. Translated by G. E. M. Anscombe. Edited by G. E. M. Anscombe and Rush Rhees. New York: Macmillan, 1953.

———. *Philosophische Betrachtungen, Philosophische Bemerkungen*. Vol. 2. Wiener Ausgabe. Vienna: Springer, 1994.

———. *Remarks on the Foundations of Mathematics*. Translated by G. E. M. Anscombe. Edited by G. H. von Wright, Rush Rhees, and G. E. M. Anscombe. Cambridge: MIT Press, 1978.

———. *Tractatus Logico-Philosophicus*. Translated by D. F. Pears and B. F. McGuinness. London: Routledge, 1961.

Workman, Daniel. "U.S. Copper Exports and Imports in 2007." *Suite101.com*, 9 September 2008. http://import-export.suite101.com/article.cfm/us_copper_exports_imports_in_2007.

Wright, Georg Henrik von. *Wittgenstein*. Minneapolis: University of Minnesota Press, 1974.

Xenophon. *The Economist of Xenophon*. Translated by Alexander D. O. Wedderburn and W. Gershom Collingwood. Bibliotheca Pastorum 1. New York: Franklin, 1971.

Zussman, Robert. *Mechanics of the Middle Class: Work and Politics among American Engineers*. Berkeley: University of California Press, 1985.

INDEX

Index

Gestalt, 109–13, 115, 215
Gift. *See* Grace
Golden Rule, 66
Good, The, 92, 114, 193, 235, 269, 273n38
Grace, 169–75, 196–99, 265–69

Habit, 41, 116, 150–69, 171, 173, 176, 178, 196, 214, 220, 227, 249, 255, 287, 288
Hammurabi Code, 66
Henri Poincaré, 27n7
Heuristics, x, 24, 28, 36–49, 69–77, 184
   defined, 44, 101, op cit.
   and following rules, 288–93
   as a mode of reading PCOE, 82–95
   and the narrative of Jesus, 225–42
   optimization, 38, 40–43
   procedures, 43–45
   as warrants, 66–77
   see Tacit knowledge
Hugh of St. Victor, 254–69

Integrity, 161–62
Internal goods, 196–97
Is-Ought Problem, 62–64
Isidore of Seville, St., 253

Jesus of Nazareth, 72, 167, 219–20, 223–41, 249, 251, 258–59, 261, 264

Know-how. *See* Tacit knowledge; Phronesis
Koen, Billy V., 14, 15, 28, 44, 45, 51, 52, 69, 77, 79, 89, 244n25

Language, 21–26, 29, 33, 79, 136, 139–46, 158, 182–93, 200, 201, 208, 222, 259, 279
   design-language, 24, 182
   object-language, 23–24

Law, ix, x, 10, 49, 66, 80, 81, 83, 84, 95, 283,
LeMessurier, William, 229–34
Limbic system, 116, 153–60, 167, 188
Local genius. *See* Genius, local

MacIntyre, Alasdair, 62, 162, 280, 281
McCabe, Herbert, 185–93, 208–10
Memory, 156, 158–59
Models, experimental vs. mental, 133–35
Moral entropy, 165–76, 196, 255–57, 266
Moral momentum, 147–50, 158
Moses, Robert (NYC overpasses), 69–70

Naturalist Fallacy, 62–64
Neuroscience and the virtues, 150–58
NSPE (National Society of Professional Engineers), 66, 81, 84, 94, 278

Palchinsky, Pyotr, 216
Phronesis, 164, 179. *See also* Practical wisdom
Plato, 22, 184, 270, 271
Practical reasoning. *See* Reasoning, practical
Practical wisdom, 156, 199, 249. *See also* Phronesis; Synderesis
Practice, xi, xiii, 163, 165, 166, 168, 175, 176, 182, 193–201 (marks of), 205n31 (definition), 208, 209, 212, 214, 218, 265, 283, 289
Professional codes of ethics (PCOE), 80–100, x, 49, 66, 194, 198, 220, 278
Professional Engineer (P.E.), 54–59, 65, 78n3, 278. *See also* NSPE

Index